P9-CFH-994

● *Pitt Series in Policy and Institutional Studies*

Democracy in

JAPAN

Takeshi Ishida and
Ellis S. Krauss

EDITORS

University of Pittsburgh Press

Published by the University of Pittsburgh Press, Pittsburgh, Pa., 15260
Copyright © 1989, University of Pittsburgh Press
All rights reserved
Baker & Taylor International, London
Manufactured in the United States of America
Second printing, 1990

Library of Congress Cataloging-in-Publication Data

Democracy in Japan / Takeshi Ishida and Ellis S. Krauss, editors.
    p.   cm.—(Pitt series in policy and institutional studies)
  Includes bibliographical references and index.
  ISBN 0-8229-3608-9. ISBN 0-8229-5414-1 (pbk.)
  1. Political culture—Japan. 2. Japan—Politics and
government—1945- 3. Japan—Economic conditions—1945- 4. Japan—
Social conditions—1945- 5. Democracy. I. Ishida, Takeshi, 1923-.
  II. Krauss, Ellis S. III. Series.
JQ1681.D45 1989
306'.2'0952—dc19   88-28057
                                              CIP

To our *sensei*

Masao Maruyama	Nobutaka Ike
Yoshitake Oka	Kurt Steiner
Kiyoaki Tsuji	Kazuko Tsurumi

Contents

Preface

This volume originated from a request by a "think tank" for a book on Japan for a series on democracy in various countries of the world. The purpose of the series was to provide both the expert and the educated layman with monographs describing and analyzing various democratic polities. We recruited some of the most knowledgeable and insightful analysts of Japan for our volume. Unfortunately, as the book neared completion, the series for which it was originally scheduled was canceled.

We and our authors felt, however, that our volume was too important and worthwhile a project to abandon. Upon its completion, therefore, we submitted the manuscript to the University of Pittsburgh Press, and after evaluation by reviewers, were delighted to have it accepted as part of the series in Policy and Institutional Studies under the general editorship of Bert A. Rockman.

Despite the change of publishing venue, we maintained our original goals for the volume: to produce a book that would explore the most important issues of Japan's democracy using and advancing the best research on Japan, thus making it useful to the scholar, but also one written in a clear and concise manner, thus making its contents accessible to the student, journalist, government official, or educated layman with little prior knowledge of Japan.

We also maintained our conception of the kind of volume that was needed in the field. Nearly forty-five years after the beginning of the American Occupation of Japan, and over thirty-five years from its conclusion, we felt it was time to evaluate objectively the outcome of that important experiment in transforming Japan into a democratic nation. Further, despite the recent spate of works on Japanese politics, few had systematically analyzed the general phenomenon of Japanese democracy in comparative perspective. Only one other book had focused specifically on issues of Japanese democracy, but we felt that its highly critical assumptions and its lack of an explicit comparative perspective limited its ability to fill the gap in the literature.[1] We attempted to use the findings of social science to place Japan in a comparative perspective in order to provide a more balanced account of Japanese democracy, one that recognized democratic accomplishments as well as failures, problems along with achievements. We leave it to the reader to decide whether we have fulfilled our aims.

We are grateful to our contributors for their patience through the long and sometimes trying process of turning our conceptions for the volume into reality. We also wish to thank the Japan Council of the University of Pittsburgh for providing financial support for parts of the final editing and production process, and all of its members for their consistent moral support for Ellis Krauss' research efforts, including this one. Our gratitude also goes to Catherine Marshall for her competence and fortitude in editing the volume, Bert A. Rockman and Frederick A. Hetzel for their support throughout the publishing process, and Barbara E. Cohen for her indexing.

NOTE

1. Gavan McCormack and Yoshio Sugimoto, eds., *Democracy in Contemporary Japan* (Armonk, N.Y.: M. E. Sharpe, Inc., 1986). This book should be consulted for a more negative view of postwar Japan based on the assumption that it has been developing as "control state" or as a form of neo-fascism.

Introduction

1 Democracy in Japan: Issues and Questions

●

TAKESHI ISHIDA and ELLIS S. KRAUSS

The Significance of Japanese Democracy

The Japanese case is particularly significant in the study of democracy in the twentieth century. Japan is the first industrialized democracy in the non-Western world. This fact alone leads to important comparative questions about the role of political culture in democracy. How is democracy conceived of and realized outside Western civilization? To what extent do the processes and problems of democracy differ when the culture and historical background vary, even if the structure of democratic governance is similar to many countries in the West?

Second, democracy in Japan after World War II was intentionally implanted and nurtured by a foreign occupying power. The American Occupation of Japan (1945–1952) attempted, through "social engineering," to create not only a democratic political system, but a democratic society and culture that would support and maintain that system. One of the most important questions about democracy in Japan must inevitably be whether the Occupation's plans for Japan were realized. To what extent does Japanese democracy today differ from those ideals based on American experience that the Occupation intended for Japan? If it does differ, does that make Japanese democracy any less "democratic"? How did the formative experience of this attempt affect the development of Japanese democracy? Can a Western political concept like "democracy" be artificially transplanted to another context? With what results?

3

Third, Japan was a totally prostrate, defeated country at the end of the war. Almost all her cities, not just Hiroshima and Nagasaki, but Tokyo, Nagoya, and the rest, were bombed-out shells. Yet in only forty years Japan has developed an economy that surpasses almost all Western nations. During that same period Japan has gone from being a predominantly agrarian nation to one of the world's most urbanized, and from poverty to affluence. In the past few years some have even regarded Japan as a model not only of economic growth but also of a successful transition to "postindustrial" society, partially because of the skillful management of its elite government bureaucracy.[1] What has been the nature of that enormous social and economic change, how "democratic" has it been, and how has it affected the development of political democracy in Japan?

These three significant facts—Japanese political tradition and culture, the experience of the American Occupation, and postwar social change—provide the frame, the context, and the significance of the specific issues of democracy addressed in this volume. After a brief review of these aspects of Japan, we will discuss the concept of democracy, the key themes that run throughout this volume, and introduce the chapters that follow.

The Historical Background of Democracy in Japan

Traditional Society

The Tokugawa regime (1603–1868), during which Japan had something like a national government led by a *shōgun* (generalissimo) who effectively ruled in the emperor's name, borrowed and used Confucian orthodoxy from China. This philosophy strongly emphasized monarchical rule under a virtuous ruler, the hierarchical stratification of society into four classes, and the obedience of the ruled to the ruler, which in China had been the scholar-official but in Japan became the samurai, the warrior-official.

The Confucian classics, however, such as the writings of Mencius, did include a concept that might have some democratic implications. This was the concept of the Mandate of Heaven, according to which if the ruler did not rule appropriately, in other words, for the benefit and welfare of the people, then the Mandate of Heaven could be lost and a revolution to change the dynasty could occur. The Mandate of Heaven, what we call today the "right to rule" or "authority," thus contained some room for the ultimate expression of popular will in its acceptance of the right of revolution against an unbenevolent ruler. Yet, despite the widespread influence of Confucianism in Japan, the concept of the Mandate of Heaven was not widely accepted by Japanese Confucian scholars. Instead, only the more paternalistic and vague idea that the ruling elite had some responsibility to govern for the welfare of the people existed in traditional Japan.

Further, the relationship between leader and follower in Japanese feudal tradition also differed from that in the feudal West. In the medieval West, retainers owed loyalty to their leaders, but the leader was specifically obligated in return to reward and take care of the retainer, a reciprocal relationship that eventually nourished the emphasis on "contract" and "right" in the Western tradition. In Japan, however, although the loyalty and obedience of the samurai retainer to his feudal lord were heavily stressed, the obligation was one way; the leader was not specifically obligated to look after his followers.[2] Though the idea of "taking care of" one's subordinates became a cultural expectation, it never developed into the basis for formal democratic or legal rights.

Two aspects of Tokugawa society nonetheless did provide some early, if limited, "democratic" tendencies. The first was the fact that the shogunal government, although powerful enough to maintain order and to rule unchallenged for over two hundred and fifty years, never established a completely centralized system. The local feudal lords continued to administer their own domains with some autonomy as long as they observed the regulations of the shogunate designed to prevent rebellion and to maintain the hierarchical class system. In addition to elements of decentralization in the relationship between feudal domains and the center, commoners at the village level were directly subject to their own indigenous leaders—village chiefs and elders who often made decisions collectively. Thus, within a system presided over by a powerful, military central government there were elements of decentralized administration, and within a system of hierarchical status and local power, there were collective and consensual aspects.

The Meiji Restoration

The rebellion of lower-level samurai from four domains that occurred in 1867–1868 swept away the shogunal government, but not under the banner of popular participation or democratic principles. Rather, the major goals of the Meiji Restoration leaders was to "restore" authority to the emperor and to protect Japan from colonization by the West. More a nationalist than a democratic movement, the idea of government *by* the people did not play a major role. Indeed, these leaders soon set about creating a centralized state, not under the control of the emperor but rather using him as a symbol to mobilize the people for unity and modernization.

Their creation of centralized institutions to penetrate and control the society provoked resistance from some who had come to be influenced by Western ideas, including the new notion of democracy and representative government. In the 1880s, a movement critical of the increasingly powerful and elitist government arose, the Freedom and Popular Rights Movement (Jiyū Minken Undō). In their petition for the establishment of a representative assembly, its leaders argued that the Meiji government was neither an imperial nor a democratic authority, but rather an oligarchy.

Pressure from this movement, as well as a desire to appear enlightened in the West, led the Meiji oligarchs to promulgate a constitution in 1889 and to establish a national assembly, the Diet, elected by limited suffrage for the first time in 1890. In practice, these two acts did not bring democracy so much as continued oligarchical rule, now legitimized by the ideology of absolute imperial rule. Sovereignty clearly resided with the emperor under the new system, not with the people, and all acts of government were technically manifestations of the imperial will. In practice, the emperor remained more or less a figurehead, and government continued to be controlled by the small group of leaders of the Restoration. These same oligarchs first monopolized the major cabinet posts under the new constitution and then, after the turn of the century, retired from official posts to act as *genrō,* elder statesmen. They chose the prime minister, one of their protégés, and continued to exercise considerable influence on government from behind the scenes, particularly during major crises.

The 1889 constitution was strongly modeled on Prussian ideas of statism. The cabinet and the bureaucracy, civilian and military, were responsible to the emperor, not to the Diet. Indeed, the Diet had only weak powers and its role was primarily to advise. It was a system in which all government agents were accountable to the emperor, who did not really rule; therefore no one was completely accountable to anyone, least of all to the people. What kept the system functioning was, within the government, the quiet coordination of the *genrō,* and, vis-à-vis society, the mobilization of popular support through the ideology of complete obedience, loyalty, and sacrifice to the emperor, propagated in the schools, the media, and the armed forces.

"Taishō Democracy"

The death of the popular and long-reigning Emperor Meiji in 1912 and the death and aging of the original oligarchs left a political vacuum. The accession of Emperor Taishō, who was both young and incapable, increasing urbanization, and the influence of ideas from abroad led to growing criticism of the oligarchical system and a desire for reform. Political parties, supported by the press and chambers of commerce, and liberal intellectuals propounding greater democracy were in the forefront of a movement "to protect the constitutional system."

One of the intellectual leaders of this movement, Yoshino Sakuzō, coined the term *minponshugi* as a label for the democracy they desired. This word for democracy implies "government for the people" rather than "government by the people" (that is, popular sovereignty) which is suggested by the word *minshushugi* used today. There is actually great political significance in this semantic difference: *minponshugi* allowed for a vague coexistence in theory between continued imperial sovereignty and greater democratic practices, whereas *minshushugi* would have forced a confrontation over where sovereignty really lay, in the people or the emperor. This basic problem, how to reconcile the irreconcilable notions of popular versus imperial will as the basic legitimizing principle of the state, was of concern to liberal intellectuals throughout the prewar period.

The death of the last original *genrō* in 1921 and the demands for reform led eventually in the mid-1920s to the "golden age of Taishō Democracy." Universal manhood suffrage widened the electorate considerably, a two-party political system had begun to develop, and the principle was temporarily established that the prime minister should at least be the head of one of the major parties in the Diet. Simultaneously, however, these democratic advances were accompanied by repression of the recently arisen leftist parties and groups through the notorious Peace Preservation Law, an instrument that was later to be turned even against liberals.

8

The End of Prewar Democracy

By the early 1930s, Japan faced several crises at home and abroad. The worldwide economic depression severely affected Japan, bringing about desperate conditions particularly in the countryside. The close connection of political parties with urban big business and the inability of the government to act swiftly precipitated a crisis of political alienation. With the invasion of Manchuria in 1931, Japan also became increasingly isolated internationally. These events and the national anxiety that accompanied them led to even greater emphasis on a mystical, emperor-centered concept of a collective, unique "national polity" and the rise of antiliberal, anti-individual, and anti-Western ideas and groups.

Political parties, with a weak mass base and an organization based on local landlords and notables in the countryside, reacted feebly in defense of democracy. Rather, in self-interested attempts to appeal to voters they competed to discredit each other with the charge of insufficient loyalty to the emperor. European fascism also contributed to the attacks on parliamentary democracy. Small right-wing groups began assassinations and terrorist attacks on government officials and leading industrialists. Sentiments for the total reorganization of the nation became current among large segments of the officer corps of the army, culminating in the abortive coup of February 26, 1936, by young military officers stationed in Tokyo.

Although none of the actions taken by the right-wing, insubordinate young officers were successful, they provided the opportunity and excuse for the army high command to gradually accumulate power within the government. With Japan's invasion of China in 1937, the army completed its takeover of the Japanese state and reorganized it along fascist lines. Thus, in contrast with Italy and Germany, Japan never experienced a successful mass fascist movement; rather, what occurred in Japan has been described as fascism from above, or the militarization of the Japanese government. In any case, the elements of democracy that had existed in Japan were eradicated by the late 1930s, and the military led Japan into the disastrous Pacific war with the allied powers.

Thus, despite sporadic grass-roots movements for democratic reform during the Meiji and Taishō periods and the establishment of democratic institutions such as elections, parties, and a parliament, the idea of popular sovereignty was never legitimized under the imperial system. Democracy was never completely institutionalized in prewar Japan.

Postwar Democracy

The American Occupation

Defeat in war and the American Occupation brought about a radical change in the postwar era. The hardships of the war and its ultimate futility prepared the Japanese people for a change of value orientations under the Occupation, and many enthusiastically endorsed both democratization and Westernization. But which democracy? Prewar conservative party politicians thought that returning to the politics of the 1920s would be sufficient to realize democracy in Japan. Marxists, who had been suppressed in the prewar period but who gained credibility in the immediate postwar era because of their lonely resistance to the war, considered American-style democracy merely "bourgeois" democracy and looked to the Communist countries as models of "democracy." Liberal intellectuals tended to accept the democratic ideas of the United States, and regarded the prewar politicians as reactionary, on the one hand, and the Marxists as revolutionary threats to democracy on the other.

Later in the postwar period, events were to diminish the appeal of these models for Japanese intellectuals. The acceptance of democratic ideals discredited a return to the prewar system; Soviet intervention in Hungary and Czechoslavakia; growing awareness of human rights problems in Communist countries; the Korean and Vietnam wars; and Watergate all served somewhat to disillusion the previous "true believers" in each system. But in the immediate postwar era these foreign democratic systems inspired conflicting visions of what democracy was and should be.

If the Japanese intellectual elite was not unified in its idea of what kind of democracy was needed in Japan, the American Occupation thought it knew. The Occupation set about constructing liberal democracy in government, and a society and political culture that would support and sustain that political democracy. A total revision of the Meiji constitution, officially adopted in 1946, made popular sovereignty the basis of the Japanese state; the emperor became a mere symbol of the state and the unity of the people. The growth of political parties was encouraged, suffrage was extended to women, and the Diet was given the same powers as parliaments in the West. The cabinet was made responsible to the Diet, and the bureaucracy responsible to the cabinet. Fundamental freedoms of speech, press, organization, and religion were guaranteed by the constitution. Local governments were given some autonomy from the center, and local executives were to be popularly elected, instead of appointed by the central government as in the prewar period. Prewar rightists and militarists were purged from official positions, thus allowing for a new political elite supportive of democracy to take power. In one of the most unique political reforms, the Occupation also included in the constitution (article 9) a clause forbidding Japan from engaging in aggressive war or maintaining an offensive military force.

Perhaps thinking of the precedent of Weimar Germany, where a democratic constitution and political system had nonetheless failed to prevent the rise of Hitler and the Nazis, the Occupation also set about thoroughly reforming Japanese society to create democratic economic and social institutions that would support political democracy. Land reform created a new class of small, independent owner-farmers; women were given legal equality; the formation of unions was encouraged; both the form and content of education was radically altered; the prewar family trusts, the *zaibatsu,* that in prewar days had concentrated economic power in their hands, were broken up.

Later chapters in this book (chapters 2 and 14) consider the long-term impact of these reforms and the extent to which they succeeded, partially succeeded, or failed to bring about the kind of political, social, and economic democracy the Occupation envisioned for Japan. Here we should mention, however, that a major change in Occupation policy took place in 1947–1948 that was to have far-reaching consequences for Japan's postwar political culture and democracy. With the onset of the cold war and the completion of the first stage of reform, the Occupation began to rethink its priorities for postwar Japan. This change involved attaching less importance to "democratization" and more to stability, less value to "demilitarization" and more to making Japan an ally of the United States in the Pacific. The latter change acquired particular significance for the United States in the wake of the Chinese Communist revolution of 1949 and the onset of the Korean War in 1950.

This change in policy, called the "reverse course" by the left and liberals in Japan, had a profound impact on political alliances and political culture in Japan. The conservatives, previously appalled by, and resistant to, the sweeping democratic reforms brought by the

Occupation, now supported the United States and the new policy enthusiastically. The left, whose main pillars were the Socialist party and allied labor unions, had previously been an enthusiastic ally of the American Occupation and its reconstruction of Japan, but it now fiercely resisted what it considered a reneging on the liberal and pacifist ideals at the heart of democracy. The result was a paradoxical polarization of Japanese political culture that has lasted to the present day. Conservatives, many of whom never completely accepted the 1946 American-inspired constitution and democratic reforms, considering them too radical and "un-Japanese," became strong allies of American foreign policy. The left became a vociferous critic of the United States and its foreign policy, but remained the staunchest supporter of the original U.S. democratic vision for Japan.

Major Trends, 1952–1985

With their electoral ascendance after the end of the Occupation, and particularly after the formation of the conservative Liberal Democratic Party (LDP) in 1955, the conservatives were able to modify some of the original postwar reforms, such as creating the Self-Defense Forces out of an Occupation-created "police reserve force." In effect, Japan now had a military force. Both the U.S. and the Japanese government interpreted article 9 of the Japanese constitution as permitting Japan to have a military so long as it was defensive in nature. Other examples of the conservatives' post-Occupation revisions included a partial recentralization of the education and police systems. These modifications, and other proposals by some conservatives to amend the constitution, have been resisted and protested by the many who see them as turning the clock back to the prewar era and as a threat to Japanese democracy.

The most important confrontation between these two political forces in Japanese democracy took place in 1960, when then Prime Minister Kishi and the governing LDP rammed the revision of the U.S.-Japan Security Treaty through a rump midnight session of the Diet which the opposition parties were boycotting to protest previous procedural machinations by the LDP. What began as an important but contained controversy over the question of Japan's alliance with the United States, then became a crisis of democracy; even many who supported the treaty became alarmed at the government's high-handed tactics and joined the movement "to protect parliamentary democracy." Massive protest failed to stop the implementation of the treaty revision, but did succeed in forcing the prime minister to resign.[3]

Following this intense confrontation, subsequent LDP governments concentrated on economic growth rather than politically controversial issues. In alliance with the elite and powerful national bureaucracy, hardly changed by the Occupation, the conservatives attempted to achieve first reconstruction from the war and then a modern industrialized economy. The successful implementation of these policies resulted in the rapid economic growth for which Japan has become famous in the West. This achievement, combined with a fragmented political opposition and an electoral system that favored the rural areas where the governing party was strongest, enabled the LDP to monopolize government power. Urbanization and generational change, however, did result in gradual and progressively declining voting rates for the LDP.

In the late 1960s, other consequences of rapid economic growth also became apparent. Urbanization brought overcrowded cities and a horrendous pollution problem; the priority given to production rather than to social infrastructure exacerbated the problem of the urban environment. As in other industrialized societies, affluence and the abundance of material goods led to concern for the quality of life. All over Japan thousands of independent citizens' movements protested the past deterioration of the environment and called for protection against further pollution.

These large-scale citizens' movements were an unprecedented phenomenon. Avoiding close ties to any particular political party, guided by no ideology, and emphasizing not only the cleaning up of pollution but also greater citizens' control over government decision making, the movements represented a changing political consciousness and a voluntaristic, nonviolent form of grass-roots participation that marked a new stage of political culture in Japanese democracy. Opposition parties at the local level soon took up the demands for improved environmental quality and their candidates were elected to local offices in most of the major urban areas of Japan. In 1970, finally heeding the demands for pollution control, the LDP passed a series of laws to clean up the environment, giving Japan probably the strictest antipollution control laws in the world.

By the mid-1970s, the LDP, usually in coalition with some of the more moderate opposition parties, managed to regain control of most local executive positions in major urban areas, but faced increasing difficulty at the national level. In the election of 1976, the combined seats of the opposition parties nearly equaled those of the LDP. Similar results obtained in the election of 1979, and this period witnessed the increasing influence of the opposition parties through the committee system of the Diet. In the election of 1980, the LDP once more obtained an overwhelming majority, but in 1983 again fell to a bare majority. To increase its voting majority, it brought into the cabinet another political party, the small conservative New Liberal Club, ushering in the first coalition cabinet since the LDP was formed in 1955. In the 1986 elections, however, the LDP regained its huge majority and once again formed a single-party cabinet.

The results of elections have become more volatile as, particularly in urban areas, voters have become more independent of political party loyalties, as well as of ideology or traditional personal ties, and tend to cast their votes on the basis of expectations of party performance in solving concrete problems, or on the basis of self or reference group interest. Nevertheless, the LDP has managed to stay in power consistently for thirty years, a record matched by no other incumbent party in the industrialized democracies in the postwar era. The implications for democracy of this one-party system, and whether it will continue into the future, are two important questions for postwar democracy in Japan.

Themes and Questions

This volume takes a wide view of "democracy." In the nineteenth century, classical liberals emphasized political democracy, often excluding the economic and social aspects, an attitude also commonly found among today's American conservatives. On the other hand, many Marxists have emphasized economic and social democracy, often forgetting the necessity for political democracy. We believe that all three elements must be given attention in any consideration of democracy in Japan. This is particularly so because the American Occupation, the starting point for postwar democracy in Japan, took such an inclusive view, attempting to democratize all aspects of Japanese society. Thus we have included in this volume articles on all three dimensions.

In chapter 2, T. J. Pempel discusses the prerequisites of democracy, evaluating the extent to which various social and political structures may help to maintain and support democracy in Japan. Then,

Ellis Krauss provides an introduction to the processes of Japanese politics and policymaking, including a general introduction to how some of the major elements in Japan's political system operate, and the role played by various social groups. In subsequent sections, our contributors analyze specific aspects of political, social, and economic democracy in Japan.

In the section on political democracy, Lawrence Beer first turns our attention to the legal framework for democracy, including basic civil liberties and freedom of the press and considers the law's connection to the social reality. J.A.A. Stockwin goes into greater detail about the Diet, political parties, and elections, and John Campbell discusses the implications for democracy of one of Japan's most important political institutions, the elite national bureaucracy. Moving the focus to the grass-roots level, Terry MacDougall looks at the system of local government, while Patricia Steinhoff takes up the question of protest and its functions in postwar democracy.

In the next two sections, we explore social and economic democracy and their connection to political democracy. Margaret McKean analyzes the basic question of social and economic equality in the postwar era, a fundamental element of the concept of democracy. Focusing on one of the major means for the creation of equality or inequality in society, Edward Beauchamp explores the educational system. The next three articles look specifically at aspects of economic democracy. The first, by Glen S. Fukushima, considers corporate power in Japan's highly developed capitalist system; the second, by Tadashi Hanami, discusses labor and management and democracy in industrial relations; and in the third, Christena Turner focuses on labor and the problems of democratic consciousness within labor unions.

We have asked each contributor to at least touch on four major questions of Japanese democracy:

1. *What are the strengths and weaknesses of Japanese democracy and what are their origins?* We are aiming here at an objective evaluation of democracy in postwar Japan in terms of the basic elements of "democracy," which we define as representation and accountability, participation, equality, and stability. To what extent are the people's views represented and their demands responded to? What are the opportunities for average citizens to participate in the decisions that affect their lives, and through what means? How politically, socially, and economically equal are individuals? How stable is Japanese democracy?

What are the trade-offs among these aspects of democracy in postwar Japan?

2. *How has Japanese democracy changed over time?* Particularly, to what extent have the American Occupation's ideals and goals for Japanese democracy been institutionalized over time?

3. *What is the congruence between formal principles and reality in Japanese democracy?* In all systems, some disparity may exist between democratic ideals and actuality, between the law and behavior, between the institutional structure and the process of democracy, between democratic goals and the means used to try to achieve them. How great or small are these disparities in various dimensions of postwar Japan?

4. *How unique or similar is Japanese democracy compared to Western democracies?* If the preceding questions attempt to evaluate Japanese democracy in terms of ideals and history, here we wish to evaluate it comparatively across nations. How much like American or European democracy is Japan? What are its unique aspects?

In our conclusion, we return to these questions, attempting an objective, critical evaluation of the dimensions of Japanese democracy based on our contributors' analyses. We will also address some of the stereotypes concerning Japan as a model of democracy and harmony for other nations, and as successfully blending "Western" and "traditional" elements.

NOTES

1. Ezra F. Vogel, *Japan as Number One: Lessons for America* (Cambridge, Mass.: Harvard University Press, 1979), chaps. 3–5, pp. 27–97.

2. See the discussion of the work of Marc Block and Takeyoshi Kawashima by Kazuko Tsurumi, *Social Change and the Individual: Japan Before and After Defeat in World War II* (Princeton, N.J.: Princeton University Press, 1970), pp. 93–94.

3. The demonstrations against the U.S.-Japanese security treaty (*anpo,* for short, in Japanese) continued for a few months in the spring of 1960 and were the largest mass demonstrations in Japanese history up to that time. The security treaty had been signed by the United States and Japan along with the peace treaty that concluded World War II in 1951, and it took effect with the end of the Occupation the following year. It provided, among other things, for the

stationing of American troops in Japan. Its provisions were not popular in Japan and were accepted only reluctantly by the Japanese government. Prime Minister Kishi renegotiated the treaty to eliminate some of its most objectionable features, such as the possibility that American forces in Japan would be used to quell internal disturbances. Consideration of the renegotiated treaty by the Diet became the opportunity, however, for the Japanese left, particularly the Socialist party, to question the remilitarization of Japan and the entire U.S.-Japanese alliance.

While there were many peaceful demonstrations against the treaty, radical left students especially engaged in more forceful protest. When Socialist representatives tried to prevent passage of the treaty with physical obstructionist tactics, the LDP passed it with a "snap vote" and in a rump session of the parliament. These actions turned a debate on the treaty into a major "crisis of democracy" and stimulated intellectuals and nonideological progressives to join the students in massive demonstrations in June 1960. The treaty went into effect as passed by the Diet, but these protests and further actions by the radical students eventually led to the cancellation of President Eisenhower's planned visit to Japan and the resignation of Prime Minister Kishi, and many observers questioned the stability of Japanese democracy. These protests proved to be the high water mark for the student movement and the left in general, who were never to reach the same level of popular support again.

For a full discussion of the background, major actors, parliamentary actions, and demonstrations, see George R. Packard III, *Protest in Tokyo* (Princeton, N.J.: Princeton University Press, 1966).

2

Prerequisites for Democracy: Political and Social Institutions

●

T. J. PEMPEL

Democracy is a term that carries heavy positive connotations. As a result, most countries in the world, despite their widely differing political, social, and economic systems, use it in some form or other to describe themselves. As John Kenneth Galbraith once put it, "Like the family and truth and sunshine and Florence Nightingale, democracy stands above doubt."[1] "People's democracies," "revolutionary democracies," "capitalist democracies," "democratic republics," "representative democracies," "liberal democracies," and "federal democracies" are but a few of the many widely applied labels attempting to link some country or group of countries to this all-popular category. The lack of agreement on just which nation-states are democratic reflects an important component in the theoretical debate about just what *democracy* really means.[2] Should it be used in a sense that is categorical or one that is relative? Many theorists hold that democracy involves certain requisites which either are, or are not, present in a particular political system and determine whether a system is, or is not, democratic. Others contend that democracy is an idealized concept reached by no actual, functioning political system; some political systems are simply closer to the ideal than others. Such a view leads to the conclusion that all countries can be scaled accordingly: country A is more democratic than country B, and both are more democratic than country C. From this perspective, even nation-states universally recognized as democratic have room for improvement.

This essay recognizes validity in each position. There is merit in distinguishing a certain group of political systems as democratic (even if they are not perfect democracies) from other systems which have dramatically different ways of organizing political life. At the same time, it is important to recognize that none of these countries represents an ideal democracy. By recognizing both the scalar categorical dimensions of democracy, it becomes possible to separate democracies from non-democracies, while at the same time comparing democracies in regard to their respectively greater or lesser adherence to democratic principles. Thus in assessing Japanese democracy, I will attempt to show the ways in which it most definitely is a democracy in the most commonly accepted sense of that term. At the same time, I will explore how Japanese democracy compares to other democratic systems and the ways in which it falls short of democratic ideals.

The key to this assessment involves the study of Japanese institutions. Institutions play an indispensable role in creating and sustaining, or conversely, in preventing or undermining, democracy. Certain institutional structures make it more or less likely that democratic principles will or will not be permanent features of a nation's politics even if the presence or absence of particular institutions in itself does not ensure the full achievement of an idealized democracy.

Before proceeding, it would be well to offer a working definition of democracy. At a minimum, democracy involves the right of citizens to determine their form of government and to choose those who will constitute that government. It also requires that government be responsive to the preferences of citizens. And finally, it requires that each citizen's preferences be weighted relatively equally.[3]

Essentially, a democratic political system exists when political institutions provide opportunities for citizens to gain and exchange information, articulate opinions, and express their political viewpoints. Potential political leaders are free to compete for the support of these citizens. And governmental institutions ensure that state policies are in some measure congruent with citizens' expressions of preference.[4] Leaving aside the question of stability, these dimensions of democracy accord closely with the basic elements of representation and accountability, participation, and equality discussed in chapter 1.

By vitually any such empirical measure, contemporary Japanese institutions are democratic. They put Japan in the company of the so-called advanced industrialized democracies of Western Europe, North America, and Australasia. This was not true of Japan prior to the end of World War II, but following the changes introduced by the American Occupation, Japan's political system took on most of the features normally associated with the Western democracies. At the same time Japan's institutions are by no means perfect vehicles to ensure the purest forms of theoretical democracy one might imagine. Even if Japan is "democratic" there is room for greater democratization.[5]

This essay begins with a discussion of Japan's two constitutions, that which set Japan on its path to modernization from the late nineteenth century until the end of World War II, and that which replaced it in 1947 and which continues to operate unchanged today. It then examines in detail the political institutions operative in three specific areas critical to political democracy. First, it looks at the institutions affecting individual citizens and their political rights. It then explores the mechanisms that allow the citizen to interact with government. Finally, it looks at the governmental institutions themselves to determine just how receptive they are to citizen control.

Constitutional Principles

The predominant philosophy of government and the principal political structures designed to fulfill them are typically articulated in a country's constitution. Under the Meiji constitution (1889–1947), democracy was neither the principal goal nor an underlying axiom of the Japanese political system. Rather, the constitution was designed to facilitate national cohesion and centralized authority. Rapid changes in Japanese society were deemed necessary by Japan's modernizers; a strong central authority was seen as the best means of carrying these out. Consequently, the constitution's drafters designed institutions which would enable a strong central government to act purposefully and with minimal opposition; they were not concerned with democratic controls over the nation's rulers.[6] With Bismarck's Prussia as its model, the constitution vested sovereignty in the emperor, as was briefly discussed in chapter 1. Indeed, the constitution was the emperor's "gift" to his people; it was neither a popularly derived nor a representatively ratified document. Under it, his word, as articulated through behind-the-scenes advisors to the throne, was supreme. The two-house parliament included one that was purely appointive, based largely on heredity and service to the state. Powers of the elective House of Representatives were severely circumscribed. Most particularly, it had no specific right to determine the composition of the executive branch; the prime minister and the cabinet were chosen by the emperor and his advisors. Although electoral strength in the lower house influenced the choice of governments during the 1910s and 1920s, votes were but one of many factors relevant to the selection of governments.[7] By far the largest number of prime ministers and cabinet officials who served under the prewar constitution were not popularly elected.[8] As became clear during the 1930s, the army, constitutionally exempt from civilian and cabinet control, was capable of becoming the major force in cabinet selection. Suffrage was sharply limited by economic status until universal male suffrage was adopted in 1925 (women only achieved the right to vote in 1947). Local governmental leaders, including prefectural governors, were generally appointed, rather than elected. A series of laws restricted the rights of citizens to organize labor unions, political parties, and interest groups; the media was subject to strict censorship; the police, the military, and right-wing terrorist groups subverted the civil liberties of citizens in numerous ways.[9] Citizens' duties to the state far outweighed the constitutional and legal guarantees of citizens' rights.

The overriding philosophy of the prewar system was summed up in the famous speech of Prime Minister Kuroda at the time the constitution was promulgated: "It goes without saying that the citizens have nothing to say either for or against the Constitution. However, as there exists political diversity and as each person has his own opinion, it is quite natural that those who have similar opinions will unite to form political parties. This being so, the government must always place itself with indifference above the political parties in order to be as impartial and just in terms of the law as it can toward everyone."[10]

Despite these restrictions on democratic control, two points are worthy of note. First, the prewar Japanese political system contained within itself the potential to become more democratic, and indeed it did so. Popular votes, political parties, and parliamentary power all became progressively more important from the late nineteenth century until at least the late 1920s. Antigovernmental interest groups, such as labor unions, did succeed in gaining greater autonomy and influence by the 1920s. Opposition parties like the socialists achieved increased popular support despite government hostility and police harassment. Some Japanese newspapers struggled to achieve commendable records of autonomy, even during the war.

The second point is that during the early part of the twentieth century, the Japanese political system was by no means unique in its restriction of democratic rights and privileges. Other countries may have been more democratic in important ways, but it is worth remembering that in the United States slavery was legal until 1862 and blacks faced severe barriers to equality in many regions until the passage of the Civil Rights Act of 1965. Catholics, Jews, and agnostics could not become members of the British Parliament until well into the nineteenth century, and the House of Lords, with its political privileges for British nobility, was a powerful impediment to democratic government until its reform in 1911. Universal male suffrage was severely restricted in Great Britain until 1884 and in much of the rest of Europe until after World War I; women did not get the right to vote in the United States until 1920, in Britain until 1929, in France until 1945, and in Switzerland until the 1970s. Union organizers had to confront hostile police, courts, and private security forces in the United States and most of Europe until well into the 1920s and later in many instances.

Such comparisons do not negate the very real institutional barriers to democracy that existed in the prewar Japanese political system. Nor do they imply that democracy was meaningless in these other countries until some liberating date in the 1920s or 1940s. Rather they suggest that while Japanese instutitions were far less than fully democratic, they still allowed for increased democratization of the political system over time. Moreover, to the extent that democratization has been an evolutionary process in all countries, Japan could be said to have trailed many other countries in its democratic development, but, in many important respects, by not more than a few decades. Consequently, the transition to far more democratic institutions under the 1947 constitution, dramatic as it was, did not involve leapfrogging over centuries but rather over decades.

When the American armies occupied Japan following World War II, they sought to establish the political, economic, and social conditions they believed would transform Japan into a democracy, and into a nonwarring state.[11] The extent to which they were or were not successful has been subject to intense debate and analysis. Even critics of Occupation policies, however, typically concede that the new political institutions, modeled on those of Britain and the United States, were far more democratic than those they replaced.

A brief overview of the major transformations may serve as a useful contrast to the prewar constitutional principles and as a basis for a more detailed examination of a number of present-day institutions. The most important change was that the political system was deliberately designed to ensure democracy. Along with "demilitarization," "democratization" was one of the two overarching goals of the U.S. Occupation.[12] Consequently, the emperor ceased to be sovereign. Instead, sovereignty was vested in the nation's citizens, and their political and personal rights were extensively expanded. Both houses of parliament were made completely subject to popular elections, and parliament became "the highest organ of state power." The cabinet was chosen by parliament, and the prime minister and at least one-half of the cabinet were required to be members of that body. Local governments were also subject to electoral control, as, at least indirectly, were the courts. In addition the civil and criminal codes were revamped in a number of ways to make day-to-day laws compatible with democratic principles and with the new constitution. A number of other changes took place which at least partially moved forward the social and economic equalities within society. In short, a broad array of institutional and structural changes were made in an effort to realize the abstract commitment to democratic governance.

Citizens and Rights in Contemporary Japan

Japan's constitution provides one of the world's most extensive catalogues of rights for citizens. Articles 10 through 40 specify the general and particular rights of citizenship. Among the most prominent are: the right to equality under law and the absence of discrimination on the basis of race, creed, sex, social status, or family origin (art. 14); freedom of conscience (art. 19); religious freedom (art. 20); freedom of residence and occupation (art. 22); academic freedom (art. 23); the right to a minimum standard of wholesome and cultured living (art. 25); the right to an equal education (art. 26); the right of workers to organize and bargain collectively (art. 28); and freedom from search and seizure without specific warrants (art. 35).

Beyond these is a series of specific political guarantees: the right to choose public officials through universal suffrage based on a secret ballot (art. 15); the right to petition for political changes (art. 16); the rights of free speech, press, and expression (art. 21); the right of access to the courts (art. 32); the right to hear charges upon arrest and to have legal counsel (art. 34); the right to a speedy trial (art. 37); and freedom from testifying against oneself (art. 38).

On balance, these rights are not simply paper guarantees; they are manifested in the day-to-day lives of Japan's citizens. At the same time, even a cursory familiarity with Japanese society will reveal many specific instances in which the concrete reality falls short of the stated constitutional ideal. Three aspects of citizens' rights deserve special attention.

The first of these concerns systematic discrimination against particular groups of citizens. There are few massive structural impediments to prevent most Japanese citizens from exercising their constitutionally guaranteed rights. Economic and social discrimination is probably no less (though probably nor more) significant in Japan than in other industrialized democracies—class counts, in Japan no less than in other capitalist societies. Yet there is no real aristocracy in Japan as there still is in Great Britain. Rather, as Margaret McKean shows in chapter 9 below, economic equality in Japan tends to be higher than in many other industrialized countries, including France, Britain, and the United States.[13] A widely cited statistic notes that 90 percent of Japanese identify themselves as "middle class." Unemployment has typically been exceptionally low in postwar Japan.[14] A number of other statistics on access to health care, high average life spans, and low and declining crime rates all suggest that the issues dividing many societies into "haves" and "have nots" or "powerful" and "powerless," while by no means absent in Japan, are far less pervasive.

At the same time, rather systematic discrimination exists in housing, employment, and social interaction against several minority groups, most notably the offspring of Japan's traditional outcastes (Burakumin or untouchables), descendants of Chinese and Korean immigrants to Japan (most of whom were born in Japan but do not enjoy the benefits of nationality and citizenship), other foreigners who have become increasingly numerous with Japan's economic successes, the remnants of the Ainu tribes in the northern island of Hokkaidō, the physically handicapped, and others. Most discrimination, through by no means all, lacks foundation in law but is nonetheless real and stigmatizes significant portions of the population (see chapters 3 and 10 below); Most important, such groups have been granted no systematic means of political or legal protection.

More significant numerically is the systematic discrimination against Japanese women, largely in educational and occupational opportunities. (It is one of history's more peculiar ironies that the American Occupation imposed an Equal Rights Amendment on Japan some thirty-odd years before it even gained serious consideration—and was defeated—in U.S. politics.[15]) Women in Japan receive on average one-half the salaries of their male counterparts. In many cases, of course, this is a consequence of differences in job category and/or seniority, which in turn is related to the fact that Japanese women more typically than men leave the work force when their children are infants and younger school children.[16] But the nation's employment patterns are also rife with examples of overt salary and promotional discrimination against women.[17] In May 1985, in part to comply with United Nations' policies, the government passed an Equal Opportunity Act. It is too early to examine the impact of the law with any seriousness, but two brief points might be noted. First, the law provides no major legal sanctions to employers found to be in violation. To Western legal scholars it lacks the teeth of civil or criminal penalties. Second, despite this flaw, there seem initially to be signs of improvement in women's employment opportunities, particularly for professional women.[18]

A second component of citizens' rights relates to educational opportunities. If the democratic citizen is expected to make informed political choices, education and literacy are critical requisites. Japan has one of the most extensive educational systems in the industrialized world, as Edward Beauchamp indicates (see chapter 10). Nearly 40 percent of eighteen- to twenty-two-year-olds attend institutions of higher education in Japan, compared to 45 to 52 percent in the United States, 26 percent in both France and Germany, and about 21 percent in Great Britain. Moreover the education is meaningful: Japanese students score extremely well on comparative international examinations; there are few dropouts; most high school programs would be the equivalent of at least one or more years of college in the United States. Throughout the society as a whole, literacy is virtually 100 percent.

Numerous criticisms can be leveled at the Japanese educational system, however. For our purposes, three deserve special attention. First, many argue that Japanese schools put excessive weight on instilling conformity and not enough on developing individuality. This, it is said, is manifested in various ways, from school uniforms, dress codes, and tight behavioral standards, to the emphasis on standardized tests as the basis for entering good schools or the stress on rote memorization instead of more creative activities. Second, there is a good deal of criticism of the government's efforts to reintroduce "moral education" into the school curriculum. Prewar Japanese indoctrination into militarism and loyalty to the imperial system remains a vivid memory for many both in Japan and in the countries with which Japan was at war. This reemerges as a warning light signaling a "return to fascism" whenever such government proposals emerge. Finally, the rewriting of Japanese history, or the censorship of textbooks, has become a source of international friction with Japan's Asian neighbors (see chapter 10).[19]

These criticisms all relate to the issue of state control over education. In effect, is the student-citizen being "educated" or "indoctrinated"? Certainly within Japan the issue is highly volatile, typically with the political left most critical of recent state changes. At the same time, it is worth noting that even the Japan Teachers Union, which has historically been left of center, has also favored an increase in moral education, though there is strong disagreement on the content.[20] This would seem to be one area where some comparisons are most helpful. Although recent efforts by the government are designed to induce greater conservatism or nationalism among the student population, the Japanese system is still a long way from its prewar predecessor, or from the unilateral indoctrination found in many of the school systems of Eastern Europe, the Middle East or even China or South Korea, the latter being among the more virulent critics of Japanese policies.

It is also worth remembering that all nations seek to instill nationalism, patriotism, and loyalty through their school systems. One would be hard pressed to find a system in Western Europe or North America that was not replete with national anthems, heroes, and mythologized pasts. History is written by the victors of wars and elections. Thus, history of the British Empire is taught far differently in Essex than in Bombay or Nairobi; Mexican children hear a very different story about the origins of Texas, Arizona, and New Mexico than do those north of the Rio Grande. That the Japanese government is attempting to instill somewhat different principles in its socialization of Japanese youth may be disconcerting; it is by no means unusual or farfetched. On balance Japan's educational system is broadly democratizing in its effects. It has been a key channel in social mobility across generations, and it has provided extensive, though by no means unfettered, opportunities for Japanese youth to acquire the knowledge required to behave as informed citizens.

Finally, a third point on citizens' rights should be considered: the Japanese citizen is free to be nonpolitical. At first glance this may seem irrelevant to democracy, but an important component of a democratic political system is that the citizen is free to have a life *without* mobilization campaigns, police surveillance, forced service to state projects, and the like. George Orwell's 1984 was certainly participatory; it was not democratic. On balance, the Japanese citizen is today free *from* the state in important ways. The government collects taxes; all citizens (and foreign residents) must be registered; several radio and television stations are only semiautonomous from government; virtually all government and semigovernmental agencies engage in public relations activities designed to convince the citizen of the meritorious nature of their work; strict laws govern various aspects of social behavior from drunken driving to safety standards for drugs and toys to inheritance rights. But most Japanese citizens are free on a day-to-day basis to escape from politics and the state and to have families, pursue hobbies, engage in sports, buy a variety of consumer goods, work, socialize, and the like without government oversight or interference. In short, there is a relatively clear demarcation between "public" and "private" that allows the citizen a wide sphere of depoliticized activity.

Again, this is not an unalloyed benefit. The tax system, for example, is widely criticized as being a 9-6-4 system. This means that wage earners pay 90 percent of their allotted taxes, the self-employed pay only 60 percent and farmers pay only 40 percent. Even if the figures are inaccurate, there is little question but that the state intrudes differently on the pocketbooks of different classes of citizens. The system of family registration has been criticized as overly Orwellian as well as discriminatory against women and nonethnic Japanese; fingerprinting of foreign residents is seen by many as an infringement of civil liberties; the Japanese police seem to many to be far more intrusive than their counterparts in England or the United States. But most such criticisms are really at the margins. There are areas where the committed democrat could easily call for improvements in Japanese institutions, but few would challenge the proposition that the Japanese citizen is free of the omnipresent state found in authoritarian systems.

Translation Mechanisms—Between Citizen and State

If the first requisite of democracy involves the rights of citizens, the second is surely the need for mechanisms that permit citizens' preferences to be translated into political choices. Four sets of institutions require comment in this area: the media, interest groups, voting systems, and political parties.

Politically independent, competitive, and widely available mass media are critical to democracy. They allow citizens access to information on the basis of which they can form reasoned opinions on matters of government. Contemporary Japan has one of the world's highest rates of newspaper readership, with three national dailies blanketing the country twice a day (see chapter 3 below).

Books and magazines appealing to a wide range of tastes and opinion are also available and sell widely. Total publications well outnumber those in most European countries on an absolute basis; on a per capita basis, Japan is roughly on a par with the United States.[21] Radios and television sets are available to virtually all families, and the general dispersion rate is on a par with most other industrialized countries. Japanese radio and television stations represent a mixture of both publicly and privately owned. Foreign works are readily translated and read broadly. Government, politics, and social problems of all sorts are among the many subjects widely and diversely covered. Certainly there is no shortage of information available to most Japanese, nor are government actions free from outside oversight.

As Ellis Krauss indicates, some see a disturbing conformity in the Japanese press (see chapter 3).[22] Despite this, one can note the overall high quality of reporting, the critical character of most editorializing, and the actual diversity in nuance among even the most similar-seeming papers. Furthermore, a number of uncensored sources of analysis and scathing criticism are readily available beyond the mass circulation material frequently examined.

Some argue that the Japanese media are too deferential to those in power. The fact that Prime Minister Tanaka's questionable business dealings were not revealed by newspaper investigative reporting but by a free-lance journalist in a magazine is often cited as evidence of this. On the other hand, the media reported extensively on the later Lockheed scandal, leading ultimately to the arrest of the prime minister. They followed similar practices of investigative reporting of corrupt officials in many other instances, both before and after. Thus, from a comparative perspective, it would appear that the Japanese media play a vigorous role in overseeing government officials and in providing critical perspectives to citizens on important social, economic, and political issues.

Interest groups are a second important component linking citizens to government. Again, the Japanese situation seems vigorously democratic. Virtually any social interest that one could imagine is organized in Japan. Although many, particularly the major agricultural, business, and professional associations, retain close ties to government, most are also fiercely independent in the pursuit of their particular vision of the national interest. They organize widely, lobby lustily, endorse or oppose political candidates, and play a major role in the politics of the nation. Furthermore, their tactics cut across a wide spectrum of generally tolerated behavior. They organize petition drives; they make political contributions; they hold public informational meetings; they boycott shops and goods; they hand out leaflets; they march on political headquarters; and in some of the more extreme instances, they occupy buildings, hold sitdowns, harangue officials, and confront police. Because a good deal of attention has been given to many of these groups, a more detailed examination seems unnecessary.[23] Suffice to say, such groups in Japan, though often criticized for their selfishness, excessive influence, and steamroller tactics, among other things, testify in precisely such ways to their vigorous and independent participation in the democratic process.

The articulation of citizen preferences in the selection of government officials is somewhat more problematic in assessing Japanese democracy. The process involves both voting and political parties. All Japanese citizens over the age of twenty can vote; registration is handled automatically by various election boards; voting is not compulsory; in most elections turnout is comparatively high by international standards, typically involving between two-thirds and three-quarters of the eligible voters for local as well as national elections.[24]

In addition, citizens have a reasonably wide choice of candidates, if not in all town and village elections, many of which are uncontested, at least in most large city, prefectural, and national elections. Over the postwar period, Japan has had from a minimum of three[25] to a maximum of seven[26] political parties competing for national office. These range from the relatively conservative probusiness, proagricultural, and pro–United States Liberal Democratic party (LDP) through moderate and more radical socialist parties to a legal Communist party. In addition, some individuals run unaffiliated or as independents. Declaring one's candidacy is a relatively simple matter of making a small cash deposit which is returned if at least 5 percent of the vote is received. There is no minimum percentage of votes needed for a party to gain national representation, in contrast to Sweden or West Germany, hence it is possible for parties to gain national representation with little national support.

In contests for the House of Representatives, the voter typically has a choice of at least five or six and often as many as twelve or fourteen candidates. In the upper house, at least that many and usually more candidates compete for seats in the local constituencies, while for the national at-large seats a party-based system of proportional representation is used. (Chapters 3 and 5 below provide more details on the election system and the parties, and chapter 7 more on local government.)

For our purposes several points need to be considered. First, there is little question but that Japanese voters have available to them a wide range of choices among candidates, parties, and approaches to governance. The party and election systems provide a greater range of choice than in single-member district systems and/or two- or three-party systems such as those in Great Britain, Germany, Australia, New Zealand, Canada, or the United States. The range of choice is close to, if not greater than, that of almost any other democracy.

Second, while all electoral systems have peculiar biases for or against various types of parties, in the Japanese case, these discrepancies are relatively small. Essentially, the larger and the smaller parties both gain slightly more seats than the actual percentage of the vote they received, while the middle-sized parties tend to get fewer seats. In addition, Japan has its regular share of vote buying, election frauds, and unsavory tactics. However, these activities are not uncommon in other democratic countries, and they only rarely have a substantial impact on the turnout.

More important than these features of the electoral system are several other specific biases. Thus, the electoral districts for the House of Representatives are vastly imbalanced in terms of the weight given to voters in some districts and not others.[27] In this sense the Japanese electoral system is significantly less democratic than many others (though by no means all).

Moreover, in the system by which the House of Representatives and the local seats for the House of Councillors is decided, several candidates are returned from an individual district, but each citizen gets only one vote. The consequence is that a candidate needs only 20–25 percent of the vote to be successful. It is thus almost impossible for a moderately large bloc of discontented voters to cast their votes effectively *against* a candidate or a party. Even if they do not vote *for* the object of their hostility, their positive votes for a different party or candidate do not automatically become negative votes denied to the target of their opposition. Support from a relatively small bloc of voters within the district can still ensure that an individual or the party does well. The target of opposition may fall from being the number one or two vote-getter in a district to being the number five vote-getter, but he is still returned to office.

In a related vein, it is difficult for voters at the local level to react to national issues. This is most especially true for parties that run two or more candidates from the same district. Even if a substantial body of citizens loathes the party in question, or wishes to punish a government party deemed to have failed in some important respect, they can not vote simultaneously against all of the party's candidates as is the case in a list system of proportional voting or in a single-member district system.

These points by no means negate the overall contention that Japan is a tolerably well functioning democracy. But in its peculiar election system there are several features that do not accord well with more common presumptions about "one citizen, one vote" and the ability to depose officials with facility once they lose favor.

Institutions of Governance

From the previous sections, it is clear that, regardless of certain important qualifications, Japan provides a number of standard institutional guarantees of democracy as they relate to the free choice of governmental officials.

Japan's postwar constitution, as was noted above, radically overhauled both the national and local systems of government to make each far more democratic. Japan has a parliamentary system of government, one in which the cabinet is chosen, not directly by voters, but indirectly through the popularly elected parliament. So long as a cabinet enjoys the confidence of a parliamentary majority, it can remain in power, even though members of parliament must stand for regular election. On the other hand, unlike presidential systems, which require periodic elections of the chief executive, in parliamentary systems, once that confidence is lost the cabinet can be forced to resign immediately through a vote of no confidence. In this broad sense, Japanese institutions are certainly far more democratic than they were before the war and are very much in line with those of other parliamentary democracies.

Local legislative bodies and local executives are restricted by national laws and regulations concerning their spheres of authority. At the same time, Japan's Local Autonomy Law accords a wide range of activities to local government. Japanese local institutions lack the specific powers found in federal political systems such as the United States, Canada, West Germany, or Australia, but they have most or more of the powers found in centralized systems such as Sweden, France, or England.[28]

Japanese political institutions are thus not dramatically different from those in many other political democracies. Yet the simple selection of certain officials, while a prerequisite of democracy, leaves unanswered at least two further questions. First, just how much actual power do the elected officials have? If those subject to popular control are not in fact the political system's real decision makers, democracy is surely circumvented. And second, once in power, just how responsive are policymakers to public control? (In addition to my discussion, see chapters 3, 5, 6, and 7 below).

Despite its constitutional role as the "highest organ of state power," the real power of the Japanese parliament is a subject of long-standing debate. Clearly, it has not been the major architect of the bulk of Japan's laws. These have been drawn up primarily by the national bureaucracy, making it, as many have argued, a major source of unelected policymaking power.[29] The animated debate over the relative power and influence of Japan's parliament and its bureaucracy has stretched over several decades.[30] Three points seem worth special mention. First, as Ellis Krauss indicates in chapter 3, there can be no question that the bureaucracy has been technically and practically subject to the policymaking controls of parliament and the LDP. There is very little evidence that the bureaucracy has been systematically acting *against* their political wishes. Unlike the military, the *genrō*, or the prewar bureaucracy, the current bureaucracy is rarely capable of acting contrary to the majority of elected officials in parliament. If it is powerful, its power lies within the arena of preferences set by the parliamentary majority.

Second, there is a good deal of evidence to suggest that over the past decade or more the policymaking influence of elected officials vis-à-vis bureaucrats has been on the rise.[31]

Third, even if the Japanese bureaucracy exercises a good deal of influence over policy formation, its influence is not significantly greater than in other parliamentary democracies where, unlike the United States, the civil service is immune to changes in the executive.

The same is true in Great Britain, France, Sweden, and most European parliamentary systems, and in all of these countries much the same debate, and relative balance, seems to prevail.

On balance, therefore, Japanese governmental institutions are weighted to ensure popularly elected officials a strong and predominant voice in policymaking comparable to other democracies.

Electoral mechanisms and voting rights play the principal role in ensuring institutional responsiveness, and as shown above, in Japan, these provide high degrees of responsiveness, though not without major qualifications. Beyond the electoral mechanisms, however, Japanese policy formation also demonstrates a relatively high degree of governmental responsiveness. Interest groups, as noted, play a big role in influencing public policy choices by officials, including non-elected civil servants.[32] And though surely they would wish to have more, opposition parties in parliament also exert considerable influence over many aspects of governance (see, for example, chapter 5 below).

Beyond regular elections, however, responsiveness can perhaps best be judged by the effectiveness of the various citizens' movements that have developed in response to environmental pollution, consumers' issues, and taxation. For the most part these movements sprang up when existing political institutions failed to deal adequately with pressing issues of concern to large numbers of citizens.[33] Using public protest, the court system, the powers of local governments, the media, and other means, such movments effectively forced an otherwise nonresponsive national government to act on their demands (see chapter 8). Such tactics by no means guarantee immediate victory for any discontented group in Japan; however, the relative success of the citizens' movements speaks volumes in favor of the ability of the citizen to squeeze responsiveness from the system.

Conclusion

Adlai Stevenson in a 1952 speech once said to a Chicago audience: "As citizens of this democracy, you are the rulers and the ruled, the lawgivers and the law-abiding, the beginning and the end." Certainly a modicum of idealism lay behind the words. Few analysts, including the most die-hard admirers of America, would be so congratulatory about the state of democracy in the United States. Yet if one recognizes that democratic realities are not quite so simple in practice as they are in the ideal, the words contain a strong ring of accuracy about the American system.

To the extent that Stevenson was correct about the United States, would his words be equally applicable to Japan? The above analysis has sought to show that in many of the most important respects, Japanese democracy is on a par with that in most other industrialized democracies in Western Europe, North America, and Australasia. It certainly has the same right as any of them to be included in the broad category of "democracies." At the same time, just as is true of all the others in the category, there are many specific areas where Japanese democracy could be improved.

NOTES

1. As quoted in Dorothy Pickles, *Democracy* (New York: Basic Books, 1970), p. 11.

2. Some of the debate over the term and its historical evolution and contemporary usage can be captured in Pickles, *Democracy;* Giovanni Sartori, *Democratic Theory* (East Lansing, Mich.: Wayne State University Press, 1962); M. Rejai, *Democracy—The Contemporary Theories* (New York: Atherton, 1967); Robert A. Dahl, *Polyarchy* (New Haven, Conn.: Yale University Press, 1971).

3. This set of categories is based on Dahl, *Polyarchy,* pp. 2–3.

4. Ibid.

5. Many critics note shortcomings in Japan's democracy, but typically they do so with no reference to other functioning political systems. See, e.g., Gavan McCormack and Yoshio Sugimoto, eds., *Democracy in Contemporary Japan* (Armonk, N.Y.: M. E. Sharpe, 1986). In fairness, McCormack and Sugimoto's treatment of democracy in Japan rests heavily on the normative and moral fulfillment of humanity, rather than on specific institutional arrangements (see esp. p. 10). And in this regard, they find the Japanese political system wanting.

6. W. G. Beasley, *The Meiji Restoration* (Stanford, Calif.: Stanford University Press, 1971), chaps. 12, 13. Particularly useful for understanding official thinking behind the constitution is Hirobumi Ito, *Commentaries on the Constitution of Imperial Japan* (Tokyo: Government Printing Office, 1889).

7. Japan was not dramatically different in this regard from many other later modernizing countries where military coups, labor union strikes, business or

financial boycotts, religious interventions, and/or foreign or international organizations, as well as popular elections, all have the potential to create or destabilize governments. Elections themselves are but one political currency among many. Until elections become the sole basis for the creation and toppling of governments, it is difficult to credit a country with being a democracy. On this point as it affects Latin America, see Charles A. Anderson, *Political and Economic Change in Latin America* (Chicago: Van Nostrand, 1967), chap. 4.

8. T. J. Pempel, "Uneasy Towards Autonomy: Parliament and Parliamentarians in Japan," in *Parliaments and Parliamentarians in Democratic Politics,* ed. Ezra Suleiman (New York: Holmes and Meier, 1986), pp. 106–53. See also Chalmers Johnson, "Japan, Who Governs? An Essay on Official Bureaucracy," *Journal of Japanese Studies* 2 (1975): 1–28, and chap. 5 below.

9. On the limits to labor unions see especially Andrew Gordon, *The Evolution of Labor Relations in Japan* (Cambridge, Mass.: Harvard University Press, 1985): Sheldon Garon, *The State and Labor in Modern Japan* (Berkeley and Los Angeles: University of California Press, 1987). On the political parties, see also Robert A. Scalapino, *Democracy and the Party Movement in Prewar Japan* (Berkeley and Los Angeles: University of California Press, 1953); Peter Duus, *Party Rivalry and Political Change in Taisho Japan* (Cambridge, Mass.: Harvard University Press, 1968); Gordon Mark Berger, *Parties Out of Power in Japan, 1931–1941* (Princeton, N.J.: Princeton University Press, 1977). On the media, see Gregory Kasza, *The State and the Mass Media in Japan, 1868–1945* (Berkeley and Los Angeles: University of California Press, 1988).

10. As quoted in Yosiyuki Noda, *Introduction to Japanese Law* (Tokyo: University of Tokyo Press, 1976), p. 98.

11. Analysis of the U.S. Occupation of Japan has been extensive. See especially Robert A. Ward and Yoshikazu Sakamoto, eds., *Democratizing Japan: The Allied Occupation* (Honolulu: University of Hawaii Press, 1987). An extensive bibliography on the Occupation is Robert A. Ward and Joseph Shulman, eds., *The Allied Occupation: An Annotated Bibliography of Western Language Materials* (Chicago: American Library Association, 1974).

12. Much of the early U.S. thinking on how Japan should be politically structured can be found in Government Section, Supreme Command of the Allied Powers (SCAP), *Political Reorientation of Japan* (Washington, D.C.: Government Printing Office, 1950).

13. See Sidney Verba et al., *Elites and the Idea of Equality* (Cambridge, Mass.: Harvard University Press, 1987). Also T. J. Pempel, "Japan's Creative Conservatism: Continuity Under Challenge," in *The Comparative History of Public Policy,* ed. Francis Castles (London: Polity Press, 1988).

14. An interesting argument on cross-national unemployment policies is found in Goran Therborn, *Why Are Some Peoples More Unemployed Than Others?* (London: Verso, 1985). Although there is controversy over Japan's official unemployment figure, there is still little question but that even if understated, Japan's unemployment rates are still quite low by international standards.

15. See Susan J. Pharr, "The Politics of Women's Rights," in Ward and Sakamoto, *Democratizing Japan,* pp. 221–52. Yet the reality is described by Beauchamp in chap. 10 of this volume: compared to their male counterparts, fewer women go on to four-year universities (many more go to junior colleges), and they face massive employment discrimination.

16. Among advanced industrial nations, Japan also shows an increase in the male-female wage differential over the ten years, 1972–82, although if one controls for education, length of service, age, and employment status, women in Japan do much better. Frank K. Upham, *Law and Social Change in Postwar Japan* (Cambridge, Mass.: Harvard University Press, 1987), pp. 126, 138.

17. One of the more interesting manifestations of this pattern took place when a Japanese multinational company based in the United States followed its domestic hiring patterns and systematically discriminated against American female employees. When employees brought suit under U.S. antidiscrimination laws the company defense was that it was *entitled* to discriminate in keeping with practices within Japan. U.S. courts ruled that its employment patterns had to comply with U.S. law, and hence could not be sexually discriminatory.

18. Upham, *Law and Social Change,* chap. 4.

19. In addition to Beauchamp's essay below (chap. 10), one can also get some of the flavor of this debate over content in the textbook by Ienaga Saburo entitled *Taiheiyō Sensō* and translated into English by Frank Baldwin as *The Pacific War* (New York: Pantheon, 1978). The book includes a discussion of some of the passages specifically objected to in Ienaga's book by the Ministry of Education.

20. William K. Cummings, *Education and Equality in Japan* (Princeton, N.J.: Princeton University Press, 1980), pp. 115–18; Robert J. Smith, *Japanese Society* (Cambridge: Cambridge University Press, 1983), pp. 121–22.

21. Kokuseisha, *Nihon no Hyakunen* (Tokyo: Kokuseisha, 1981) p. 330, and *Nihon no Kokusei Zue, 1984* (Tokyo: Kokuseisha, 1984), p. 476. In publications Japan ranks fourth in the world behind the United States, the Soviet Union, and Germany.

22. See Nathaniel B. Thayer, "Competition and Conformity: An Inquiry into the Structures of Japanese Newspapers," in *Modern Japanese Organization and*

Decision Making, ed. Ezra Vogel (Berkeley and Los Angeles: University of California Press, 1975).

23. One of the more important new studies is Muramatsu Michio et al., *Sengo Nihon no Atsuryoku Dantai* (Tokyo: Toyo Keizai, 1986).

24. This compares favorably to figures in noncompulsory democracies.

25. In 1955, the Liberal and Democratic parties merged to form the Liberal Democratic party, following the earlier merger of the two wings of the socialist movement to form the Japan Socialist party. These two were joined by the Japan Communist party.

26. In the early 1980s, the LDP, the JSP, and the JCP faced competition from the Democratic Socialist party, the Clean Government party, the New Liberal Club, and the Socialist Democratic Federation.

27. See chaps. 3 and 5 below, and T. J. Pempel, *Policy and Politics in Japan: Creative Conservatism* (Philadelphia: Temple University Press, 1982), p. 38.

28. This point has been subject to a good deal of debate and analysis both in the English and Japanese language research. Among the more insightful works in English see Terry E. MacDougall, "Political Opposition and Local Government in Japan," Ph.D. thesis, Yale University, 1975; Kurt Steiner et al., *Political Opposition and Local Politics in Japan* (Princeton, N.J.: Princeton University Press, 1980); Richard J. Samuels, *The Politics of Regional Policy in Japan: Localities Incorporated?* (Princeton, N.J.: Princeton University Press, 1983).

29. I have made such an argument at greater length in several places. See T. J. Pempel, "The Bureaucratization of Policymaking in Contemporary Japan," *American Journal of Political Science* 18 (November 1974): 647–74; and "Uneasy Toward Autonomy." See also Johnson, "Japan, Who Governs?" and chap. 6 below.

30. See Pempel, "Bureaucratization of Policymaking," and "Uneasy Toward Autonomy"; Ellis Krauss and Michio Muramatsu, "Bureaucrats and Politicians in Policymaking: The Case of Japan," *American Political Science Review* 78 (1984); Michio Muramatsu and Ellis Krauss, "The Conservative Policy Line and the Development of Patterned Pluralism," in *The Political Economy of Japan,* vol. 1: *The Domestic Transformation,* ed. Kozo Yamamura and Yasukichi Yasuba (Stanford, Calif.: Stanford University Press, 1987), pp. 516–34.

31. Krauss and Muramatsu, "Bureaucrats and Politicians"; Muramatsu and Krauss, "Conservative Party Line"; Inoguchi Takashi, *Gendai Nihon Seiji Keizai no Kōzō* (Tokyo: Tōyō Keizai, 1983); John C. Campbell, "Policy Conflict and Its Resolution with the Governmental System," in *Conflict in Japan,* ed. Ellis Krauss et al. (Honolulu: University of Hawaii Press, 1984);

Seizaburo Satō and Tetsuhisa Matsuzaki, *Jimintō Seiken* (Tokyo: Chūō Kōronsha, 1986).

32. See Muramatsu and Krauss, "Conservative Party Line," and also Muramatsu, *Sengo Nihon no Atsuryoku Dantai,* both of which show the extent to which interest groups claim relatively high degrees of satisfaction with their ability to exert influence over lawmaking and the creation of bureaucratic regulations.

33. See especially Margaret A. McKean, *Environmental Protest and Citizen Politics in Japan* (Berkeley and Los Angeles: University of California Press, 1981); also Upham, *Law and Social Change,* chap. 2.

3 Politics and the Policymaking Process

●

ELLIS S. KRAUSS

In the preceding chapter, T. J. Pempel has outlined the social and political institutions that support Japan's democratic system. To understand the specific aspects of Japanese democracy discussed below, this chapter provides further background on the structure of the postwar Japanese government and the process of politics and policymaking.

The National Diet and Elections

The American-inspired postwar constitution of Japan designated the Diet (parliament) as the "highest organ of state power" in order to make clear that ultimate political responsibility rested with a popularly elected legislature, rather than with the emperor or with a cabinet not responsible to parliament as in the prewar period. The Diet's actual political role, however, has been more modest than this elevated constitutional phrase might indicate. Because of the perpetual dominance of one party in power in a parliamentary system and the role of the bureaucracy in postwar Japanese politics, as I describe below, the Diet's political functions often have been more formal than real; it has ratified policy rather than initiated it. Nevertheless, the Diet remains the formal promulgator of law and the arena for political debate and conflict, and its members, at the preparliamentary stage if not in the formal legislative process, play important roles in representing the people and creating public policy. It is therefore important to understand the nature and structure of this institution.

There are two houses in the Diet, an "upper house," the House of Councillors, and a "lower house," the House of Representatives. The House of Councillors has 252 members elected for six-year terms, with half the body coming up for reelection every three years. One of the rather interesting aspects of this chamber is that 100 of its members are elected at-large, that is, by the nation as a whole rather than by local districts. Until recently, this was accomplished by listing all the candidates on a ballot, giving each voter one vote, and declaring the top 50 vote-getters to be elected (only half were chosen in each third-year election). Under this system, naturally, people with nationwide visibility and reputations, or those with national networks of organizations behind them, had a distinct advantage. As a result, many councillors were media personalities—what the Japanese call *tarento* or "talent"—actors and actresses, television anchormen, and so forth, or key leaders of agricultural, labor, or other interest groups that could mobilize their members nationwide.

In 1983, however, this system was changed to one of proportional representation similar to that used by many Western European democracies. Political parties choose candidates and list them in a rank order prior to the election; the voter votes for one of the parties. Each party is then awarded a certain number of seats roughly proportional to the percentage of votes it received, and the candidates on its list up to the awarded number of seats are elected. It was hoped that this new system would reduce the financial costs of elections by permitting parties to run coordinated campaigns for all their candidates instead of costly nationwide individual "personality" campaigns. It was also hoped that the parties would pick candidates with "serious" backgrounds. At the very least, this new system should strengthen the role of the major political parties in the upper house where their representation and discipline had been somewhat looser than in the lower house (see chapter 5 below).

The relationship between the House of Councillors and the House of Representatives has certain similarities with both the British and U.S. systems. The House of Councillors, like the Senate in the United States, but unlike the British House of Lords, has substantial formal legislative powers. Unlike Congress, however, and more like the British Parliament, the lower House of Representatives in fact is the more important body. Procedurally, it has constitutional priority over budgets and treaties and can override a decision by the House of Councillors regarding a bill or the selection of a prime minister. Politically, most cabinet ministers have come from the ranks of representatives rather than of councillors, and the smaller districts from which representatives are elected put them closer to the voters' practical concerns and attention.

The House of Representatives now consists of 512 members. As in other parliamentary democracies, general elections are held when the prime minister dissolves the Diet and calls a new election, but constitutionally at least once every four years. Historically, general elections have been called on average every two to three years.

The occupational background of representatives differs from the pattern found in some Western democracies, including the United States, in that there are few lawyers. The greatest number of representatives are former local politicians or former bureaucrats (in the case of the governing party, about a quarter of each, respectively). This does not mean the absence of legal expertise, however. Local politicians gain experience in their local legislatures, and bureaucrats are legal experts by virtue of their undergraduate education (usually by majoring in law) and experience in formulating bills (see below). Businessmen and journalists are also found in the lower house.

In the socialist parties, which are supported by union federations, former trade union leaders are well represented. A recent trend, especially in the Liberal Democratic party (LDP), is the increasing number of relatives (sons, sons-in-law, nephews, etc.) or aides who have "inherited" the seats of former Diet members. Women are greatly underrepresented, occupying only a bit more than 3 percent of both chambers (most in the upper house), a percentage about the same as in the British House of Commons or the U.S. House of Representatives in the mid-1970s, but significantly below the percentage found in West Germany's lower house and Canada's Parliament. This percentage would be even lower were it not for the Japan Communist party (JCP) which makes a greater effort than the other parties to recruit women candidates to the Diet, particularly to the lower house. For example, in 1985, of the eight female members of the lower house, five were JCP representatives and none were LDP; in the House of Councillors, five of the nineteen women were Communist representatives, with seven from the ruling party (LDP).

Elections to the House of Representatives

Japan has an election system for its lower house which is unlike that of any other major Western democracy, but is similar to its prewar system: a "multimember" district system. From two to six, but usually three to five, representatives are elected from each local electoral district. Since the number of seats in each district is supposed to be apportioned according to population, the massive urbanization of postwar Japan should therefore have resulted in large-scale changes in the number of apportioned seats and/or the drawing of district boundaries. But because the conservative LDP, the governing party since its formation in 1955, has stronger support in rural than in urban areas, no major reform has taken place. Consequently, malapportionment has been severe. In the worst cases, it has taken four or five times as many votes to elect a representative in an urban district than in a rural district.

The media constantly and vociferously call attention to this political inequality that makes one citizen's vote worth less than another's, and there has been a string of court cases challenging the electoral system. The Supreme Court, however, has thus far failed to support a "one-man, one-vote" ruling, as in the famous *Baker v. Carr* decision in the United States. Although it has declared inequalities in some extreme cases to be unconstitutional, it has supported their constitutionality in other less extreme but still substantial cases. In no case, however, has it required a new election as a result of inequalities nor has it ordered the Diet to thoroughly revise the entire system.

The ruling party, when pressured by the courts, the media, or the public, has made certain changes. It has raised the total number of Diet seats by adding a few to the most densely populated urban districts, but without substantially subtracting seats from the rural districts, as occurred in 1976. In response to a 1985 Supreme Court ruling that the 1983 election was unconstitutional due to the imbalance of seats, the party added eight seats to urban districts and substracted seven from rural ones. This reform still leaves the most underrepresented urban districts with about one-third the representation of the most overrepresented rural constituencies, a ratio the Supreme Court seems willing to tolerate. Thus redress of this problem has ranged from marginal to only slightly better, leaving the basic inequalities intact.

The political implications of redistricting are at the heart of the lack of action: a Japanese newspaper once calculated that if the lower house had been fairly apportioned in the mid-1970s, the ruling LDP would have lost twenty-seven seats, and the largest opposition party, the Japan Socialist party (JSP), would have lost seven, these going to the smaller, urban-based opposition parties. With both the governing majority party and its chief opposition party in the Diet standing to lose by fair reapportionment, and with the Supreme Court unwilling to force a wholesale reform, the reasons for the continuation of this democratic inequality are obvious.

The system of multimember districts has further consequences for how the public's representatives are chosen and who they are. A large party with substantial popular support, like the LDP, runs more than one candidate in many districts. Thus two or more conservative candidates may run against each other, competing for the support of conservative and independent voters. In this situation, the voters focus on the person, not on the party, and election campaigning revolves more around the individual—his personality and what he can do for the district—than on the party or its ideology or policies (much as in American primary elections). Identification with political parties is weak, and a higher percentage of people than in many other democracies vote for the individual instead of the party. One study of this phenomenon concluded, however, that "if the electoral system were changed, voting on the basis of candidate in national elections should recede overnight to about one-third of the population, a level similar to candidate-based voting in other nations."[1] A major study of voting in Japan also indicates that while strong party identification may be lower than in other industrialized democracies, "party image," a somewhat vaguer orientation toward political parties, is an important determinant of the vote.[2]

Vote mobilization is carried out by the candidates themselves rather than by party organizations. The LDP lacks a mass organization at the grass-roots level. Even if it had such an organization the party would have to remain out of the process in districts where it had more than one candidate—or support all candidates equally. Left on their own to get out the vote, candidates form *kōenkai,* personal support organizations, to help them win elections. The leadership of the *kōenkai* consists of the Diet candidate, his aides, and allied local politicians in his district, but it is also a mass membership organization of constituents that stays in existence even between elections. For a nominal fee, individuals are enrolled as members. The *kōenkai* usually sponsors numerous social and recreational activities for its members and keeps the candidate salient to them by such activities as mailing them New Year's calendars and inviting him to give speeches. *Kōenkai* staff also serve as conduits of requests to the candidate for favors and aid. Thus when election time rolls around, the candidate has a built-in campaign organization that can be mobilized on his behalf.[3] The *kōenkai* may be said to take the place of the local party organization or the temporarily mobilized volunteer organization of American elections but to bear some resemblance to the vote mobilization of the old-fashioned political machine.

Campaign funds for LDP candidates come from various sources. Again, the competition among LDP candidates in the same district means an equitable distribution of party funds to each. Candidates must supplement these with funds from other sources, and of course each candidate tries to gain an advantage over his party rival(s) in the district by raising more money. One source is the businesses and other interest groups who support candidates. Another is leaders of LDP factions (see below) who, in return for loyalty and support in their pursuit of the party presidency (and thus the prime ministership), help the politican running for the Diet get party endorsement and also give him campaign funds for his race. Thus the electoral system and the competition among LDP candidates in the same district also contribute to the factionalism of the LDP.[4]

Opposition parties' candidates often also form *kōenkai* to help them get elected, but rely to a greater extent than LDP candidates on grass-roots party organization or on activists affiliated with supporting interest groups. The JSP, for example, relies heavily on union activists and the campaign contributions of its supporting trade-union federation.

A final point about election campaigns for the Diet is the strictness of campaign regulations: much of what is taken for granted in the United States as integral to a campaign, such as door-to-door voter canvassing, is illegal in Japan. The American Occupation, afraid of the potential for manipulation of the individual in Japan's "group culture," forbade such practices and gave the Japanese strict rules about the conduct of campaigns, which are still in effect. The number and location of election posters is strictly regulated, for example, as are the number of sound trucks a candidate may use. No campaigning is allowed prior to the officially declared campaign which lasts only one month.

Those who believe that the seemingly never-ending election campaigns in the United States promote voter apathy, or who have visited Japan during an election and found even the limited number of sound cars to be a major form of noise pollution, may feel these restrictions should be applauded. Because they are so strict, however, they are frequently sidestepped by the aides or supporters of the candidates. For example, a future candidate may speak prior to the actual beginning of the campaign as an educational rather than political activity, advertising the speech with picture posters, or campaign workers may go to the door of a voter's house during a campaign and ask the resident to step outside for a chat before raising the subject of the election campaign. Outright violations of the regulations are not uncommon either. A general election usually winds up with the police arresting about a thousand people on election violations, and this is probably but a small number of the actual violations. Combined with the widespread practice of not reporting much of the money received and spent by candidates, a case could be made that these strict, "clean" election regulations may actually contribute to a cynicism toward democratic elections by setting unenforceable standards of campaign behavior.

The mass media do not play as large a role in Japanese elections as in the United States. Political advertising was permitted on television for the first time in the 1969 election, but it is strictly regulated by a law which allows only a limited number of fixed time commercials, and these are allocated equally to the parties and candidates. The ads are paid for by public funds. Consequently, candidates with more campaign funds cannot use them to gain an advantage over their rivals.

The Prime Minister and the Cabinet

Legally, the prime minister of Japan has powers and limitations similar to leaders of other parliamentary democracies. He is the chief executive elected by members of the Diet (but in case of disagreement between the two houses, the decision of the House of Representatives is the determining vote). He has the power to dissolve the House of Representatives and call an election and to select the cabinet, without having to have his choices confirmed by the Diet. Within the prime minister's office, further, are located various agencies, ranging from relatively insignificant information gathering ones such as the Statistics Agency to more important ones such as the Economic Planning Agency and the Defense Agency.

The prime minister, his cabinet, or an individual minister is responsible to the Diet through the device of "no confidence" resolutions; a successful vote necessitates within ten days either the calling of a new election or the resignation of the cabinet. In addition, to avoid the prewar situation in which prime ministers or cabinet ministers were military or ex-military men, the prime minister and a majority of the cabinet, must be Diet members, and all must be civilians. The prime minister's chief aide is the chief cabinet secretary, who serves as something equivalent to a combination of head of the White House staff, chief press secretary, liaison to the party, and political advisor.

The major limitations on the otherwise legally powerful office of prime minister are political, not constitutional. It is the way the prime minister is selected and the nature of the perpetually ruling LDP that limit the power of the office. No politician can become prime minister unless he is a leader of one of the major factions in the party and forms alliances with other faction leaders. The prevalence of factionalism in the party has many origins, including the multimember district electoral system which encourages members of the same party to run against each other and to give loyalty to a faction leader in exchange for support at election time. But as Nathaniel Thayer has pointed out, perhaps the chief cause of factionalism is the way in which the prime minister has been selected.[5]

After the formation of the LDP in 1955, the president of the party, who would now be certain to be confirmed as prime minister since the party controlled a majority of seats in the Diet, was chosen by a party convention of Diet members as well as two representatives from each prefectural chapter of the LDP. In order to guarantee the loyalty and vote of the Diet members at that convention, organized factions gradually formed around key leaders of the party and contenders for the prime ministership. A politician who wanted LDP endorsement to run for the Diet or to serve in the cabinet could not do so without joining a faction once he became a representative, and thus most LDP Diet members eventually became members of a faction. Factions came to be organized hierarchically, with the faction leader and his lieutenants at the top and the position of faction followers being greatly determined by seniority (not so much by age as by the number of times the person was elected to the Diet and when he or she joined the faction). When a faction leader retires or dies, usually one of his senior lieutenants succeeds him.

For most of the postwar period there have been five major factional lineages, as well as a number of smaller ones from time to time. No single faction has ever had a majority of Diet members by itself, and therefore faction leaders must form alliances and gain the support of other factions in order to win the party presidency and thus the prime ministership. Takeshita Noboru, who became prime minister in November 1987, was the leader of the largest faction; his predecessor, Nakasone Yasuhiro, led one of the smaller factions, but was supported by two of the larger factions. As Michael Leiserson has noted, the LDP in this respect really resembles a "coalition government" except that the only parties that have a chance of joining the coalition are the factions within the LDP.[6]

Factions have been widely criticized on many grounds. They are said to weaken the unity of the party and thus hurt the LDP's image with the voters; to breed corruption and the financial dependence of the party on big business (the faction leader needs a great deal of money to get his followers elected and thus increase his chances of becoming the prime minister); and to undermine the power and stability of the prime minister's office.[7]

Efforts have been made at reform, most especially during the mid to late 1970s. The resignation of Prime Minister Tanaka over allegedly unusual dealings involving his business career, and the subsequent Lockheed scandal in which he was accused of having accepted a bribe, focused public and media attention on the problems of corruption and the LDP political leadership, including the evils of factionalism. At one point, factions were even declared to be "abolished," although this proved to be but a temporary and doomed exercise in reform.

Most important, the LDP finally revised the procedures by which the party president was selected and put these into effect for the first time in the 1978 party presidential contest. The reform created a two-stage selection process. The first stage was essentially a party primary election involving a complicated voting system but in which all LDP members and "associate members" were entitled to participate. The top two vote-getters from that party "primary" would then engage in a "run-off" vote only among LDP Diet members with the winner becoming party president. In its first test, hundreds of thousands of new members joined the party to be able to participate in the voting, and the new system caused a stunning upset: incumbent Prime Minister Fukuda, a strong supporter of the reform, came in second to the then-party secretary-general Ohira, and Fukuda decided not even to compete in the run-off but to allow Ohira to succeed him.

The revised system, however, did not succeed in eliminating factions; it merely extended them to the grass roots of the party and "massified" them. Ohira beat Fukuda because former prime minister Tanaka's faction, with whom Ohira had an alliance, mobilized its political machine to register party members and get out the vote for Ohira. Furthermore, after this first experiment, the system was modified to provide that the "primary" stage would only be used if there were four or more candidates for party president. If there are three or less, then only the LDP Diet members select the winner, essentially making factional coalitions again the determining factor in who becomes party president and thus prime minister. Factions therefore remain the core of the process by which Japan's chief leader is chosen.

Because factions are based on personal loyalty and political self-interest, distinctions among the factions usually are not significant in deciding policy matters (although there have been some exceptions). But factions are crucial in other respects. First, the coalitions and relations among them obviously determine who becomes prime minister. Second, the necessity to make political deals and gain the support of other faction leaders in order to win office limits the independence of the prime minister. He must always consult and reach agreement with his allies and their factions lest he jeopardize his majority coalition within the party. Despite the inherent powers of his office, therefore, the prime minister politically is like the head of a rather collective leadership. Furthermore, the factions that were not part of the coalition that put him in office are constantly trying to maneuver against him, criticize him, and create an opportunity for one of their own leaders to take his place. For these reasons, although it is something of an exaggeration, some LDP politicians and students of Japanese politics say that the real limitations on the ruling party and the most effective "opposition" in the Japanese system comes from *within* the LDP, rather than from the other parties. Factions thus provide a check on monolithic power, partially substituting for the lack of alternation of parties in government.

Finally, factions are important because they have a great deal of influence on who is selected for the cabinet. The cabinet consists of about twenty people: the heads of the twelve ministries and eight other ministers who are usually given posts as heads of some of the various agencies in the prime minister's office. There is no real difference between the heads of ministries and the heads of agencies—all are considered of cabinet rank.

The ultimate aim of most Diet members is to attain that rank, where a post provides prestige and the opportunity to do something for one's constituency. Here, too, factions are important if not decisive. When the new prime minister forms his cabinet, one of the primary considerations in the distribution of portfolios is factional politics. Cabinet positions are used to reward a few members of one's own faction, and they provide another incentive for faction members to remain loyal and work hard for their leader through the years. But more important, they also are used to reward the leaders of factions that supported the prime minister in his successful bid to capture the prize and may also be seen as a "down payment" on continued support in the next race. In effect, cabinet posts are an integral part of the exchange relationship within factions and among the factional coalitions.

A wise prime minister will also distribute a few posts in his cabinet even to the factions that opposed his candidacy. Such largesse may help to convince enemy factions to switch sides next time and in the interim may help to mitigate their maneouvering and dampen their criticism. After all, it is hard for factions to criticize the actions of a cabinet in which they hold office. The art of cabinet-making in Japan consists of being able to distribute just the right number and type of posts to satisfy one's factional allies, one's own faction, and opposing factions in the party.[8]

If factional balance is so important in who gets a cabinet post, then one may wonder how qualified Japan's cabinet ministers are to govern the country and preside over the specialized ministries they head. The truth is that some may not be "qualified" in the narrow sense of having detailed expertise in a particular policy area. But some are, perhaps being senior Diet politicians with long careers on Diet and party committees in that area. Expertise is not as necessary for a cabinet post in the Japanese system where, as we shall see below, a highly skilled career bureaucracy can manage the details of administration and policy. The job of a cabinet minister has less to do with detailed administration and policymaking than it does with approving bills that are hammered out in the party and bureaucracy, representing the interest and view of one's ministry vis-à-vis the other agencies of government, and managing conflicts that arise within the party and the government. For these tasks, the skills of a senior politician are more useful than those of a technocrat.

Even if the cabinet member wanted to learn the details of administration of his ministry or agency, he would hardly have time. Cabinets are typically shuffled by the prime minister about once a year (he doesn't need the approval of the Diet for cabinet appointments). This frequent shuffling gives the prime minister that many more posts at his disposal during his tenure in office to distribute as part of the factional game. It also allows that many more LDP Diet members to take their turn in the cabinet, a not unimportant means of providing incentive to them to continue to do their best for the party and their factions. The rapid turnover of cabinet ministers has allowed a large number of LDP Diet members in the postwar period to be part of the government.

Bureaucracy and Parties in Policymaking

Party factions are a common phenomenon in many democracies, although the Japanese version certainly has its unique aspects. This is also true of the bureaucracy. In modern democratic societies, the expertise of bureaucracies has become a usual and indispensable part of the process by which policy is made and implemented. But the role of the Japanese bureaucracy may be especially prominent. Its influence in policymaking will seem surprising to Americans, but rather more familiar to Europeans, where bureaucracies often play a more active and consequential part in the decisionmaking process.

The Japanese government bureaucracy consists of twelve ministries and various agencies (many of them technically part of the prime minister's office), organized along functional lines. Thus, there is a Ministry of Finance; of International Trade and Industry; of Labor; of Construction; of Transportation; of Foreign Affairs; of Agriculture, Forestry, and Fisheries; of Education; of Health and Welfare; of Posts (which also has jurisdiction over much of telecommunications); and of Local Autonomy (local government).

All together, there are about half a million central government employees, of which over a fifth are connected to the Ministry of Education. The size of the central and local bureaucracies in Japan is the *smallest* per population of the democracies in the industrialized world, with 45 government employees for every 1,000 citizens, compared to 77.5 in the United States, 74.4 in West Germany, and 104 in England.[9]

There are generally two types of government bureaucrats, the higher civil service and technical (*gikan*) bureaucrats. Generally, it is the higher civil service that has the most prestige and the most influence on policy. As John Campbell points out (see chapter 6 below), higher civil servants are an elite group, accorded high status (but not very high pay), and are recruited disproportionately from the nation's most prestigious university, Tokyo University, particularly the Faculty of Law. Of the over 50,000 persons who take the higher civil service exam each year, only about 1,300 pass. Thus, the Japanese bureaucracy can truly be said to comprise many of the "best and the brightest" in Japan.

The bureaucracy plays two major roles in policy in Japan: policymaking and policy implementation. It is in the latter role that the Japanese bureaucracy has become famous in the West, particularly for its practice of "administrative guidance" (*gyōsei shidō*). Administrative guidance is a general term that encompasses formal and informal methods of implementing policy, from the issuing of formal administrative ordinances that have the force of law, to informal communications that attempt to persuade social groups to go along voluntarily with a policy.

These practices have become an issue of much controversy in the case of "industrial policy," in which some have argued that the Ministry of International Trade and Industry's administrative guidance has been responsible for selecting the industrial sectors with the most competitive futures and helping them to achieve that potential.[10] The extent to which this practice occurred, how it occurred, and how much it was responsible for Japan's economic growth is a matter of much debate among Japanese specialists and economists. For our purposes, we should only note that in all countries bureaucrats have to interpret general laws and policy guidelines and use various means to enforce their interpretations. And although it may be true that in Japan bureaucracies have more discretion in implementing laws than in countries like the United States, compliance with administrative guidance often succeeds in Japan either because it is in the best interests of the group anyway or because they trust the bureaucrats in the long run to mitigate any great hardships the group incurs as a result of "going along."

The bureaucracy's role in policymaking is less well known in the West, but perhaps more important. The policymaking and legislative process usually *begins* in the bureaucracy in Japan, with most government-sponsored legislation being formulated by the bureaucrats. A proposal would then go to the LDP's Policy Affairs Research Council (PARC) and its myriad divisions, subdivisions, and committees for discussion, review, modification, and approval by the Diet members of the LDP. During these party deliberations on policy, bureaucrats often participate by informal communication to the politicians and even by appearing at PARC meetings to discuss the policy. This unusually close relationship of a government bureaucracy with a political party's internal decision-making process is undoubtably the result of the long rule of the LDP.

If PARC approves a proposal, it would then go to the higher executives of the LDP for approval and finally to the cabinet for discussion and approval as cabinet-sponsored legislation. Although bills sponsored by the cabinet represent a minority of the bills introduced into the Diet, they have a much higher chance of being enacted into law than those introduced by individual Diet members.

Once the cabinet approves it, a bill goes to the Diet Strategy Committee of the LDP which decides upon the priority and timing of the bills introduced into the Diet. Once introduced, they are referred to specific committees where they are discussed and, if approved, voted upon by the full house. Here too, higher bureaucrats may be active in providing information to committees or to their ministers when the latter are questioned by the committees.

The governing party consistently has had a majority of the House of Representatives for the past thirty years, and it enforces party discipline: once a bill is approved by the party all LDP Diet members must vote for it. Theoretically, therefore, the LDP should be able to pass any legislation it wishes without negotiating with or making concessions to the opposition, as in other parliamentary democracies. Despite this theoretical power, however, because of an anomaly in the procedure for the distribution of committee seats and chairmanships in the lower house, when the LDP's majority slips below a certain proportion of seats, opposition parties may gain a majority of voting members or the chairmanship of a committee. This occurred between 1976 and 1980 in the lower house, giving the opposition parties more influence than previously on legislation through the committee system.

Even before 1976 the opposition parties had used various techniques to delay or obstruct the deliberations of committees or the full house. Despite their minority of seats, these parties can force the LDP to negotiate with them over the content and wording of bills. Because of opposition resistance, some legislation is postponed until the next session, amended, or shelved completely by the governing party. As a result, only about three-quarters of government-sponsored bills actually have been passed since 1955, and about a quarter of these have been amended once introduced into the Diet.[11]

The policymaking process in Japan thus displays some rather distinctive features. One is the large role played by the bureaucracy, being involved in the process from the formulation of legislation, through its discussion in the LDP, to its consideration by the Diet. (The consequences for Japanese democracy of having an influential elite bureaucracy are analyzed further in chapter 6.) The role of the bureaucracy in policymaking, the close relationship between the LDP and the bureaucracy, and the fact that about a quarter of LDP politicians have been bureaucrats before running for office has led many observers to emphasize the power of the bureaucracy relative to politicians in Japan. It should be remembered, however, that no bill will even be introduced into the Diet unless it has been thoroughly discussed and approved in the LDP. In this sense, ultimate power for what becomes law rests with the governing party.

Additionally, in recent years the role and influence of LDP politicians in policymaking has been increasing. As they have acquired expertise from their long service on specialized committees, they have been able to rival the bureaucrats in their knowledge of particular kinds of policy and their connections to interest groups in that policy area. This has enabled them to play a more active and influential role in policymaking. One of the most salient debates in recent years among those who study Japanese politics is the question of whether LDP politicians or bureaucrats have the most influence in policymaking. Whichever group does, however, may be less important than the fact that *both* are very influential and have become highly integrated and interdependent during the long-term rule of the LDP.

Furthermore, as we have seen, even opposition politicians have some influence on policy through their committee activities or their ability to force the LDP to negotiate and compromise on certain aspects of a bill. This point brings up a second distinctive characteristic of the Japanese policymaking process: a perpetual majority party in a parliamentary system that nevertheless does not get all of its legislation passed. Rather than one-party dominance leading to completely impotent opposition and the automatic enactment of all the government's legislation, the process does allow for input from the opposition parties. Thus, although the Diet has not lived up to its constitutional role as the "highest organ of state power" because most substantive policymaking occurs in the bureaucracy and the LDP *prior to* its introduction into the Diet, it has provided an important forum for the legitimation of policy and for the opposition to exert at least some influence on legislation even though it is a perpetual minority.

The combination of these distinctive elements of Japan's policy-making process may well be unique in the democratic world. For each specific one, however, we may find a counterpart in other democracies. Americans may find the power of the bureaucracy in policymaking surprising, but the French would find it less so; Britons would find strange the majority party having to negotiate with the opposition to get its legislation passed, but an American considers this natural in Congress. J.A.A. Stockwin analyzes the issues posed for democracy by the lack of alternation in power of political parties (see chapter 5 below), but these same issues have had to be faced in Sweden (where the Social Democratic party held power for over forty years uninterruptedly until 1976, and has again since 1982) and in Italy (where the Christian Democrats have been the dominant party in the cabinet for most of the postwar era).[12]

Social Groups in Politics

As in other democracies, various social groups also play a major role in politics and policymaking. The most important is big business (see chapter 11). Business's influence in politics stems from various factors. The most important is the close connection between the business community and the LDP. Big business provides most of the funds for the LDP as a party, as well as for the factions, and thus gains access to and a hearing from the ruling party. In 1984, big business corporations reported almost 5 billion yen (about $20 million) in contributions to the political parties, with 90 percent of it going to the LDP.[13] As this figure represents only officially reported contributions, the actual figure is probably even larger.

When made through legitimate channels for the purpose of supporting the ruling party and the only major political party that is thoroughly probusiness in orientation (the major opposition parties are either socialist, Marxist, or welfare-state oriented), such contributions merely represent the Japanese version of interest-group politics found elsewhere. When individual business firms attempt to influence policy on behalf of their own particular interests, a more unsavory form of politics has often resulted: corruption. The Lockheed scandal—Prime Minister Tanaka was indicted and convicted of accepting a bribe from a

Japanese corporation acting as agent for an American airplane manufacturer that was trying to influence procurement decisions—is only the
most notorious of such cases of the alleged corruption of "money
politics" in Japan.

Another reason for the influence of business on the government is
its organization. Four or five major associations, the most important
of which is Keidanren (the Federation of Economic Organizations),
attempt to achieve a consensus about policy among business organizations and then to influence government to adopt policies favorable to
business, particularly in the area of macroeconomic policy. Whereas
earlier in the postwar period, big business was somewhat subservient
to and dependent on the bureaucracy, with Japan's economic success,
business has become much more autonomous and has pushed for a
more laissez-faire attitude on the part of government. Indeed, the
hand of large enterprise can be seen clearly in the call for "administrative reform" on the part of the LDP, the key political issue of the early
1980s, under which the size of government would be further decreased and some large public corporations would be privatized.

Another key interest group with close connections to the LDP is
agriculture. Most of Japan's 8 million farmers belong to Nōkyō
(Union of Agricultural Cooperatives). More than just an agricultural
cooperative federation, however, Nōkyō provides many nonagricultural services to rural families, from supermarkets to insurance firms
and banks. One of its most important functions is to act as a pressure
group on the LDP and government. The exchange between Nōkyō
and the LDP is clear. The farm cooperatives help mobilize the rural
vote for the LDP, on which an important portion of its Diet seats
depend, and in return the farmers get favorable agricultural policy.

The most important part of this policy has been the perpetuation
of a system by which the government sets the price of the rice crop
that it will buy from the farmers. This has kept rice prices artificially
high and thus benefited farmers. Subsidies for various growing programs and protection from foreign imports (most notably in the citrus fruit and beef industries) have also been part of the "pay-off" to
Nōkyō and the farmers for their crucial support for the LDP. Although Japanese industry has a well-earned reputation for efficiency
in the West, agriculture is an important exception. Government programs have perpetuated a relatively inefficient and expensive (to the
taxpayer and the consumer) farm industry for political reasons, a
phenomenon not unknown in the West, most especially in the Euro-

pean Economic Community. On the positive side, this attention to farmers has resulted in agricultural policy functioning as a sort of rural "welfare" policy which has kept Japan's income and wealth distribution among the most equitable in the industrialized world (see chapter 9 below).

There is a wide range of other interest groups that over the years have come to support the LDP, financially or with votes, in return for favorable policy. Professional groups, such as doctors (represented by the powerful Japan Medical Association), educators, small businesses, local development associations, and even some welfare groups are known to have close connections to the LDP and the bureaucracy. Indeed, one of the reasons that the LDP has been able to perpetuate its tenure as the ruling party has been its nature as a "catch-almost all" party with connections to and support from many social groups.

The most important group not represented among the LDP's supporting coalition is labor. Organized labor is divided, being represented by several major federations, but the two most important of these each supports one of the opposition parties. Sōhyō (General Council of Trade Unions) is the largest and most important federation and is closely linked with the JSP, providing it with most of its funds and activists at election time. It is also the most leftist of the union federations, and its leaders and activists include some very orthodox Marxists.

The union structure in Japan is rather unusual. Most unions are enterprise unions confined to a particular company, rather than craft or industrial unions organized on a wider basis. Unions also usually include both the blue- and white-collar workers at the company. This helps account, of course, for the rather unmilitant nature of Japanese unions compared to their Western counterparts: the union's interests are inextricably bound up with the fate of the company. One exception to this generalization are public employee labor unions, where the employer is the government. The leftist proclivities of Sōhyō are in part explained by the fact that it contains many public sector rather than private enterprise unions, and thus it sees political action against the conservative government as its main goal.

One situation in which a union may become more militant is when a company violates the ground rules for treatment of workers in Japan, one of which is the expectation that full-time, permanent employees will not be fired or laid off. Once the company violates such norms, even workplace disputes can become quite intense.[14]

Dōmei (Japan Confederation of Labor) has been the other large union federation with heavy political involvement. It is one of the main supports of the Democratic Socialist party (DSP), a party whose moderate socialism, support for parliamentary democracy, and pro-Western alliance policies causes it to resemble such Western European parties as the Socialist party in West Germany. Dōmei is composed primarily of private enterprise unions and therefore, like American labor unions, believes that political activity is but a supplement to its main goal of improving its members' economic benefits through negotiation with employers directly.

By supporting the opposition parties, the main labor federations are cut off from political influence through the LDP, although they do maintain connections to government through the bureaucracy and through policy advisory councils to the government on which labor union representatives sometimes sit. Labor's lack of influence on government, compared to business or agriculture, is only one of its political problems. The fragmentation of the labor movement also has hurt politically. The economic and cultural obstacles to expression of demands in private enterprises when the union is coterminous with the company is yet another major stumbling block to union power. And finally, internal union democracy is often far from ideal, leading to alienation toward the unions even among some workers (see chapter 13). All of these factors have contributed to making labor unions somewhat less powerful in politics than they are in the United States and in many European countries.

Many of these problems of organized labor, along with a declining unionization rate (about 28 percent of the work force, down from 56 percent in 1949), led in November 1987 to a major new initiative to bring about greater labor unity, and thus political clout. The Japanese Private Sector Trade Union Confederation (Rengo) was formed, in part by the formal dissolution of Dōmei and another independent labor federation and their incorporation into the new organization. In 1990, Sōhyō is expected to dissolve itself and also join. Now composed of sixty-two labor unions with a total membership of over five and a half million workers, Rengo holds the potential for having far-reaching effects on Japanese politics. Whether the new organization will actually bring about a significant increase in labor's political influence and a reorganization of relationships among labor's political allies remains to be seen.

Like labor, religious groups have some influence on Japanese politics, but again to a lesser extent and in a different way than in the United States. Many Japanese are nominal Buddhists, but religion does not play a central role in the daily life of the average Japanese. Centuries of religious eclecticism and tolerance have left their mark on the present. Many Japanese will be married in a Shinto (the indigenous "religion" of Japan) ceremony and have their cremation and funeral according to Buddhist ritual, but lead most of their lives in a relatively secular fashion. The most important exceptions to these generalizations, however, are the devout and enthusiastic adherents to the so-called new religions that usually are relatively modern offshoots of Buddhism.

Politically, the most important of these new religions is the Sōka Gakkai, the Value Creation Society. Sōka Gakkai is the secular arm of the Nichiren Shoshū sect of Buddhism and has worldwide chapters and followers. In the mid-1960s, the society established its own political party, the Kōmeitō or Clean Government party (CGP), to help attain its objectives of world peace through the spread of Nichiren Shoshū beliefs, the elimination of corruption from politics, and a social welfare society in Japan.

This party grew rapidly in the 1970s and became one of the leading opposition parties, capturing around 10 percent of the votes and seats in elections for the lower house. The party is now separate from the religious organization, but Sōka Gakkai members remain a goodly part of the CGP's voters and activists. During many periods since its formation, the party has been in bitter conflict with the Communist party, not only over issues of principle, but also in competition for voters not identified with either the LDP or the JSP. The two parties have the only mass party organizations in Japan. As one of the major center parties in the Diet, the CGP plays a crucial "swing" role between the Democratic Socialists on the right and the socialists and communists on the left in the ideological spectrum of the opposition.

The relationship between the Sōka Gakkai and the Kōmeitō represents another example of a universal tendency of social interest groups and political parties in Japan. Some of the other major opposition parties are similarly dependent on one particular interest for votes, funds, and energy: the JSP on Sōhyō labor federation, the DSP on Dōmei labor federation. Interest groups in the United States, however much they may incline toward one party, may support or endorse candidates who will work on their behalf, regardless of party affiliation. Not so in Japan. Interest groups have tended to ally themselves closely with only one party.

The mass media's political role is somewhat less clear than that of interest groups. As Lawrence W. Beer indicates (see chapter 4), freedom of the press is supported by law and defended actively by the media in Japan. Japanese newspapers tend to see their political role very explicitly as educating public opinion, on the one hand, and acting as its representative and guardian, on the other. Whether they actually play these roles as much as they believe they do is open to question; but there is no doubt that in a nation where the three major newspapers (the *Asahi, Mainichi,* and *Yomiuri*) are read nationwide and have a combined circulation of over 15 million per day, and where television broadcasting consists of one mammoth public broadcasting agency, NHK (like the BBC in Great Britain), plus a full range of commercial networks, these media are politically significant. Indeed, one survey of elite groups in Japan found that all of them except the media itself tended to rank the media as the most powerful group in Japanese society.[15]

The political implications of the ubiquitous Japanese media are ambivalent, perhaps more so than in other democratic countries. On a daily basis the newspapers especially can be fairly critical of government in their editorial positions and in the issues they choose to highlight. Some people consider them more important as an "opposition" than the opposition parties themselves, raising issues that would otherwise not get on the government's agenda. The national press, for example, was instrumental in maintaining interest in the pollution issue in the late 1960s and early 1970s. On the other hand, it has been argued that despite fierce commercial rivalry, the Japanese press tends to be rather conformist, with little variation in content at any particular time.[16] Moreover, it is highly dependent on government sources and has a close, institutionalized relationship with them. The fact that journalists for the national papers have elite educational backgrounds similar to politicians and bureaucrats also serves to make the politician-journalist relationship in Japan as incestuous as it is adversarial. It is probably not an accident that the business dealings of former Prime Minister Tanaka were revealed not by a daily newspaper but by one of the more independent and influential monthly magazines. The press in Japan is particularly Janus-faced, therefore, being simultaneously a critic of the "establishment" and a part of it.[17]

Further outside the establishment in opposition are two groups which have played major roles in politics at various times: students and minorities. Edward Beauchamp discusses the accomplishments and drawbacks of Japan's precollege educational system (see chapter 10). The very strenuous competition and high standards of that system contributes to alienation among many students that manifests itself primarily during their college years. The university period is perhaps the freest of any in a Japanese person's life, a rather relaxed transition between the excruciating demands of the "examination hell" to enter a good university and the great pressure for conformity to social roles expected of both company employees and housewives. The politicized atmosphere of the university campus in Japan leads some to discover a political identity and to express their alienation ideologically during this period.

Leftist student organizations, usually highly fragmented and mutually hostile, coalesced to influence national politics in Japan, as they did in Western democracies, in the 1960s. Both the wing affiliated with the Japan Communist party and the even more radical "anti-JCP" revolutionary wing were key opponents of the U.S.-Japan security treaty in 1960.[18] In 1968–1970, student groups ranging from relatively nonideological ones to extreme Marxist ones managed to close down over a hundred campuses. Their protests resulted in new legislation to enable riot police to be more easily introduced into universities, but also in some rethinking among educators and the public about the pressurized and rigid college entrance examination system. (In chapter 8 below, Patricia Steinhoff concisely describes the context and techniques of, and government countermeasures toward, protest movements in Japan.)

The visibility of the student movement as an actor in politics declined noticeably in the 1970s, as it fragmented even further and students' concerns became less political. During that same decade, however, the protest of minority groups became important for almost the first time in Japanese history. Japan is a relatively homogeneous society culturally, compared to the pluralist, multiethnic, multiracial societies of many Western countries. Few outside Japan realize that it has two fairly large minority groups: Koreans and Burakumin, or outcastes.

Over half a million Koreans live in Japan. They came, or were brought by force, when Korea was a Japanese colony before and during World War II, and were subsequently marooned there by the division of Korea and the failure of the Koreas and Japan to work out a program of resettlement. Despite several generations of residence and the fact that the descendants of the original migrants have lived in Japan since birth and are often raised speaking Japanese, many are still legally resident aliens without citizenship rights, including the right to vote.

Koreans are frequently discriminated against by majority Japanese in marriage, employment, and in interpersonal relations. Until the 1980s, however, their political views were expressed, if at all, through either the pro–South Korean or pro–North Korean associations that polarize the Korean community in Japan. Now, however, the issue of alien registration has galvanized a protest movement and created a disturbing issue for the government. All aliens in Japan must register with local ward, town, or village offices, a procedure that includes fingerprinting. Some Koreans refuse to be fingerprinted, considering it to be both discriminatory and insulting. Many of these registrants have consequently found themselves in legal difficulties. Interestingly, some local governments, which register aliens as part of their delegated functions for the national government, have sided with the protesters and, much to the chagrin of the Ministry of Justice, have registered even those who refuse to be fingerprinted. This illustrates one aspect of the complicated relationship in which some local autonomy can be found even in Japan's basically centralized system.

The "outcastes" represent another cultural and political problem. Although racially, ethnically, and linguistically "Japanese," between one and three million citizens are seen as part of a separate, "unpure" caste and are systematically discriminated against. This group was referred to as Burakumin (hamlet people) because historically they had been forced to live in separate villages. The origins of this caste system remain somewhat obscure, but may have begun after the introduction of Buddhism in Japan over a millennium ago when killing or eating cattle, or even working with hides and leather were frowned upon and those who engaged in these occupations came to be seen as "unclean." The descendants of the original Burakumin still suffer from discrimination. Intermarriage between an outcaste and a nonoutcaste is often difficult (middle-class Japanese families will hire special agencies to investigate the family histories of prospective sons- or daughters-in-law to check for just such bloodlines), and many large companies avoid hiring outcastes. "Ghetto" neighborhoods exist in many large cities in Japan.

In the early 1970s, the Burakumin became particularly active politically, pushing for recognition, an end to discrimination, and more funds and programs to redress their material grievances. The situation was complicated, however, by the fact that outcaste activists were split between an organization close to the Japan Communist party and one close to the Japan Socialist party. Competition between these two organizations was bitter, and in a few instances broke out in incidents of violence, as when JSP-affiliated activists beat up and tortured high school teachers who were JCP supporters.

The outcastes' movement did result in central and local programs for better housing and changes to the educational curriculum in some locations. Despite the goal of many outcastes for full integration (*dōwa*) into Japanese society, however, personal and institutional discrimination remain. Unlike the U.S. civil rights movement, which eventually forced Americans to confront the problem of discrimination, the issue of outcastes is rarely discussed publically by the Japanese, and they often pretend that the problem does not exist. It is interesting, though, that in the conflict between the United States and Japan over the further opening of Japanese markets to U.S. agricultural products, it was sometimes argued that a major reason for the Japanese government's resistance to rapid opening of the beef market was the negative economic effect of such import competition on an industry in which numbers of outcastes are employed.

Democratic Politics

Much of what I have described above in this introduction to the process of politics and policymaking in Japan will seem familiar to American readers: electoral competition, the politics of representation, party rivalry, interest group pressures and political influence, legislative bargaining, a critical yet establishment press, dissent, and minority grievances. Other aspects, such as one party continuously in power, electoral malapportionment, the larger role of the bureaucracy, *kōenkai,* interest groups' exclusive ties to one party, a militant Marxist student movement, an outcaste minority, and others, undoubtedly seem quite different.

I would warn the reader, however, against too readily concluding that the unfamiliar aspects of Japanese politics make Japan "exotically unique" or that the differences with U.S. politics must inevitably be the result of Japanese cultural differences. As I have tried to show, some of the more unfamiliar aspects of Japanese politics and democracy have equivalents in Western European politics. On a number of dimensions of politics, it is the United States (for better or worse) that is really the unique democratic political system when compared to Europe and Japan. Also, in some of the cases where Japanese politics differ from America or Europe, the disparities can be explained by causes other than "culture." A different electoral system or a more active Supreme Court, for example, would bring about significant changes in some of the unique aspects of electoral politics in Japan. Culture does matter, but it is not the only factor determining differences in political processes.

NOTES

1. Thomas R. Rochon, "Electoral Systems and the Basis of the Vote: The Case of Japan," in John Creighton Campbell, ed., *Parties, Candidates, and Voters in Japan: Six Quantitative Studies,* Michigan Papers in Japanese Studies 2 (Ann Arbor: The University of Michigan Center for Japanese Studies, 1981).

2. See Bradley Richardson et al., *The Japanese Voter,* esp. chap. 10 (forthcoming).

3. The most comprehensive study of *kōenkai* is Gerald L. Curtis, *Election Campaigning, Japanese Style* (New York: Columbia University Press, 1971).

4. On campaign funding and factionalism, see ibid., and Nathaniel Thayer, *How the Conservatives Rule Japan* (Princeton, N.J.: Princeton University Press, 1969), chaps. 2 and 5.

5. *Conservatives,* pp. 21–26.

6. Michael J. Leiserson, "Factions and Coalitions in One-Party Japan: An Interpretation Based on the Theory of Games," *American Political Science Review* 62 (September 1968): 770–87.

7. Thus, in the eleven years between the end of Sato Eisaku's eight-year tenure as prime minister in 1972 and Nakasone Yasuhiro's ascension to the post in 1983, there were five prime ministers. LDP prime ministers are now limited to two, two-year terms by party rules. Nakasone, like Sato an exception to the trend, served five by convincing the party to give him a special one-year exemption.

8. On how cabinets are made and on what basis, see Thayer, *Conservatives,* chap. 7.

9. PHP Kenkyusho, *The Data File, 1984* (Kyoto: PHP Kenkyusho, 1984), p. 35.

10. Chalmers Johnson, *MITI and the Japanese Miracle* (Stanford: Stanford University Press, 1982).

11. On the use and frequent success of opposition obstruction in the Diet in the postwar era, see T. J. Pempel, "The Dilemma of Parliamentary Opposition in Japan, *Polity* 8 (Fall 1975): 63–79.

12. T. J. Pempel's forthcoming edited volume, *Uncommon Democracies* (Ithaca, N.Y.; Cornell University Press), analyzes and compares the various cases of this interesting democratic variant.

13. *The Japan Times Weekly,* September 21, 1985, p. 4.

14. Tadashi Hanami, "Conflict and Its Resolution in Industrial Relations and Labor Law," in *Conflict in Japan,* ed. Ellis S. Krauss, Thomas C. Rohlen, and Patricia G. Steinhoff (Honolulu: University of Hawaii Press, 1984), pp. 107–35.

15. Kabashima Ikuo and Jeffrey Broadbent, "Referent Pluralism: Mass Media and Politics in Japan," *Journal of Japanese Studies* 12 (Summer 1986): 335–41.

16. See Nathaniel Thayer, "Competition and Conformity: An Inquiry into the Structure of Japanese Newspapers," in *Modern Japanese Organization and Decision-making,* ed. Ezra F. Vogel (Berkeley and Los Angeles: University of California Press, 1975), pp. 284–303.

17. This ambivalent role of the Japanese media is a major theme in Susan J. Pharr, ed., *Media and Politics in Japan* (forthcoming).

18. George K. Packard III, *Protest in Tokyo* (Princeton, N.J.: Princeton University Press, 1966).

Political
Democracy

4 Law and Liberty

●

LAWRENCE W. BEER

A critical part of Japan's democratic core since 1945 has been a comparatively successful system of law and constitution. Japan was forced into unequal international relations under Western treaty law in the 1850s; by 1900 it had developed new Westernized forms of law and government that were intelligible and acceptable to the West, an unavoidable condition for achieving full independence and legal equality in the West-dominated international relations of the day. Opting for continental European models and theories, Japan put down roots in the civil-law tradition and continues today in that most influential of the world's legal families. Democratic notions of constitutionalism, individual rights, and freedom derived from varied Western sources also became widely known in Japan in the latter decades of the last century, but remained subordinate and suspect.

Until the cataclysmic defeat of August 1945, what counted most in modern government, law, and society was not individual rights and civil liberties, but dedicated service to the sovereign emperor and the "divine land" over which he presided as a benevolent father in quasi-mystical union with his nation-family. Or such was the ever-more-insistent ideological basis for sociolegal restraints and aggressive calls for loss of self in service to the state, at home and abroad. Prewar repressive ultranationalism involving inventive warping of traditions regarding the emperor and the military was instilled over time through modern techniques of mass education, mass media, policing, and administration; that spirit brought utter national failure.

The nature of Japan's constitutional commitment to democracy is unintelligible without reference to its rejection of the systemic foundations of that failure.

Many well-established forms of law and government continued after World War II, but the contents were fundamentally altered, as in East and West Germany. A constitutional revolution began in 1945, when the American-centered Allied Occupation (1945–52) forced Japan's government to forge stong new links among law, society, and liberty. The dignity of each person and popular sovereignty replaced the emperor and his state as the critical alloy, and a constitutional prohibition of militarism in 1947 fused with the new state vision. By "constitutional revolution" I mean a long-term, essentially nonviolent process in which a different set of constitutional values achieves legitimation throughout a national society by such means as laws, administrative and political actions, judicial decisions, and education through family, religions, schools, the mass media, and other community institutions. In early autumn 1945, Occupation directives (SCAPIN) were promptly implemented in Japanese law through ordinances; within months of surrender, the structure of repressive laws came tumbling down.[1]

It seems doubtful that Japan would be a democracy today in the absence of catalytic intervention from above at that time of unprecedented failure; the first two years of the Occupation were especially crucial. Throughout Japanese history, fundamental changes had been wrought by victorious groups without reference to representative processes; so constitutional change from above was not a new or strange phenonmenon. Can a constitution written primarily by foreign conquerors be a good and workable document? Japan's experience suggests a clearly affirmative answer. How a constitutional democracy begins is much less important than the level of support it comes to enjoy among the affected populace. In Japan, the overwhelming majority are quite content with their democratic structures, individual rights and freedoms, and constitutionally restrained military (article 9). The Constitution of Japan (*Nihonkoku Kempō,* 1947) is the institutionalized basis for legitimate law, policy, and public values in postwar Japan.[2]

"Revisionist" efforts to alter constitutional arrangements in order to legitimize more extensive military development, restore the nominal powers of the emperor, and/or deemphasize civil rights and liberties have met with ample publicity but little success. Barring international catastrophe, the present constitutional consensus seems likely to continue; but so will Japan's search for nonmilitary means of shouldering the "political responsibilities" of a world economic leader. The occasional American intrusions in Japan's internal constitutional politics on the side of fuller rearmament seem insufficiently sensitive to the intimate historic relationship among militarism, antidemocratic repression, and emperor-centered ultranationalism; but this linkage between internal constitutionalism and foreign policy is admittedly unique among the world's democracies.

Naturally enough, many American scholars have focused more on the roles of the American Occupation in the establishment of Japan's democracy than on its status after independence. Scholars and journalists tend to measure Japan's politicolegal system in terms of American understandings of democracy during the Occupation. The American model, however, seems a less appropriate basis for evaluation than democratic principles that transcend a particular issue. To understand Japanese law, one must comprehend how various elements of European, American, and Japanese legalism and constitutionalism are stirred together in distinctive democratic legal practice.

Constitutions

Venerable Constitution?

To appreciate the relative success of Japan's constitutional democracy, it helps to look briefly at the constitutional map of the world and to analyze Japan's performance in light of criteria that are "transcultural," that is, applicable across diverse legal cultures. As of mid-1988, the Constitution of Japan is one of only 22 out of 165 single-document constitutions in the world which date from the 1940s or earlier.[3] The idea of setting forth a single authoritative statement about a country's fundamental principles and structures of government as the supreme legal basis for legitimacy first found expression in the Constitution of the United States (1787), the only single-document constitution dating from the eighteenth century. A few constitutions, such as that of Norway (1814), continue from the nineteenth century. Most thought-provoking, over 100 constitutions today had their beginnings in 1970 or later, and others are in the process of reconsideration in this unprecedented age of constitutional experimentation and—in many countries—constitutional "pre-stability." All but a very few nations, such as the United Kingdom and Islamic nations that use the Koran as a constitutional document (Saudi Arabia, Oman, Libya), consider a single-document constitution indispensable.

Today, as during the Tokugawa period (1603–1868) and under the Meiji constitution (1889–1947), Japan is unusual for its constitutional stability. Neither modern constitution has been amended even once; but the present constitution is quite superior to its predecessor in channeling law and politics along paths which protect democracy and respond to national need without formal amendment. By comparison to other Asian nations, Japan is unique in the stability of its legal, constitutional forms and practices in the postwar era.

The critical importance of constitutional stability may be too much taken for granted in nations like the United States and Japan which have it. Whatever the reasons for its enjoyment of this type of stability, Japan is indeed fortunate. Many have suggested economic prosperity as a major reason for Japan's postindependence political peace; more attention might well be given to a converse interpretation: without its solidly supported infrastructure of democratic law and constitution, the nation's economic performance since 1950 would have been far less impressive.

Transcultural Perspectives on Democratic Constitutionalism

Analyses of democracy and constitutionalism in a foreign country may best be grounded less in theory than in detailed knowledge of the specific country's way of concretizing its principles in the everyday workings of public and private law and institutions. One should assess another system in terms of the broadest transcultural principle and in terms of the country's own stated constitutional foundations. For example, John Locke and Chief Justice John Marshall may be well known in Japan, but it seems more useful to discuss Japanese constitutionalism according to theoretical presuppositions that are less culture-specific than the historical course of judicial review and individualism in the United States, and more applicable to culturally varied contexts.

A basic transcultural assumption for constitutional democracy compatible with statements in the preamble and provisions of the Constitution of Japan is the following: the inherent dignity of each person is the foundation for popular sovereignty and for public values reflected in law and policy. Constitutional documents, philosophical and religious leanings, and legal histories of nations may dramatically differ without conflicting with this fundamental principle. Nondemocratic constitutional systems, on the other hand, look elsewhere for legitimacy: the emperor in prewar Japan, the Communist party's monopoly on the understanding of historical laws through Marxism in Communist countries, God's will as perceived in the Bible or the Koran by individuals variously selected as authoritative interpreters by their communities in Islamic countries, and so forth.

Ultimately, however, a *democratic* constitutional system must assume the individual person is the primary public value. Whatever the other variations in cultural assumptions and ideals, governmental and legal service reflecting that ultimate value seem to require, formally or informally, institutionalization of the following or equivalent features:

1. A constitutional division of governmental power among two or more organs. Independent courts with an adequate range of jurisdiction over public rights cases are a common necessity, for example, whatever the shape of the state structure may be in other respects, federal or unitary, with two or more branches of government.

2. Clear limits on the amount of governmental power possessed by anyone and on the length of time power is legitimately possessed. For example, in large democratic systems, elections and other legal procedures are used to bring peaceful, routine passage from one national leader or group of leaders to the next.

3. Governmental authority and means of coercion under the constitution and pursuant laws sufficient to maintain public peace and national security within limits defined by the human rights of citizens and others in the community.

4. Government involvement in socioeconomic problem-solving to assure citizens' subsistence needs and a life compatible with human dignity when the private socioeconomic sector fails to provide this minimum.

5. Legally protected and encouraged freedoms of peaceful expression and silence regarding personal or group belief or opinion, and regarding information. A transcultural theory of freedom must be an integral part of a human rights theory, not separate from it, as is too often the assumption in American law and scholarly commentary.[4]

6. Procedural rights in criminal and civil justice for each citizen equal to the rights of all others within the national community. All must be equally subordinate to the law regardless of sociopolitical position. No system's leaders would accept such practices as torture, for example, as legitimate procedure in their own regard.

Human Rights and Law in Japan

In general, Japan's present constitution reflects the above transcultural theoretical presuppositions; but as elsewhere, commitment to rights, freedom, and justice is in certain areas deficient. Here I briefly note a few characteristics of the legal system and human rights categories under the Constitution of Japan, before focusing in more detail on freedom of expression.

Modern Japanese law has been evolving distinctly for over a century and now manifests links with indigenous, European, and Anglo-American traditions. Japan's nonindividualist, group-oriented system of sociopolitical values and organization bears traces of the pre-1868 feudal era, as do the perennial use of conciliation to resolve disputes and the important but less crucial element of Japanized neo-Confucianism. Indigenous legalism has also been affected by European constitutional theories and code legalism and, since 1945, by American ideas of constitutional rights in a judicial setting.[5]

As in other civil-law systems, the most authoritative laws under the supreme constitution are five codes (hōten) with a degree of consistency, clarity, and completeness not characteristic of American law: the Civil Code governing legal relations between private parties, the Code of Civil Procedure, the Criminal Code, the Code of Criminal Procedure, and the Commercial Code. Each code provides a comprehensive framework of rules into which all other levels of legalism must fit. Other very basic laws (kihonhō) lay out the ground rules for broad areas of legislative concern, such as education and labor relations, or implement constitutional directives on government structures such as the Diet, the judiciary, and local government ("local autonomy units"). Japan is unitary, not federal, in structure, and only the Diet can pass statutory law; but under national law, local governments enjoy limited taxing and ordinance-making authority. The broad outlines of the codes are also filled in by cabinet orders, administrative rules, court regulations, and other administrative legalisms, but not, at least in theory, by "judge-made law."

Civil lawyers sometimes view the field of law in American common-law jurisdictions as in a state of sprawling disorder repugnant to the clear and rational ordering appropriate to law. And some see American legal scholarship as too preoccupied with cases and lacking in theoretical sophistication and broad principle. As a matter of fact, it is often quite difficult for an American to know his or her legal rights without the assistance of a local lawyer familiar with federal, state, county, and town statutes. The ordinary citizen in a civil-law country finds law more easily, often through small specialized collections of rules published to help people with particular occupations or interests; for example, compendia of laws affecting a taxi driver or a public employee or dealing with women's rights or pollution problems. Whatever their focus, these authoritative guides fit logically into a legal system that is an intelligible whole.

As a civil-law country, prewar Japan had courts as units administered by the Justice Ministry and staffed by judges who were a type of higher civil servant; the judiciary was not constitutionally separate and had only limited jurisdiction, especially with respect to civil rights and liberties. In democratic civil-law jurisdictions generally, the function of judges is to faithfully and fairly apply the written statutory law passed by democratically elected parliaments, with deference to the constitution and the codes; but judges are not supposed to make law or policy—as they occasionally do in the United States—with inventive legal interpretations in decisions which may serve as binding precedents in future cases. Furthermore, European constitutional history from before the French Revolution of 1789 established a long-lasting bias in civil-law countries against viewing courts as defenders of individual rights.

The view of the law and of the limited role of the judiciary had been absorbed by most democratically inclined legal professionals in 1946 Japan. Into this world view came the quite different American notion that the judiciary should be an independent branch of government with broad powers. Ever since, judges in Japan have been deciding legal disputes guided by a mixture of civil law and American theory, judicial precedent, and their sense of duty as custodians of individual rights. In this perception, law and constitutional principle are best sought not in neat codes or in the results of sometimes tumultuous parliamentary debates, but in the context of judicial decisions on real controversies brought before a court. Thus, within Japan's constitutional law, two democratic conceptions of judicial role have vied for influence since 1947, with a modified American plan regarding the judiciary gradually attaining full integration into the civil-law framework. Neither civil law nor common law is inherently more democratic. Had Japan's postwar revolution of freedom been instigated by a democratic European conqueror, for example, the role of the courts and judicial review might be much less important than they are today, and arguably at least, without a loss of democratic thrust.

However, under the Constitution of Japan (chapter 6), an institutionally independent Supreme Court has authority over all other courts, comprehensive jurisdiction, and the judicial review "power to determine the constitutionality of any law, order, regulation or official act" (article 81).[6] The Supreme Court contains fifteen justices who divide into three Petty Benches in deciding most cases. Only occasionally, as for major constitutional cases, do all justices join in deliberation as the Grand Bench. Today the courts enjoy their increased autonomy and influence as settlers of disputes and, in effect, as participants in societal policymaking. Precedent is not binding as law in future cases, but judges pay due regard to the substantial body of accumulated prior decisions, and the mass media and scholars have, by their reports and comments on cases, vastly expanded public awareness of the courts and democratic legal issues in the past forty years. Judges are major actors in some human rights dramas; but some critics fault some courts, especially the Supreme Court, for being too deferential at times to law passed by democratically elected legislatures.

The scope of justiciable constitutional rights in Japan is quite broad under chapter 3, articles 11–40. Article 97 proclaims: "The fundamental human rights by this Constitution guaranteed to the people of Japan are fruits of the age-old struggle of man to be free; they have survived the many exacting tests for durability and are conferred upon this and future generations in trust, to be held for all time inviolate."[7]

In broad terms, chapter 3 provides a more adequate constitutional basis for theoretical discourse on human rights law and policy than the constitution of the United States with its amendments; but the American authors of chapter 3 may well have been setting forth what they considered an appropriate understanding of *American constitutionalism* in 1946. The enumeration of rights in Japan's document reflects well-integrated views of the rights many Americans felt should be explicitly honored in American constitutional law. In the idealistic days after the New Deal and World War II, a year and half before the United Nations adopted (with major American input) the rather comprehensive Universal Declaration of Human Rights, Americans wrote into a historic and lasting foreign constitution an understanding of American constitutional rights which American scholars and lawyers might well look to for perspective when interpreting related law in the United States. The extensive Japanese case law on constitutional rights accumulated since 1947 in a quasi–common-law manner, and the solid knowledge of American constitutional law which many Japanese legal professionals bring to their consideration of a case, make Japan's experience in this area an apt object of American attention. Moreover, since Japanese law may integrate European civil-law approaches with Anglo-American common law and constitutionalism more systematically than any civil-law or common-law country, Japan serves as a laboratory of living non-Western comparative law and a possible bridge for better mutual understanding between nations of civil-law and common-law legalism and constitutionalism, particularly with respect to human rights.

Japan's learned and large corps of constitutional lawyers has written voluminous commentary—too little of it known outside Japan—on the constitution and on each important judicial decision. They commonly categorize different sets of human rights as follows:[8]

1. Equality of rights under the law. Article 14 prohibits "discrimination in political, economic, or social relations because of race, creed, sex, social status, or family origin," as well as inherited honors or nobility (except in the case of the powerless dynastic monarchy). Article 24 recognizes "the equal rights of husband and wife" in all matters. The governing interpretive principle of private law is "the dignity of individuals and the essential equality of the sexes" (Civil Code, article 1-2).[9]

2. Economic freedoms and property rights (articles 22 and 29). Japanese have the freedom to choose their occupations and to engage in business, and the right to use property within limits "in conformity with the public welfare."

3. Rights related to the quality of socioeconomic life (*shakaiken*). This category includes rights to welfare assistance, social medicine, compulsory education (article 26), "minimum standards of wholesome and cultured living" (article 25), and workers' rights. Workers have the right to work under laws that set reasonable conditions of wages, hours, rest, and working environment (article 27), and "to organize and to bargain and act collectively" (article 28), unless they fall within the broad category of public employee.

4. The right to participate in election politics (*sanseiken*) by standing as a candidate, campaigning, or voting (article 15). Articles 44 and 14 ban discrimination in connection with a person's candidacy and election to office. Japan's most serious constitutional problem seems

to be malapportionment of seats in the House of Representatives. In the face of recent Supreme Court findings of unconstitutionality, the Diet may be moving, ever so hesitantly and reluctantly, toward a reassignment of seats to constituencies which will assure the citizen of densely populated areas that his or her vote has more than one-third the value of a vote in sparsely populated election districts, the very modest standard discussed by the Supreme Court.[10]

5. Procedural rights (articles 31–40). A full array of such rights is guaranteed by law and generally assured by highly professional judges, prosecutors, and police. Article 31 sets the basis: "No person shall be deprived of life or liberty, nor shall any other criminal penalty be imposed, except according to procedure established by law."

6. Rights and freedoms of the spirit (*seishinteki jiyūken*), such as thought, conscience (article 19), religion (article 20), expressions (article 21), and professional academic activity, the world's first such provision (article 23); and the right to choose occupation and place of residence (article 22). All the above exist within the limits of and with the expressed civic duty to further "the public welfare" (articles 12 and 13), which has been judicially defined as the maintenance of public order and human rights.

Although some of these rights may seem only glowing guidelines without legal bite, such is not the case; they have proved justiciable in court. Japan's system of constitutionally guaranteed human rights and democratic government does measure up to the transcultural criteria suggested earlier. And, in general comparative terms, its human rights record emerges as rather strong, especially perhaps in the areas of civil liberties and criminal justice.

Freedom of Expression

Freedom of expression, like constitutional stability, tends to go unnoticed when it exists, but it may well be the most demanding test of healthy constitutional democracy in any country, because it presupposes the level of institutionalized respect for the individual necessary to enforce tolerance for the active coexistence of every individual's opinions, beliefs, convictions, and knowledge. The content of expression varies tremendously in inherent and social value, ranging from the trivial and absurd to the philosophically seminal and aesthetically magnificent. Thus, a persuasive theory of freedom must rest not on attribution of a magical quality to freedom to utter or express, but rather on tolerance; not on a mythical "free marketplace of ideas," but on active protection and encouragement of diversity in discourse. Respect for the relative weights of ideas and for the truth precludes tolerance for error and ethically repugnant ideas as such. The proper object of tolerance is the individual person, not ideas; as a consequence of his or her inherent dignity, the individual has a rightful claim on respectful treatment. Respect dictates societal and legal tolerance for the individual's utterance even of valueless or repugnant views, insofar as such expression does not itself result in intolerant or other disrespectful treatment of others. "Mutualism," with an implied openness to community awareness, seems a better way to describe the reciprocal relationship between individuals' rights than "individualism" or "collectivism."[11]

In the decades before defeat, Japan manifested little tolerance for ideas or for people holding unorthodox views. With the Occupation, a close, repressed, ultranationalist society experienced what might be termed a nuclear flash of freedom and openness. The aftershocks and fallout altered law and politics, and a closed society began a long process of opening. Article 21 of the constitution is central: "Freedom of assembly and association as well as speech, press and all other forms of expression are guaranteed. 2. No censorship shall be maintained, nor shall the secrecy of any means of communication be violated."[12]

Two subsectors of freedom of expression seem most critical: media freedom and the freedoms of assembly and association. Mass media freedom is central because the Japanese media, especially the press, is one of the world's most extensive and technically proficient communications systems (though not always impressive in investigating sensitive issues) and constitutes the only major national, reasonably coherent, and organized center of power counterbalancing the government. The press mediates diffuse linkages among official and private elites, diverse interest groups, and the general population.

The freedoms of assembly and association are crucial because Japan's political culture is group-oriented. Organized groups, and individuals as members of groups rather than alone, most naturally and freely express interests, demands, expectations, and grievances and provide coherent, lasting social existence to a great variety of viewpoints. Assertive groups in informal league with the media seem to form the backbone of freedom of expression under the law.

Before presenting a few cases to illustrate the law and socio-

politics of freedom, mention must be made of the officially sponsored promotion of free speech and human rights by means of lay
volunteers, the Civil Liberties Commissioners and the Local Administrative Counselors.

Rights imply the availability of remedies to vindicate or protect
them, but "remedies" may include a wide variety of sociolegal mechanisms; courts of law can be costly, slow, intimidating, and in the end
less effective than other means. The social ideal in Japan is not so
much the "justiciable rights" which are stressed in the United States,
as "conciliable rights."[13] Civil Liberties Commissioners are unpaid
men and women meticulously selected for their credibility and commitment to human rights. They assist local citizens by conciliatory,
noncoercive, low-cost, quick, and effective resolution of human
rights problems and disputes.[14]

In the 1980s, about eleven thousand five hundred commissioners
(13 percent women) in a broad range of working and living environments throughout Japan have assisted annually in about fifteen thousand cases of rights violation and with some three hundred sixty
thousand rights consultations. They also play a major role in human
rights education in the schools and in annual local and national observances of Human Rights Day (December 10, the anniversary of the
United Nations Universal Declaration of Human Rights) with public
assemblies, panel discussions, debates, poster and essay contests, and
other modern means of diffusing ideas and information about human
rights ideals.

Local Administrative Counselors, average age sixty, are limited
to dealing with grievances against public officials. In 1982, roughly
five thousand of these respected, unpaid local citizens connected
with the Administrative Management Agency handled some two
hundred thousand complaints on a confidential and impartial basis.
Most cases are settled to citizen satisfaction by explanation, discussion, or conciliatory remedial action in consultation with appropriate
authorities.

Such lay people have helped in the transition from the prewar
arrogant functionary of the imperial government to the postwar official who is a "servant" of the people. Together with the courts, Diet,
mass media, and schools, the commissioners, counselors and other
volunteers have institutionalized constitutional rights. They personify
the official promotion of free expression of grievances and heightened
awareness of human rights at the sidewalk level among a people

traditionally reticent and suspicious about egocentric assertions of individual right.

The Freedoms of Assembly and Association

Rigid prewar suppression of the rights to assemble and to form associations has given way to a vigorous and well-established postwar tradition of rather flamboyant exercise of the freedoms to organize into common-purpose groups, to hold public political rallies, and to march in demand or protest down city streets. The issues and groups behind collective actions are as varied as life in a large, urbanized, technologically advanced, and internationally powerful and sensitive society. A day without a demonstration in Tokyo is indeed hard to imagine. In Japan's group-oriented society, such a custom may not be too surprising; but the rarity of violence is remarkable, in comparison with other democratic and nondemocratic legal cultures (see also chapter 8 below). Customary law appropriately restrains group violence, and the Mobile Police (*kidōtai*) are very well trained to keep confrontations to a minimum. However, group exuberance, passion, or political intent have led, on relatively few occasions, to arrests and a long line of judicial decisions on the law of demonstrations and freedom of expression. Demonstrations are regulated primarily by some sixty local "public safety ordinances" (*kōanjōrei*) and the Road Traffic Law.[15]

The most important judicial decision in Japanese legal history on freedom of assembly was the Supreme Court's 1960 Grand Bench judgment in the Tokyo Ordinance case. The case grew out of the "security treaty crisis"—the enormous mass movement engendered by revision of the U.S.-Japan treaty relationship. Subsequent decisions have been glosses, aimed at applying and refining *Tokyo* doctrine, or modifying some of its less palatable aspects. In November 1959, early in the Security Treaty drama, a Tokyo district court, following other recent Tokyo court decisions, refused to allow police detention of students who had demonstrated without a permit. The case went directly to the Supreme Court along with two other ordinance cases. With Chief Justice Kotaro Tanaka, a former professor at Tokyo University, presiding, the court reversed the decision, upheld the ordinance, and set forth in some detail a classic account of its jurisprudence at that juncture.

In summary, the justices held that: (1) The guarantee of freedoms such as freedom of assembly "is the most important feature that distinguishes democracy from totalitarianism." (2) Citizens must not abuse such rights of expression, and should exercise these, like all constitutional rights, for the public welfare. (3) Courts are required "to draw a proper boundary between freedom and the public welfare," to guarantee the freedom of peaceable assembly, and to decide whether and to what extent legal restraints on public gatherings are appropriate. (4) The proper degree and kind of legal restriction depends on the nature of the "expression" at issue. Collective activities such as demonstrations have a potential for group violence which justifies public safety ordinances as "the minimum measures necessary to maintain law and order." (5) In deciding whether measures taken are minimum and necessary, judges should not be distracted by debate on whether an ordinance must establish a prior notification system or a permit system in order to be constitutional, but should instead "consider the spirit of the ordinance as a whole, not superficially, but as a functional entity." (6) The Tokyo Ordinance is constitutional because the Public Safety Commission is clearly required to grant a permit unless "it is clearly recognized" that the demonstration at issue "will directly endanger the maintenance of the public peace." (7) The Public Safety Commission must use its discretion in balancing "maximum respect to freedom of expression" with "its responsibility to the inhabitants to maintain law and order" after thorough study of the particular situation. The ordinance is not "entirely free from the danger" of abuse, but the problem does not justify holding it invalid. (8) Under the ordinance, if the commission puts off deciding on a permit application until after a set time before the planned demonstration, the applicants may not assume they can go ahead with the gathering, and this restraint does not amount to an unconstitutional "general prohibition." (9) Debating about whether the law is too general in referring to places where gatherings may be regulated is "profitless." "In streets and other places" and "in any place whatsoever" are not unconstitutionally general.

The *Tokyo* decision has proved to be a powerful precedent; but judges over time have refined the procedural standards and set concrete guidelines for applying ordinances to places and circumstances, and there is very little legal restraint on vigorous public protest. Since the late 1960s, many judges have taken a more relaxed view of the dangers of demonstrations. The Supreme Court seemed to approve of this stance with its 1975 Grand Bench decision in the Tokushima Ordinance case.

The accused, Teramae, a union official and antiwar activist, was arrested for demonstrating in 1964 against visits by U.S. nuclear submarines, for leading a snake-dance down city streets in 1968 to protest the presence in Japan of B-52 bombers, and for attendant violence. Teramae was convicted under the Road Traffic Law, but article 3 of the Tokushima Public Safety Ordinance was found unconstitutionally vague in requiring demonstration leaders to "maintain orderly traffic." On appeal, the Supreme Court held that although article 3 was not clear enough, it was not unconstitutional, because "a person of ordinary common sense" could figure out how to apply it "in a concrete case."

A decision by Judge Terao of the Tokyo high court in 1977, upheld by the Supreme Court in 1979, showed more appreciation of group political activities and labor campaigns than *Tokyo* and other decisions. Judge Terao upheld 1966 convictions for illegal demonstrations dating from 1961; but he reduced the sentences from imprisonment to mild fines and wondered about the constitutionality of the prior restraint established by the Tokyo ordinance's permit system. Moreover, he criticized those who see danger in demonstrations held by unions and other groups. The Supreme Court sustained the holding in law and society and saw no need to comment on Terao's reasoning, which raised eyebrows in conservative circles.

The status of the freedoms of assembly and association is quite sturdy, and political protest in public is perhaps less restricted than in the United States. On the other hand, there seem to be too many restraints on public employees' rights of expression. Early in the Occupation, government workers were given the same rights as private-sector union members; those rights were suddenly taken away later in the 1940s. Even today, the labor movement remains bitter over this peremptory denial to public employees of freedoms enjoyed by other workers. Special restraints on the freedoms of civil servants and the right to strike are commonplace in democracies, though easily justified only with respect to people who make policy. The Japanese Supreme Court has consistently upheld restrictions on *all* classifications of workers under the National Public Employees Law and related legislation. No distinction is recognized in law, for example, between janitors and vice-ministers. In the famous *Sarufutsu* case (1974), a postal worker was convicted by the Supreme Court, reversing an acquittal, for putting up six political posters on a public bulletin board during his leisure hours, on grounds that public officials must be politically neutral to retain public trust in the impartiality of government administration. The law does not intend to restrict expression of opinion, the court said, but that may be an inevitable side effect. As of 1988, no distinctions between types of public employees have been judicially allowed at the highest level. However, denationalization of industries such as tobacco and communications in the mid-1980s freed large numbers of workers from what may be the least warranted of burdensome restraints on free speech in Japan.[16]

Mass Media Freedom

The mass media in Japan are free, technically competent, diverse, and, taken as a whole, as informative, entertaining, and educative as any nation's system.[17] Sustained investigative newspaper and television reporting on sensitive matters is, as in many democracies, uncommon. Whether one lives in a small mountain village or a great metropolis, one has access to a varied fare of national and local newspapers, magazines, books, films, radio, and television. The media are a major force for further national integration of a people already unusually homogeneous; the noteworthy exception is the million Okinawans, who read their own newspapers and not Japan's nationwide papers. Most important in the communication of opinion and news are a few national newspapers, such as the *Asahi Shimbun, Mainichi Shimbun, Yomiuri Shimbun,* and *Nihon Keizai Shimbun,* each with a daily circulation of millions; in number of copies of newspapers disseminated per thousand people, Japan leads the world. A few of the leading papers also publish books and magazines. Elements of the media are at times entangled in legal disputes over invasion of privacy and defamation, and recurring obscenity debates mirror public and parental concerns.[18] A right of privacy inspired by American conceptions was first recognized as law in a 1964 Tokyo court case concerning Yukio Mishima's political novel *After the Banquet,* which depicts a veiled version of a Tokyo politician's marital affairs. Local governments have passed ordinances assuring both citizens' access to information on official matters and privacy regarding data on individuals in official records; but Japan does not have statutory law on freedom of information or privacy rights.

Each sector of the mass media has one or more systems of self-regulation and attendant industry codes of ethics; such systems count more than laws in the daily balancing of freedom with industry responsibility. Three of the most important Supreme Court decisions on media freedom are the Hakata Station Film case (1969), the Nishiyama State Secrets case (1978), and the Hokkaidō Newsman's Privilege case (1980).[19] In *Hakata,* a district court ordered four local television stations to present for use as evidence film taken in 1968 during a student-police encounter at a train station. The broadcasters refused to comply, even after a unanimous Supreme Court upheld the order; so portions of the film were seized by the police in 1970. (Courts in Japan do not have strong powers of subpoena and contempt; the only thing judges can do when someone refuses to submit evidence, as here, is to issue a seizure warrant.) The students had clashed with police at Hakata (Fukuoka) on their way from demonstrations protesting the visit of a nuclear-powered aircraft carrier, the USS *Enterprise,* in southwest Japan. Little violence occurred and none of the four students arrested was convicted; but numerous lawyers and opposition politicians joined the students in bringing charges against some 870 police officers for allegedly abusing their authority during the scuffles. In the absence of other testimony, and long after the reports had been broadcast, the district court asked the TV companies for footage of the events. With the backing of virtually the entire mass media industry, the companies refused to comply on grounds that "the use of this film as court evidence might render free and impartial newsgathering and reporting impossible"; but the Grand Bench disagreed. The court held that the constitution guarantees the freedom to gather news and to report facts and ideas in service to the public's right to know. But once they had used the film in news programs, the stations had accomplished their purpose in newsgathering; so the court order was not directly related to newsgathering freedom. The court admitted that use of film for another purpose might possibly lead to someone refusing to cooperate with some reporters in the future. However, this freedom has to be balanced against the need for evidence to assure a fair trial, when other sources of evidence were inadequate. While noting that any disadvantage to the media must be kept to the minimum, the court held that the film in this case was virtually indispensable evidence for determining guilt or innocence. The case is noteworthy for many reasons: for judicial endorsement of new aspects of media freedom and democracy, for example, but also for the industry's remarkable cohesion (in an appeal of questionable legal merit) in the face of challenge from the nation's court system. The mass media temporarily took on the cohesion of a small in-group and became a coherent feudal alliance of public and private concerns under perceived threat from a competing power center, the judiciary. In August 1970, the district court upheld the students' contention that an abuse of police authority had occurred, but dismissed their case on grounds of insufficient evidence—the videotapes did not in the end clearly show the identities of individual policemen.

In the mid-1980s, a major political controversy erupted over a state secrets bill proposed by the ruling Liberal Democratic party. The bill was successfully opposed by a coalition of scholars, media people, and politicians on grounds that it could be used in repressive ways and was proposed without prior clarification of citizens' rights to government information. In 1978, when the Supreme Court made its first ruling on newsgathering and state secrets in the *Nishiyama* decision, there was no anti-espionage law. Takichi Nishiyama, a *Mainichi Shimbun* political reporter, violated a solemn promise to his source and leaked to a Diet member information obtained from a lover (K. Hasumi) working in the Foreign Ministry. The revelation concerned the terms under which Okinawa reverted to Japan from the United States in 1972. The government of Prime Minister Eisaku Sato had assured the public that no secret arrangements had been made, but Japan had apparently agreed secretly to pay $5 million to Okinawans in land-damage claims. Nishiyama and Hasumi were found out as sources, arrested, and convicted. Hasumi had violated the prohibition in the National Public Employees Law (article 100 [1]) against leaking secrets learned in the course of carrying out official duties. Nishiyama was guilty of inducing a public employee to commit a crime. The maximum sentence in this case was a year in prison and a small fine; the same maximum could apply to an instance of major treason.

The Supreme Court held: (1) that the courts have the authority to determine what is a state secret and what is merely a political secret; (2) that the government's maintenance of secrecy in these negotiations was proper; (3) that the government's failure to bring the facts in this case to the Diet did not violate the constitutional order or constitute illegal secrecy; and (4) that although free newsgathering and reporting are crucial to the people's right to know and freedom of expression, Nishiyama engaged in illegal inducement in his ethically questionable dealings with Hasumi (both were married). Generally, scholarly commentators felt that Nishiyama should have been acquitted because he was involved in newsgathering activities, but questioned his ethics. Less often noticed was the fact that the *Mainichi Shimbun* "chose to remain silent about the controversial issue of public importance despite its own brave words about a 'people's right to know.' "[20]

In a final relevant case, a "newsman's privilege" not to divulge confidential sources was first recognized by judicial decision in 1979. In 1952, the Supreme Court had denied a claim to professional confidentiality under article 105 of the Code of Criminal Procedure; but in 1980 the same court let stand a 1979 Sapporo district court decision hailed by the media. The court applied provisions on "occupational secrets" in article 281 of the Code of Civil Procedure to the situation of newspaper reporters. Hideshige Shimada, a reporter for the *Hokkaidō Shimbun,* wrote in 1977 that parents had complained about child abuse in a local nursery. M. Sasaki, the alleged object of complaints, brought a civil suit against Shimada and his paper for false and defamatory reporting, asking for damages and a published apology. Under cross-examination, Shimada would not divulge his sources, claiming his right and duty to maintain confidentiality. The district court ruled that the identity of a newsman's confidential sources should be honored under article 281 unless it blocks access to evidence necessary for a fair trial, which was not the case here. Revelation of his sources, the judge held, would impair Shimada's future professional ability to gather and freely report news.

Conclusion

The strengths and problems of civil liberties and constitutionalism in Japan appear in the daily interplay of a hybrid legal system and a group-oriented society which might be termed a "communitarian feudal democracy." As in other democracies, it no longer seems helpful to assume that government and law are more likely to be sources of threat or assistance to the individual than the private sector. Government seems neutral, so vigilance about civil rights needs to be omnidirectional. Japan's non-Western, non-individualist sociolegal culture provides a useful counterpoint for nations like the United States which are in need of a more transcultural understanding of constitutional democracy for the next century. Perhaps it is time for people everywhere to look less at their own democracies and other forms of government through the glasses of Western political theory and constitutional experience, and to begin afresh to induce new democratic legal theory with eyes focused on some of the rich evidence coming from non-Western areas such as Japan.

The evidence from Japan's constitutional culture suggests: (1) that a mutualist understanding may more adequately protect the individuality and the rights of each person than a self-centered individualism blind to the rights and needs of other individuals and the community; (2) that one or both legal traditions of the West—civil law and common law—can be transplanted successfully into the radically different cultural soil of other world regions and yield a distinctively new and healthy flowering; (3) that the trappings of democracy—for example, a parliament or independent courts—may vary in their operation from country to country; but the foundation of constitutional democracy is the same (and is not a Western property but a powerful force in Japan as well as in many other non-Western nations): a recognition of the inherent value of each person everywhere and the duty of the state and society to preserve and serve that human dignity under law; (4) that with respect to religion or ideology and the state, Western democratic and Communist understandings of issues are sometimes irrelevant in other regions, because State Shinto and the emperor in Japan and distinctive indigenous constitutional realities elsewhere (Thailand, Tibet, and Indonesia, for example) do not fit Western analytical frameworks; and finally, (5) that, for the postwar period, it has been politically possible for a major world power to refrain from flexing major military power and to take as one of its guiding constitutional principles that "the Japanese people forever renounce war as a sovereign right of the nation and the threat of use of force as a means of settling international disputes" (article 9) so that "never again shall we be visited with the horrors of war through the action of government" (preamble).

NOTES

1. Lawrence Ward Beer, *Freedom of Expression in Japan: A Study in Comparative Law, Politics, and Society* (Tokyo: Kodansha International, 1985), pp. 71–82.

2. For the text in English of the Constitution of Japan, see Hiroshi Itoh and Lawrence Ward Beer, *The Constitutional Case Law of Japan* (Seattle: University of Washington Press, 1978), pp. 256–69. This book contains major Supreme Court decisions in translation.

3. Information on dates of constitutions was kindly provided by Professor Albert P. Blaustein, Rutgers University Law School, January 1988.

4. Beer, *Freedom,* chap. 1.

5. On Japan's modern law, see ibid., chaps. 2 and 4; also Itoh and Beer, *Constitutional Case Law,* and the journal *Law in Japan* published by the Asian Land Program, University of Washington, Seattle. On the evolution of the postwar courts, see David J. Danelski, "Judicial Review and Democracy in Japan," a paper presented at the Congress of the International Political Science Association, Paris, 1985.

6. Itoh and Beer, *Constitutional Case Law,* p. 266.

7. Ibid., p. 268.

8. Ibid., pp. 258–61. For examples of Japanese categorization of human rights, see the authoritative *Kempō Hanrei Hyakusen,* special issues nos. 68 and 69, published by the leading law journal *Jurisuto* (Tokyo: Yuhikaku Publishing Company, April and May 1980).

9. Civil Code of Japan, Law 89 of 1896, as amended.

10. On the malapportionment issue, see Lawrence W. Beer, "Japan's Constitutional System and Its Judicial Interpretation," in *Law and Society in Contemporary Japan,* ed. John O. Haley (Dubuque: Hunt Publishing Company, 1988), pp. 26–28. Other Japanese law professionals support a 2–1 discrepancy as the most allowed by the constitution, or even "one person, one vote" as the standard.

11. Beer, *Freedom,* pp. 30–36.

12. Itoh and Beer, *Constitutional Case Law,* p. 259.

13. Beer, *Freedom,* pp. 109–10, 139–40; and Dan Fenno Henderson, *Conciliation and Japanese Law: Tokugawa and Modern,* 2 vols. (Seattle: University of Washington Press, 1965).

14. For more detailed discussion of lay commissioners and counselors, see Lawrence W. Beer, "Human Rights Commissioners (*Jinken Yogo Iin*) and Lay Protection of Human Rights in Japan," Occasional Paper No. 31, International Ombudsman Institute, Alberta, Canada, October 1985.

15. Beer, *Freedom,* chap. 5.

16. Ibid., chap. 6.

17. Ibid., pp. 281–89.

18. Ibid., chaps. 9 and 10.

19. Ibid., chap. 8.

20. Ronald Brown, "Government Secrecy and the 'People's Right to Know' in Japan," *Law in Japan* 10 (1977):138–39.

5

Political Parties and Political Opposition

●

J. A. A. STOCKWIN

Democracy, Opposition, and One-Party Dominance

The failure of the opposition parties to take power in Japan over a very long period raises questions of fundamental importance, not only about the politics of Japan, but also about parliamentary democracy in general.[1] Between 1945 and 1955 the national government was controlled by various groups that in 1955 joined to form the Liberal Democratic party (LDP) which has monopolized national political office since that time. (For about eighteen months in 1947–48 there were two successive coalition governments which included the Japan Socialist party; and from December 1983 to July 1986 the LDP ruled in coalition with a tiny conservative fragment, the New Liberal Club.) Conservatives and conservative independents have formed a majority in every election since the war for both the lower and the upper houses of the National Diet. Japan, to borrow Giovanni Sartori's terminology, has a predominant party system which is of unusual longevity.[2] Sweden provides a somewhat comparable example of longevity in power by a single party (the Social Democrats), but Japan is arguably the industrialized world's only unambiguous example of *conservative* longevity.

The most important question which this raises for the understanding of parliamentary democracy is whether it really matters. Can a predominant party system like that of Japan sit easily within the category of "parliamentary democracy" or should it be a matter of serious complaint that the party in power does not change over several decades? If parties in opposition never take office, does this mean that the system ceases to be genuinely democratic?

Two contrasting kinds of answers may be given to these questions. The first would deny that a predominant party system is necessarily undemocratic: even though the same party always takes power, this occurs on the basis of the freely expressed will of the electorate, which has the freedom to dismiss the government and replace it with the opposition should it so wish. The electorate, however, has not so chosen, and this ought to be interpreted as indicating electoral satisfaction, rather than a defect in the system. Reinforcing this argument is the suggestion that continuity in power creates continuity, and thus consistency, in administration. Government based on one-party dominance may thus plan from a long-term perspective, without having to adjust traumatically to elections which change the party or parties in power.

The opposite kind of answer is that predominant party politics fails to provide access to power (or the prospect of access to power) for those parties and their supporters which are permanently out of office. Thus a very substantial part of the electorate, and a major segment of those who enter politics, are deprived of the opportunity to participate—or elect those who participate—in the control of government. The argument is reinforced by the more empirical consideration that predominant party politics may lack the stimulus provided by fairly regular alternation in power. Alternating politics—according to this argument—is rather like the effect of the tide on a beach: by a regular tidal process of flushing and cleansing, the beach is kept pristine, fresh, and free of detritus and jetsam. A beach not subject to tidal action needs cleansing by other mechanisms if it is to stay pure and function properly as a beach.

A further related set of questions concerns the role of opposition parties in a predominant party system. To what extent, if at all, are opposition parties able to exercise influence despite having little or no possibility of taking office? Does the fact that opposition parties are effectively excluded from office impel them to seek alternative channels of influence? Is this likely to mean that they will resort, out of frustration, to such "extraparliamentary" activities as the fomenting of riots and demonstrations? Will they, more broadly, seek to exercise veto power against government policies of which they particularly disapprove, or will they rather tend eventually to become clients of those in office?

Comparative Perspectives

Before measuring a predominant party system against a model of alternation in power, we should note that the latter has rather few actual examples. The British political system is most often cited as an example of alternating "swing of the pendulum" politics, but an examination of past history shows that it is an imperfect example, at best. The Conservatives won three successive general elections, each with a larger majority than the last, and formed governments continuously between 1951 and 1964, while Labour appeared to be the dominant party (despite losing the 1970 election) from 1964 to 1979. Moreover, the establishment of the Alliance between the Liberals and the Social Democratic party (formed as a Labour breakaway in 1981) has now imparted a three-party, or even four-party, character to British politics which squares ill with the principles of alternating politics.[3]

When we look at parliamentary democracies other than the British, we see a bewildering variety of possibilities, from predominant conservative parties facing occasionally successful labor party challenges, such as Australia and New Zealand, through fluid multiparty systems with a marked conservative predominance, such as Italy, to social-democratic predominance facing conservative challenge, as in parts of Scandinavia. The United States exhibits features of alternation in elections both to the presidency (restricted to two four-year terms) and to Congress, but the system is so different in operation from that of a European-style parliamentary democracy that comparison is problematic.

Anything like a "pure" example of alternation in power is thus extremely hard to find. Nevertheless, in most parliamentary democracies the parties in office do change from time to time. France is an interesting example of a country where a long period of ascendancy by center-right forces was replaced between 1981 and 1986 by a Socialist/Communist ascendancy (from which the Communists excluded themselves in July 1984). Even in Italy, where the Christian Democratic party has ruled, alone or in coalition, for nearly four decades, the composition of coalitions changes and, as in 1983–85, it is even possible for a non–Christian Democrat (the leader of the small Socialist party) to be prime minister. Japan is close to the extreme end of a spectrum ranging from systems where no change in the party composition of governments takes place over several decades to systems where governments and oppositions have exchanged places from time to time and will possibly do so in the future.

The absence of "pure" alternating systems thus should not blind us to the fact that in democratic politics a situation of no change whatsoever in the party composition of cabinets is unusual, and change as an unsurprising, if irregular, expectation of political life is closer to the "norm." What then is the basis for belief in regular alternation and single party predominance respectively?

The "classic" justification for regular alternation on what was thought to be the British model was that it was a method of spreading effective representation to diverse sections of the society and thus binding it together. Supporters of the party currently out of power could realistically expect that in the foreseeable future their party would attain office, and therefore they were not disinclined to follow the parliamentary road. A further justification was that so long as defeat at the polls was a real and not just a theoretical possibility, a government was likely to be kept on its toes, would be careful to avoid so far as possible inept or grossly unpopular measures and would be constantly concerned to maintain its reputation for probity and effectiveness. In other words, responsible and representative government was likely to ensue.[4] For two-party alternating politics in a parliamentary democracy to work well, a necessary condition, in this view, is that it should be centripetal, that is, the two major parties should both compete electorally for the "middle ground of the electorate," or in other words for moderate opinion that in some way lies between the mainstream ideological positions of the two parties themselves. These "moderate" electors are (according to this theory) a pragmatic, nonideological lot, so that if they hold the key to which party wins elections, governments themselves should be less ideologically committed than the activists in each party would like.

In order for these conditions to obtain, however, three further conditions must be fulfilled. First, government and opposition must alternate *in practice* with reasonable regularity. A party cast into long-term opposition is likely to experience the kind of disillusionment that in political terms tends to create a centrifugal, rather than centripetal system. Second, and more important, the party leadership must both be committed to pursuit of power by appeal to moderate electoral opinion, and also be able to control and avoid being controlled by partisan activists in its own ranks. Third, policies must be crowned by a reasonable degree of success. If substantial sections of the electorate begin to perceive that reasonable, middle-of-the-road policies are failing to stem a drift into national economic decline, then the legitimacy of centripetal alternating politics is likely to recede. Instead of being seen as the politics of sweet reason, it comes to be regarded by dissatisfied elements as the politics of "Tweedledum and Tweedledee."[5]

In the British case, the political center of gravity of both major parties had by the late 1970s moved conspicuously toward their respective extremes and away from middle-of-the-road consensual politics, which despite much confrontational rhetoric had prevailed since the 1950s. The rise of the Alliance of Liberals and Social Democrats in the early 1980s stemmed from widespread dissatisfaction with the polarization of the two major parties under diverging leadership. Ironically, however, the effect of the Alliance's emergence was to split the opposition to the radical Conservative government of Margaret Thatcher, and, given the highly nonproportional electoral system based on single-member constituencies, the inability of either the Labor party or its centrist rivals to eliminate the other could perhaps permit the long-term continuation of Conservative rule.

Changing Japanese Perspectives

During the late 1950s and early 1960s many political observers within Japan believed that Japanese politics were likely to travel down a road leading to alternating politics and that such a system as it operated in Britain and elsewhere had merits that were readily transferable to Japan.[6] Today in contrast, it has become quite fashionable to present Japan as an example demonstrating the merits of nonalternating politics.[7] Several factors appear to be at the root of this remarkable change in approach.

From a Japanese point of view, lack of appeal in British-style alternating politics (whatever it may have meant in practice) reflected in part the perception that the British economy was in relative decline. A common belief in Japan about the British (and other European) politicoeconomic systems was that conflict between antagonistic and well-organized social classes served to inhibit economic progress. Alternating government therefore was seen as essentially the political reflection of (or at best, an attempt to manage) a fundamentally class-divided society from which Japan is happily distinct.

The other side of this coin was that domestic criticism of Japan's own politicoeconomic arrangements declined as belief in Japan as an economic success story capable of overtaking in economic competitiveness regions such as Europe, became widespread.[8] Political continuity and stability, allied with social discipline, diligence, resourcefulness, and communal striving for group goals on the part of a technologically educated work force were seen as highly desirable features of the system.

The specifically political part of this evaluation contains some interesting nuances. Defenders of the system are perfectly prepared to criticize (often in forthright terms) particular politicians or decisions or even institutions, but assume as a matter virtually beyond argument that the LDP will and should continue more or less to monopolize the right to form cabinets. The opposition parties are dismissed as incapable of governing in their own right, although it is conceded that one or other of the smaller middle-of-the-road parties might be brought into government as a junior partner. (This has already happened with the New Liberal Club (NLC) that in 1986 was reabsorbed into the LDP from which it defected, in a protest over corruption, in 1976.)

There are certain tacit assumptions here of great importance. One is that there is no point in upsetting the channels of communication that have been built up over a long period between the LDP government ministries and a range of interest groups. In the main, these relationships are thought to work well and result in policy outcomes which are both realistic and forward-looking.[9] Another is that the opposition parties have shown little evidence of their capacity to undertake responsible government. They are badly fragmented and do not effectively cooperate because each is seeking increased parliamentary representation at the expense of the others. The quality of their leadership is generally low and they lack the depth and extent of contacts and experience that the LDP possesses. Third, and at a deeper level of analysis (or rather, feeling), the concept of alternation of power, or even the idea that the opposition parties might have a realistic chance of governing at rare intervals, runs counter to the sense of a unified Japanese polity, in which so far as possible a patron-client relationship is maintained between the central government and other elements within the system, whether these be interest groups (other than those semi-incorporated into central government), local government authorities, or political parties in opposition.

The opposition parties themselves are taking on some of the characteristics of government clients. Essentially this is because a party permanently out of office is still faced with the necessity of effectively representing its supporters, even though it has no chance of doing so by attaining office and seeking to put its proposals into law. Except in the case of parties whose ideological opposition to the established government is uncompromising, parties in permanent opposition must over a long period be strongly tempted to be drawn into a client role vis-à-vis government, including the party in office. There is evidence that faction leaders in the LDP actively pursue contacts for their own purposes with leaders of some opposition parties, which have been developing a relationship with the LDP smacking of clientelism. In any case, the parties in opposition occupy a largely peripheral position in the political system, and this has come to be widely accepted as their natural situation. The LDP, by contrast, has become a kind of "Japan-party," in other words, the party whose natural role it is to run Japan.

Opposition Parties and their Position in the Japanese Party System

We now turn to the principal focus of this chapter, which is why the opposition parties have been so unsuccessful since the 1950s in attaining office at national level, and whether this really matters. Let us examine first why the opposition has failed in what should presumably have been its primary task, that of attaining office.

The opposition as a whole has had some successes since the 1950s, but the picture is one of progressive fragmentation and proliferation. The LDP, on the other hand, despite rumors of splits, has only once suffered an organized defection, that of the New Liberal Club in 1976 (though individuals have occasionally defected).[10] At the general elections for the House of Representatives held in May 1958, 97 percent of seats were taken by the two major parties, the LDP and the Japan Socialist party (JSP), with the JSP winning 35.5 percent. In 1988 there were five parties in opposition, none of which had even been in government since the LDP was formed in 1955. How they have all fared in successive elections can be seen in table 1.

Of them, the JSP remained the largest parliamentary party throughout, but its strength was declining or at least remaining static, its image was generally regarded as poor, and from its status in the late 1950s as

TABLE 1

Opposition Party Performance in the House of Representatives, 1958–1983

(votes in units of one thousand)

		JSP	DSP	Kōmeitō	JCP	SDL
22/5/58	Seats	166 (35.5%)			1 (0.2%)	
	Votes	13,094 (32.9%)			1,012 (2.6%)	
20/11/60	Seats	145 (31.0%)	17 (3.7%)		3 (0.6%)	
	Votes	10,887 (27.6%)	3,464 (8.8%)		1,157 (2.9%)	
21/11/63	Seats	144 (30.8%)	23 (4.9%)		5 (1.1%)	
	Votes	11,907 (29.0%)	3,023 (7.4%)		1,646 (4.0%)	
29/1/67	Seats	140 (28.8%)	30 (6.2%)	25 (5.1%)	5 (1.0%)	
	Votes	12,826 (27.9%)	3,404 (7.4%)	2,472 (5.4%)	2,191 (4.8%)	
27/12/69	Seats	90 (18.5%)	31 (6.4%)	47 (9.7%)	14 (2.9%)	
	Votes	10,074 (21.4%)	3,637 (7.7%)	5,125 (10.9%)	3,199 (6.8%)	
10/12/72	Seats	118 (24.0%)	19 (3.9%)	29 (5.9%)	38 (7.7%)	
	Votes	11,479 (21.9%)	3,661 (7.0%)	4,437 (8.5%)	5,497 (10.5%)	
5/12/76	Seats	123 (24.1%)	29 (5.7%)	55 (10.8%)	17 (3.3%)	
	Votes	11,713 (20.7%)	3,554 (6.3%)	6,177 (10.9%)	5,878 (10.4%)	
7/10/79	Seats	107 (20.9%)	35 (6.3%)	57 (11.2%)	39 (7.6%)	2 (0.4%)
	Votes	10,643 (19.7%)	3,664 (6.8%)	5,283 (9.8%)	5,626 (10.4%)	368 (0.7%)
22/6/80	Seats	107 (20.9%)	32 (6.3%)	33 (6.5%)	29 (5.7%)	3 (0.5%)
	Votes	11,401 (19.3%)	3,897 (6.6%)	5,330 (9.0%)	5,804 (9.8%)	402 (0.7%)
18/12/83	Seats	112 (21.9%)	38 (7.4%)	58 (11.8%)	26 (5.1%)	3 (0.5%)
	Votes	11,065 (19.5%)	4,130 (7.3%)	5,746 (10.1%)	5,302 (9.3%)	381 (0.7%)
6/7/86	Seats	85 (16.6%)	26 (5.1%)	56 (10.9%)	26 (5.1%)	4 (0.8%)
	Votes	10,412 (17.2%)	3,896 (6.4%)	5,701 (9.4%)	5,313 (8.8%)	499 (0.8%)

SOURCE: *Asahi Nenkan*, various issues.

JSP = Japan Socialist party (Nihon Shakaitō)
DSP = Democratic Socialist party (Minshatō)

JCP = Japan Communist party (Nihon Kyōsantō)
SDL = Social Democratic League (Shaminren)

the only significant party in opposition, it has become merely primus inter pares. The Democratic Socialist party (DSP) was formed in 1960 as a splinter from the JSP. The defectors were unhappy about what they regarded as pro-Communist tendencies in the JSP leadership during the political crisis over revision of the Mutual Security Treaty with the United States. The DSP, backed by the Dōmei federation of labor unions, has considerable support among certain categories of private sector workers, but has never managed to win more than thirty-eight lower house seats (its total at the elections of December 1983).

The Kōmeitō (sometimes called in English the Clean Government party)[11] is based on the Sōka Gakkai sect of Nichiren Buddhism and was formed as a political party contesting parliamentary elections in the early 1960s. Although it broke formal links with the Sōka Gakkai in the early 1970s, those who vote for it are still largely sect members. The sect has a tightly knit organization, and the Kōmeitō is able to calculate with remarkable accuracy the number of its voters in advance of an election. Its support is heavily concentrated in big cities and among workers in small firms and their wives. It attracts about 10 percent of the vote and its policies are generally moderate.

The Japan Communist party (JCP) is by far the oldest party in Japan but has only been legal since 1945. After a brief flowering during the occupation, when it fought (unsuccessfully) to control the labor union movement, it entered a period of persecution and internal dissent in the 1950s, when it lost nearly all its parliamentary representation. Under more united and resolute leadership in the 1960s, however, the JCP built up its grass-roots organization to a point where it was able to gain as much as 10 percent of the vote[12] and more than thirty seats in lower house elections. It has since declined slightly in support.

The Social Democratic League (SDL; also sometimes called in English the United Social Democratic party) was a right-of-center breakaway from the JSP at the time of the latter's leadership troubles in 1977–78. It is a miniparty which once engaged in some parliamentary and electoral cooperation with the NLC.

Several points emerge from our analysis of the process of opposition party fragmentation. First, since the 1950s both the LDP and the JSP have declined considerably in strength in the big cities of Japan's eastern seaboard where concentrations of people live. In those areas in the 1960s and 1970s the JSP suffered even more serious losses than the LDP, as the two of them saw their votes eaten into by a JSP splinter (the DSP), a new religious party (the Kōmeitō) and an old party revived (the JCP). To some extent the electoral situation now appears to have stabilized with the opposition stuck in this fragmented condition.

Some indication of the difference in vote catchments of the various parties may be seen in table 2. In this table, the vote totals for the eight prefectures containing the biggest cities have been listed in descending order for each party. From this it may be seen that the LDP and JSP are similar in concentrating the big-city prefectures exclusively at the bottom end of the table; in other words, they perform most poorly in metropolitan constituencies. This is in extreme contrast to the Kōmeitō, JSP, and NLC-SDL (the last two miniparties combined their meager strength in that election), whose performance in the eight metropolitan prefectures lies toward the top end of the table. Only the DSP has a fair spread, though with marked urban concentration in the Nagoya area and in Kansai.

This appears to reflect the establishment of new loyalties with the rapid postwar urbanization, together with a notable increase in the urban protest vote. From this, however, the JSP with its old-fashioned and unappealing image signally failed to profit. On the other hand, in the remoter rural prefectures of Kyūshū, Tōhoku, and elsewhere, where the LDP is overwhelmingly strong, the JSP remains the only opposition party with any substantial following.

This picture is extremely interesting when we contemplate the differences in electoral behavior that have led to this result. To oversimplify, whereas the countryside is the two-party preserve of the LDP and JSP, with the former outclassing the latter, the big cities are an arena of political competition among five or six roughly equal political parties. It is common in metropolitan constituencies for no party to win more than one seat (each constituency elects several members), whereas in rural constituencies the LDP regularly wins two, three, or even four. In other words, the impact of urban protest against government policies is severely blunted by the babel of voices against the LDP even though the LDP itself has lost much ground in city areas. When to this is added the failure substantially to redraw constituency boundaries to take account of population shifts,[13] we come closer to an explanation why the LDP remains so entrenched in power. In order, however, to penetrate to the deeper reasons why this so, we need to look at the electoral system, especially that for the lower house.

Electoral Politics

The electoral system has two key features: it is based on multi-member constituencies, and the voter has a single nontransferable vote. Until 1987, all constituencies for the House of Representatives (except one) elected either three, four, or five members. The 1987 reform created, in addition, one six-member and four two-member constituencies. Each voter has one vote, and there is no possibility of vote transfer or preferential voting. This system (or something very like it) has been in use in all House of Representatives elections between 1925 and World War II, and in all such elections since 1947. Its correct designation is "single nontransferable vote (SNTV) in medium-sized constituencies."

Since the system has been in use for the bulk of Japan's electoral history, and since it is rare outside Japan, we may well call it "the Japanese system of voting." The system has several important effects. First of all, it is possible for a candidate to be elected in a five-member constituency with as little as 10 percent of the total votes (two-, three-, and four-member constituencies are naturally less permissive). This makes it easy for small parties, for factions within large parties, and for individual candidates with a personal base of support, to be elected. Conversely, it creates conditions inimical to the imposition of tight party discipline such as is required for the development of a (pre-Alliance) British-style two-party system. For instance, a party able to muster, say, 15 to 20 percent of the vote in all of the forty-three five-member constituencies would have a quite reasonable chance of electing one member in most of them. Under the British system candidates are rarely elected with less than 30 to 35 percent of the vote in a given constituency. This makes things very hard for small parties without a regional base. In the Japanese but not the British system a dissident group within a party has considerable incentive to defect and establish a new party.

Another effect of the Japanese system is that it does not encourage the voter to think of party rather than personality. The voter knows that several members will be elected from his constituency but he merely has a single vote, which he cannot transfer in any preferential way. He also cannot vote for a list of candidates.[14] It is possible, therefore, for individual candidates (including candidates for big parties such as the LDP in the many constituencies where several of them are standing) to cultivate a strictly personal, strictly nontransferable

TABLE 2
Urban Support for Parties by Prefecture in the National (PR) Constituency: House of Councillors Elections, 1983

Order of Voting Strength per Prefecture	LDP		JSP		DSP		Kōmeitō		JCP		NLC-SDL[a]	
	Const.	% vote	Const.	% vote	Const.	% vote	Const.	% vote	Const.	% vote	Const.	% vote
1					Aichi	16.28	Ōsaka	22.89	Kyōto	20.97	Kanagawa	8.52
2					Hyōgo	14.17			Ōsaka	16.70	Saitama	7.39
3					Ōsaka	11.63					Tōkyō	5.19
4							Hyōgo	19.77	Tōkyō	11.92	Chiba	2.94
5												
6					Kanagawa	10.08						
7												
8												
9							Tōkyō	17.89				
10							Saitama	17.51	Hyōgo	10.41	Kyōto	2.01
11									Saitama	10.47	Ōsaka	1.96
12							Kanagawa	17.40				
13									Kanagawa	8.79		
14											Hyōgo	1.84
15							Chiba	16.55				
16							Aichi	15.98	Aichi	8.28		
17												
18					Kyōto	8.46					Aichi	1.65
19												
20									Chiba	7.77		
21												
22					Tōkyō	8.04	Kyōto	14.86				
23												
24												

Order of Voting Strength per Prefecture	LDP		JSP		DSP		Kōmeitō		JCP		NLC-SDL[a]	
	Const.	% vote	Const.	% vote	Const.	% vote	Const.	% vote	Const.	% vote	Const.	% vote
25												
26					Chiba	6.92						
27												
28					Saitama	6.48						
29												
30												
31												
32												
33												
34												
35												
36												
37			Kanagawa	14.07								
38			Hyōgo	13.68								
39												
40	Chiba	33.21	Chiba	13.27								
41	Kyōto	31.79										
42	Aichi	31.09	Saitama	11.99								
43	Saitama	29.05	Aichi	11.69								
44	Tōkyō	27.62										
45	Hyōgo	27.34	Kyōto	10.25								
46	Osaka	24.94	Tōkyō	9.98								
47	Kanagawa	22.67	Osaka	9.18								

SOURCE: *Nihon Keizai Shinbun*, 27 June 1983.

Note. The eight most urban prefectures are listed.

a. The New Liberal Club and the Social Democratic League were in alliance for this election.

local base of support (in Japanese *jiban* or *jimoto*). This in turn tends to promote, though it is by no means the only factor promoting, factionalism within the larger parties.

We are here faced with a considerable analytical dilemma, which is also of importance for our study of Japanese democracy. Put in crude terms, does the Japanese system of voting simply reflect the norms of Japanese society, being thus the "natural" system for Japan, or is it, on the contrary, an "introduced" system which itself has structured the party system and created its features of one-party dominance, fragmented opposition, factionalism endemic in big parties and so on? The problem is that most of the evidence could lead more or less equally plausibly to either conclusion. For instance, does the fact that the system has lasted so long mean that it fits in with social and political norms which may be regarded as "given," or does it, on the other hand, mean that it has persisted because it is convenient for the ruling LDP establishment?

Fragmentary and incomplete evidence leading to suggestive conclusions does exist, but it is insufficient to produce a clear general answer. In the 1986 House of Councillors elections (as in previous elections) twenty-six out of the seventy-six seats available in prefectural constituencies were fought as contests to elect a single member, or in other words as British-style contests. Of these every one was contested by a single LDP candidate, all but five were contested by the JSP, all but one were contested (hopelessly) by the JCP, and two were fought by the DSP. Twenty-three contests resulted in LDP victories, and three were won by independents. In this example, therefore, LDP multiple candidacy (and therefore much of the rationale for factionalism) was eliminated, only one party (the JSP) presented a serious opposition candidate in nearly all the constituencies, and the JCP only ran because of its longstanding policy of contesting all constituencies, however hopeless. The JSP did so badly because nearly all the upper house single-member constituencies are in rural prefectures where the LDP has a natural majority. The system, however, largely eliminated overt manifestations of LDP factionalism and most minor party candidacies apart from the Communists. In other words, it is at least arguable that it forced the LDP and the opposition in general to behave not unlike major parties in Britian.

Another tantalizingly incomplete piece of evidence comes again from the 1986 upper house elections, where for the second time fifty seats were contested in a nationwide constituency using list system proportional representation (PR). (Before 1983 these seats had been contested at each upper house election based on the single nontransferable vote.) The LDP vote was 38.58 percent, or substantially below the national LDP total in the simultaneous 1986 lower house elections (elected under SNTV in medium-sized constituencies) of 49.4 percent. It seems at least a plausible hypothesis that when voters were confronted with an impersonal list of names and an instruction to vote for a party, fewer of them were inclined to vote for the LDP than in the cosier constituencies of the House of Representatives which gave ample opportunity and incentive for personality voting.

On the other hand it also seems to be true that the lower house electoral system survives because it is, or has become, an integral part of the political system. Whether this means that it is the "natural" system for Japan is a metaphysical question which is beyond our capacity to resolve. It seems, however, that it survives because it is in the interests of most of the participants in politics that it should survive. It is convenient for the LDP for several reasons: it fosters personality voting, which is advantageous in rural constituencies where the party presents several candidates; it perpetuates opposition fragmentation by allowing minor parties to survive; the failure to rectify imbalance in the value of a vote between rural and urban constituencies (the "negative gerrymander") gives the LDP more seats than it deserves from its vote percentage and so helps it win elections; at a more abstract level, fostering the proliferation of parties in opposition has perpetuated an LDP monopoly of power which has gradually sapped opposition morale in the sense of determination to take power. The notion of a natural, experienced, and responsible party of power is then easy to promote, with its counterpart, a fragmented, irresponsible, inexperienced opposition, bereft of serious political ideas, which it would be foolish to admit to the corridors of power.

More surprisingly, the present system is also convenient, to a greater or lesser degree, to the opposition parties themselves. That it is convenient for the DSP, Kōmeitō, JCP, and other minor parties, is easy to understand. They would probably be eliminated from Parliament in a British-style system. The JSP too, however, has opposed change on more than one occasion. Apart from the fact that it appears to reap a marginal advantage from the "negative gerrymander" (see table 1), its loss of votes to minor parties in the big cities means that it would have virtually no safe seats in present circumstances if the British system were adopted. Its distribution of support has diverged greatly from that of the British Labour party, which concentrates its support in inner city and mining areas, particularly in the north of England, Scotland, and South Wales.

A similar exercise to that just attempted in relation to a change to the British electoral system might also be essayed with various systems of proportional representation. Here we have some concrete data to analyze, because PR has now partially been introduced into elections for the upper house. Limited though it is, this reform might be seen as revolutionary in its implications because the voter votes for a party, not a single candidate. He still, however, only has a single *nontransferable* vote, and therefore is unable to express his preferences beyond one party list. The results of the experiment in 1983 and 1986 show a reduction in the LDP vote percentage, and a further proliferation of small parties.[15]

If we return, however, to the British system of election, we should note that JSP objections might not prove valid in the long term. Much would depend on whether that party were able to seize the initiative in the creation of a new effective second party in the aftermath of the electoral elimination of most of the minor parties. A whole new political game would have emerged, with far-reaching implications for all parties and politicians. Whether a two-party system with frequent or infrequent alternation were to emerge would depend on a fairly long-term series of initiatives and developments following the reform. Unfortunately political scientists do not possess laboratories where these things can be tested through experimental procedures.

Japanese electoral politics has achieved a position of relatively stable (perhaps even extremely stable) equilibrium. Few people believe that a change of government (except in the sense of "incorporation" of minor parties) will take place in the foreseeable future. Without a radical change in the electoral system (and perhaps not even then) the only event likely to precipitate a serious change in the party composition of cabinets would be a split of the LDP into two parties of roughly equal size as a result of factional quarreling. Even then it seems quite possible that they would form a coalition government with each other, which would scarcely constitute much of a change.

The Opposition's Role in Japanese Politics

The stable equilibrium of Japanese politics (which should not be confused with illusory "metastability"[16]) favors the LDP at the ex-

pense of the opposition and excludes the opposition from most meaningful participation in policymaking. On the other hand, the opposition since the 1950s has managed to exercise a certain degree of veto
power, the results of which are to be seen in particular in defense
policy. The "no war" clause (article 9) of the 1946 constitution would
seem, according to a literal interpretation, to render armed forces
("military potential") illegal. Although the LDP has patently not been
inhibited by this article from building up the quite impressive military
force euphemistically described as the Self-Defense Forces, it has
never been able to revise the article (nor any other article in the
constitution) because the opposition has blocked the two-thirds majority of both houses of the Diet required before a proposal for constitutional revision can be put to a referendum of the people. So far as
actual defense policy is concerned, the fact that it has been developed
in an atmosphere of controversy about the legal status of the Self-
Defense Forces may be seen as some measure of the opposition's
effectiveness. The LDP itself, however, has been divided on defense
matters, with some influential groups being strongly in favor of restraint.[17] On the other hand, there has been some erosion of anti-
defense thinking on the part of oppposition parties.

The National Diet has been a forum for the exercise of a limited
amount of opposition influence though the manner of its exercise has
changed over time. During the 1950s and 1960s there were set-piece
confrontations over contentious issues, in which the opposition (at
that time largely the JSP) would resort to filibustering and boycotts in
order to block government legislation. The filibuster was used because the government lacked complete control of the parliamentary
timetable. The opposition was sometimes able to force a delay to the
point where contentious legislation would lapse at the end of the
session. There was a limit to the extent to which extraordinary sessions of the Diet could defeat these tactics. Boycotting the Diet (or its
committees) also had some success because the LDP was at times
inhibited from resorting to the "forced vote," where it would pass the
legislation on its own votes in the absence of the opposition.

For several years during the 1970s, known as the *hakuchū* or
"parity" period, the opposition parties had sufficient parliamentary
strength to deny the LDP control of key committees of both houses.
This was a time of greater give and take in relations between government and opposition, partly because of changes within the opposition itself: it was now not one party but several, with the small

centrist parties favoring a conciliatory approach. It is doubtful whether the fragmented opposition parties even during the *hakuchū* period, with their narrow clienteles, were ever able to make much of a *positive* impact on policy. Since the end of the *hakuchū* period in 1980, government-opposition relationships have still been notably less confrontational than in the 1960s. The LDP is able to buy off the opposition with minor concessions on many issues, which makes less surprising the frequency with most of the opposition parties vote with the government. The publicity given to noisy confrontation on certain issues ought not to obscure the backstage deals on many others.

All this, however, is less important than the overwhelming fact that the opposition remains a weak and rather minor force in political decision making. It has faced the unenviable dilemma of other long-term oppositions—whether to adopt a strategy of confrontation or assimilation. In postwar Japan, confrontation used to be crucially important, but has tended to give way to assimilation. The tendency is aided and abetted by the mechanisms of clientelism, put into operation by sections of the LDP with a view to "subverting" sections of the opposition. Most of the opposition parties, but not the Communists, have virtually opted out of serious policy formulation on "hard" issues of economic choice. Civil servants admit that they only take serious note of policy proposals emanating from the LDP and are able to forget about most of what comes from the opposition, which they would say is hardly "policy" in any case.[18]

Conclusion

In conclusion, let us return to the principal questions posed by the "predominant party" character of Japanese politics since the 1950s, and the weakness of the opposition faced with the impressive political success of the LDP.

Why the system has evolved in this way is a question best answered by comparison with other nations. Where something approaching the alternating politics model has operated, the major parties have been able to stay reasonably close to the "middle ground" of political opinion. Also, related to this, they have continued to represent the interests of broad sections of the community, rather than confining their appeal to narrow groups. This in turn has contributed to their general moderation of approach. They have for the most part avoided severe polarization based on region, religion, class, or ideology, even though these factors have played some part. In addition, the major parties have remained reasonably intact and have avoided excessive fragmentation.

In Japan, from the late 1950s onward, one major party, the JSP, rather than following the "aggregative" path of the German Social Democrats or the British Labour party, turned inward on itself and sought to appeal to the ideologically committed and to what the party itself defined, somewhat unrealistically, as the working class of Japan. This led to various evils from the party's point of view. Talented people of moderate views were forced out of the party, its base of support narrowed, and much of its electoral support, especially in the cities, was eroded by minor parties, notably the Kōmeitō, the DSP, and the JCP.

To an extent this would have been understandable had Japan been a society severely divided along class lines. It was difficult, however, to view the nation in the 1960s and 1970s in this way, and indeed many commentators have noted that contemporary Japan appears to be remarkably homogeneous. While not accepting the more extreme versions of this view, it is nevertheless difficult to understand the rationale behind the direction of the JSP appeal in that period. Minor parties were able to erode its support as a result, though it is worth noting that none of them succeeded in aggregating widely different sources of support and evolving into major parties. It is true that rapid economic growth tended to erode the JSP's appeal, but that ought to have dictated evolution toward the more mundane and practical concerns of the electorate, rather than a retreat to narrow Marxist rhetoric. However we state the problem, the rationale behind the JSP approach in the 1960s and 1970s is difficult to understand. The net effect of JSP failure combined with limited success by the minor parties has been to weaken the opposition, even though, as we have seen, it is not entirely impotent.

Our final concern, raised in the introduction to this chapter, is whether the weakness of the opposition has really mattered. A respectable case can be made for the view that it has not. Essentially the argument is that the LDP has brought good government to Japan. In face of this one salient fact, what some might regard as blemishes, such as factional struggle, corrupt dealings, personality rather than party voting, opposition clientelism, and so on, pale into insignificance. Politics in Japan has developed in such a way as to avoid for the most part the economically debilitating effects of strong horizontally organized unions confronting employers. The governability problem besetting European politics in the 1970s has been rather less salient in Japan. The Japanese way of conducting politics has evolved in the direction of strong central government able to stay in control without stifling local and private initiative. It is true that some decision making is characterized by immobilism, though there are subtle ways in which immobility is paraded as an argument against foreign pressure in issues of trade and defense.[19] Indeed it is quite possible to construct an argument that policy immobilism has actually contributed to the national interest, in particular by slowing down foreign-induced change in ways that enable the domestic economy to adjust to them more easily.

On the other hand, a largely impotent, fragmented, and in part clientelist opposition is a feature of the Japanese system of politics which is difficult to reconcile with notions of democracy as generally understood.[20] It is true that there are pluralistic as well as corporatist features of the system, irrespective of weak political opposition. To some extent factions in the LDP provide opposition, but their operation has a personalistic and money-centered, rather than policy-oriented, character.

Governments before 1940 changed frequently in a kaleidoscopic process of competing elites, none of which had sufficient power to dominate. The occupation reforms provided greater clarity and simplicity in the location both of sovereignty and of power. This had the salutary effect of enabling the political system to evolve in the direction of "fusion-of-power" politics where power and responsibility were fairly clearly located. It is also true that the establishment of political stability and accountability was facilitated by the formation and consolidation of the LDP.

The system, however, as it has evolved in the three decades since 1955, shows distinct signs of stagnation and self-satisfaction. In the words of Robert Dahl:

> If high consensus societies can profit from the advantages of incremental change, they run an opposite danger. Where there is little dissent, both political leaders and citizens escape the compulsion to weigh the relative advantages offered by a comprehensive, large-scale change, even when a large-scale change might prove less costly in the long run than either the status quo or a

series of incremental changes. The history of politics is writ large with the results of costly timidities that have produced too little too late.[21]

Dahl, it is true, goes on to warn against "ideological" conflict as in postwar France and Italy,[22] but the essential point still stands.

It is obvious that for a range of reasons it would be difficult to create a viable opposition in Japan, capable of responsibly taking power. Many observers, Japanese and foreign, will remain unconvinced of the desirability of trying.

Nevertheless, we conclude with three points. The first is that changes of government do not necessarily mean loss of national "consensus." To an extent the belief that a loss of "consensus" would ensue dervies from European and other class-conflict models that are largely inappropriate for Japanese conditions. Second, the assumption that the present electoral system is "natural" for Japan needs to be subjected to close scrutiny. I have suggested in this chapter that in several crucial respects it is an outdated and inefficient system that serves to perpetuate without much intellectual justification a status quo that strongly favors the present political establishment. Finally, no real change in the system is likely to occur unless the opposition parties themselves will it (though a change in the electoral system may be required to help them rethink).

Healthy democratic politics for Japan depends on a willingness on the part of government and opposition alike to rethink the system creatively and with a long-term perspective. Many aspects of Japanese life since the war have proved extraordinarily creative and successful. Why should this not happen in politics also?

NOTES

1. See for instance T. J. Pempel, "The Dilemma of Parliamentary Opposition in Japan," *Polity* 8 (1975): 63–79; Terry E. MacDougall, "Asukata Ichio and Some Dilemmas of Socialist Leadership in Japan," in *Political Leadership in Contemporary Japan,* ed. Terry E. MacDougall, Michigan Papers in Japanese Studies 1 (Ann Arbor: Center for Japanese Studies, 1982), pp. 51–91; Gerald L. Curtis, "Domestic Politics and Japanese Foreign Policy," in *Japan and the United States: Challenges and Opportunities,* ed. William J. Barnds (London: Macmillan, 1980), pp. 21–85.

2. Giovanni Sartori, *Parties and Party Systems: A Framework for Analysis* (Cambridge: Cambridge University Press, 1976).

3. So long as the Alliance fails to replace the Labor party but itself fails to be eliminated, the Conservatives could well continue as the predominant party.

4. See A. H. Birch, *Representative and Responsible Government* (London: Allen and Unwin, 1964).

5. See R. Catley and B. McFarlane, *From Tweedledum to Tweedledee: The New Labor Government in Australia* (Artarmon: Australia and New Zealand Book Co., 1974).

6. For instance, the LDP politician Ishida Hirohide in 1963 predicted that the Socialists (JSP and DSP) would attain a parliamentary plurality by 1970, an argument based in part on the British model. "The Vision of the Conservative Party," *Chūō Kōron*, January 1963, pp. 88–97; an abbreviated translation is in *Journal of Social and Political Ideas in Japan* 2 (August 1964): 55–58. For an early account of the JSP which broadly assumed that an opposition capable of taking power was inherently desirable, see Allan B. Cole, George O. Totten, and Cecil B. Uyehara, with a contributed chapter by Ronald P. Dore, *Socialist Parties in Postwar Japan* (New Haven, Conn.: Yale University Press, 1966).

7. See, for instance, Satō Seisaburō and Miyazaki Tetsuhisa, "Jimintō no chō-chōki seiken no kaibō" (Analysis of the Ultra-Durable LDP Regime), *Chūō Kōron*, November 1984, pp. 66–100.

8. A Japanese visitor to Oxford in 1984 cited Oswald Spengler's *Decline of the West* as prescient of the decline of Europe and rise of East Asian and Pacific region in world affairs.

9. There are conspicuous exceptions where policymaking shows less than optimum effectiveness. For a recent study of protest against the siting of Narita airport see David E. Apter and Nagayo Sawa, *Against the State: Politics and Social Protest in Japan* (Cambridge, Mass.: Harvard University Press, 1984).

10. It is important to remember, however, that the conservative side of politics was as much subject to fragmentation before 1955 as the progressives.

11. "Fair Play Party" would be a better translation.

12. This figure exaggerates JCP support by comparison with the Kōmeitō because the JCP always contests virtually every seat whereas the Kōmeitō fights only those it can win.

13. In 1984 the difference in the value of a vote in the most overrepresented and most underrepresented constituencies was approaching five to one, but in 1986 a constituency reform reduced the discrepancy to about three to one.

14. A list system has now been introduced for the national constituency of the House of Councillors.

15. Apart from the parties previously mentioned, seats were won in the 1983 upper house elections by Second Chamber Club, a grouping of Independents, the Non-party Faction (similar), the newly formed Salaryman's party and the newly formed Welfare party.

16. Zbigniew Brzezinski, *The Fragile Blossom: Crisis and Change in Japan* (New York: Harper and Row, 1972), pp. 14–17.

17. See Ōtake Hideo, *Nihon no Bōei to Kokunai Seiji* (Japanese Defense and Domestic Politics) (Tokyo: Sanichi Shobō, 1983).

18. Discussion with group of civil servants, 1983.

19. See the discussion in "Government Decisionmaking in Japan: Implications for the United States," submitted to the Committee on Foreign Affairs, U.S. House of Representatives (Washington, D.C.: Government Printing Office, 1982).

20. This assumes that "democracy" is a concept of general applicability. Extreme nationalists in Japan (as elsewhere) argue that democracy is not a Japanese concept anyway, but this does not appear to represent mainstream political thinking in Tokyo.

21. Robert A. Dahl, *Political Oppositions in Western Democracies* (New Haven, Conn.: Yale University Press, 1966), p. 392.

22. Ibid.

6 Democracy and Bureaucracy in Japan

JOHN CREIGHTON CAMPBELL

Democracy and bureaucracy are fundamentally antithetical. Democracy is bottom-up political process devoted to responsiveness. Bureaucracy is top-down administrative structure devoted to rationality. Modern democratic governance is based on the premise that the two can work together. The governments of Japan, the United States, and the nations of Western Europe hardly resemble the Athenian senate or the New England town meeting, but they are just as different from a "pure" bureaucracy like an army or a corporation. They are mixtures of both elements, both represented by large organizations: governmental ministries and institutionalized political parties. As Aberbach, Putnam, and Rockman observe, the "problematic relationship between these two institutions is perhaps the distinctive puzzle of the contemporary state, reflecting as it does the clash between the dual and conflicting imperatives of technical effectiveness and democratic responsiveness."[1]

In this as in so many regards, Japan has long been perceived as rather a special case. While the postwar Japanese political system is clearly democratic in the formal sense of popular sovereignty, free elections, and so forth, many have seen it as tipped heavily toward bureaucratic domination. For years most Japanese writers deplored this apparent tendency as a "feudal remnant" which must be overcome if Japanese politics were to become truly modern.[2] In contrast, foreign observers have hailed the successes of the Japanese political system and ascribed them specifically to an elite bureaucracy free to make good policy without excessive political interference. As Ronald

113

Dore puts it, "One of the conditions for the effectiveness of the bureaucracy is that you have lousy politics."[3] In short, both the critics and the celebrators agree that the imperatives of "technical effectiveness" have predominated over those of "democratic responsiveness" in postwar Japan, as compared with the United States and other advanced nations.

In this chapter I will explore several themes relating to the assumption that bureaucratic elements outweigh democratic elements in the Japanese polity: To what extent is the Japanese bureaucracy a social elite standing above the mass population? To what extent is Japanese internal bureaucratic organization based on democratic principles, and how does that relate to democracy in the entire political system? To what extent has the bureaucracy been able to dominate its environment—particularly the ruling Liberal Democratic party—and what is the direction of change along that dimension? To what extent has the overall pattern of public policy in Japan reflected bureaucratic influence as compared with that of other political actors?

These questions were not derived from a precise and comprehensive definition of "democracy"—a matter which political theorists have discussed for centuries without reaching much agreement. I selected them because they are relevant in a more general way to our sense of what democracy means, and more particularly because they are among the most crucial issues in contemporary Japanese politics. This has to do with Japanese modern history.

The Bureaucratic Legacy

The tradition of bureaucratic dominance is stronger in Japan than in any other contemporary democracy. Civil and military bureaucrats were the direct heirs of the samurai "oligarchs" who carried out the Meiji Restoration in 1868. They were well entrenched before the political parties began to gain influence in the early twentieth century, and they regained dominance when party politicians subsequently proved unable to run Japan effectively. The prewar Japanese government was hardly a monolithic or totalitarian structure—for one thing, power was too fragmented among multiple bureaucracies for that—but the era is well typified by the phrase *kanson minpi,* "exalt the officials, despise the people."[4]

When the American Occupation took over Japan in 1945, two of its key goals were "demilitarization," eliminating the military bureaucracy, and "democratization," establishing the rights of the people vis-à-vis government and, not incidentally, assuring their sovereignty over the civil bureaucracy. The Diet was established as the supreme organ of state, and the prime minister it elects was put in charge of the cabinet and ministries.

The Americans also attempted to carry out reforms within the civil bureaucracy itself, by purging a few top officials, abolishing the Home Ministry, creating a National Personnel Authority, and establishing a variety of administrative standards. These reforms did not go as far as initially intended, however, because the Occupation authorities themselves had to depend on the Japanese bureaucracy to administer the nation and implement broader political, economic, and social reforms. The Americans could not easily discard their own tools. Most ministries thus emerged from the Occupation essentially intact, led by officials recruited before the war, imbued with the traditions and organizational missions developed over the decades, and ready to play an important role in rebuilding Japan.[5]

Bureaucrats as an Elite

The typical Japanese national-level upper civil servant is a graduate of the Law Faculty of Tokyo University, a fact which automatically makes him the elite of the elite. A Japanese mother has no higher ambition for her most talented son than for him to enter this faculty, which in fact had been established back in the Meiji period precisely to train bureaucrats. Moreover, while many of the best and brightest university graduates have recently been choosing to apply to large corporations instead of a governmental ministry, bureaucratic careers clearly bring higher status in Japan than the United States. Education is the predominant measure of status in Japan, and by that measurement bureaucrats today stand head-and-shoulder above the general population.

This fact is not at all unusual. In every advanced nation, higher level bureaucrats are much better educated than the average, and in many countries most are the product of special schools. The French *grandes écoles* are the obvious example, but Oxbridge has long played a distinctive role in supplying British civil servants, and more generally, education in public law is characteristic of officials in continental Europe, as in Japan. Moreover, these European elite institutions generally have more of an upper-class bias in their student body than historically has been true of the "meritocracy" of Tokyo University, which along with other national universities charges relatively low fees and has been a traditional channel of rapid upward mobility. It is worth noting, however, that the proportion of students from relatively advantaged backgrounds has been increasing in Japan's top universities recently, partly because their parents can afford extra schooling.[6]

A more subtle point might also be mentioned. In most countries, only a small proportion of young people advance to higher education, particularly four-year universities. Uniquely among the advanced democracies, Japan and the United States have achieved mass higher education, with over one-third attending post-secondary schools. The gap between the officials and the public is therefore narrower in these countries than elsewhere.

The question of bureaucrats as an elite hinges on more than educational advantages. Many Americans believe that bureaucracy should be "representative" in the sense of including all segments of society, perhaps by actively recruiting women and minority groups. This idea is known only in academic circles in Japan. No effort is made to bring minority groups into the bureaucracy, and officialdom remains overwhelmingly male, although a few posts, such as chief of the Women and Young Workers' Bureau in the Ministry of Labor, are generally reserved for women.

Are such facts important? Presumably, attracting the best students from the best universities makes the Japanese bureaucracy more effective in terms of sheer talent, and public respect encourages self-confident leadership. A strong continuity with the prewar period is that Japanese top officials are much more likely than their counterparts in the West to believe that they have the chief responsibility within their areas of jurisdiction for defining the national interest and determining major public policies.[7] At the attitudinal level Japanese bureaucrats do not appear very democratic. Still, real political democracy is more a matter of structure and process than of attitudes.

Bureaucratic Organization

Japan's twelve ministries (*shō*) have much the same titles and jurisdictions as American departments—Foreign Affairs, Health and Welfare, Finance, Transportation, and so forth—and they are similarly divided into specialized bureaus and sections. Each ministry is headed by a cabinet minister, virtually always a senior member of the Diet from the Liberal Democratic party (LDP). A large umbrella structure called the Prime Minister's Office (Sōrifu) incorporates several other agencies (*chō*) with lower status than the ministries, though their heads also serve in the cabinet—the Economic Planning, Environment, and Land Agencies are included, as is even the Defense Agency, the equivalent of the Pentagon in the United States. Under the prewar system, formal control of the bureaucracy lay ultimately in the emperor, but the lines of effective authority were unclear, a source of serious confusion. Today, the bureaucracy is unambiguously responsible to the Diet through the cabinet and the prime minister.[8]

In comparison at least with their American counterparts, Japanese ministries appear better able to maintain autonomy by controlling their own organizations. A notable indication is that political appointments are limited to ministers and parliamentary vice-ministers—the latter is a negligible position—and even cabinet ministers, though formally quite powerful, are usually in office so briefly that they cannot dominate policymaking. Each ministry is really managed by its administrative vice-minister, a few top staff personnel, and the bureau chiefs, all of whom are permanent civil servants who have spent their entire careers (except perhaps for some temporary assignments) in the same ministry.

A key to understanding any organization is how it handles its people. Since recruitment, socialization, promotion, and specialization practices link individual and organizational goals, they largely determine how well the organization will perform. My impression is that this point is unusually well understood in Japan—or at least that Japanese bureaucratic organizations have shaped these practices to promote effectiveness through organizational cohesion to an extent rarely found elsewhere. In one sense, these benefits of organizational cohesion and effectiveness have been gained through some sacrifice of democracy. I will return to that point after a brief description of the ministerial personnel system.

Recruitment and Socialization

Japanese governmental agencies are very selective in picking their future leaders. A written test similar to the university entrance examination is administered first, and those who score well are then interviewed intensively by ministry officials. What the ministry looks for, beyond intelligence, is the man who is organizationally minded, ambitious, and willing to work hard.

The new recruit is thus promising material, but no more; before becoming a full-fledged member he not only acquires new skills and specialized knowledge, he must also be imbued with the traditions, values, norms, and way of life of his organization. Each ministry has an "apprenticeship" period of five to ten years during which the young official is rotated every year or two among posts with diverse functions, plus a spell of classroom instruction either within the ministry or at a university (sometimes overseas). Jobs that require supervising a staff of clerks, interacting with local officials, and mastering various substantive fields within the ministry's domain of knowledge are successively assigned.

Promotion

At every stage of the training process, and still more intensively in the years following, each official is carefully watched by the more senior bureaucrats, who are trying to pick winners. Gossip in a ministry often centers on whether a particular "class" (a single-year cohort of twenty or so higher civil servants) looks promising or disastrous, and which officials within a class seem likely to rise to highest office. Differential treatment within a class does not really become apparent until after the training period, but then some will get the more desirable jobs—assistant chief in a general affairs rather than a specialized or routine section, a regional office in Tokyo rather than Hokkaidō. Those on the "escalator"—we would say "fast track"—have more chance to show off their dedication and talent, while their less talented or fortunate colleagues must work extraordinarily hard (or happen into some opportunity to shine) if they are to have much hope for the top jobs.

These differences sharpen over time, since only a few in any class will become bureau chiefs, and just one official from two or three adjacent classes can serve as administrative vice-minister. The "losers," however, are neither forced out nor left in low-status jobs under former colleagues. For most of their careers they will be promoted at only a slightly slower pace, usually to jobs that have equal formal status and pay but are not quite as close to the mainstream of ministry functions. Those left out at higher levels become "counsellors" or "advisors"; they receive considerable deference but do not have line responsibilities. At the final stage, however, when a new vice-minister is appointed everyone else in his class (and earlier classes) retires—the general principle is that supervision should always be by higher seniority. This promotion system engenders strong competition, based on who can best carry out the ministry's mission, but it also mitigates the consequences of losing to prevent less-favored officials from becoming embittered and unproductive.

After "retirement," typically around age fifty-five, bureaucrats usually move on to comfortable second careers in public corporations or private firms within their ministry's jurisdiction. A few even run for the Diet, and in fact many postwar prime ministers and cabinet members have been ex-bureaucrats. This "descending from heaven" (*amakudari*) is often seen as a mechanism for extending bureaucratic influence over the Japanese economy, society, and polity. As is true as well of the shuttling of executives between the Pentagon and big defense contractors in America's "military-industrial complex," influence probably runs both ways—the companies who hire former bureaucrats seek access to the ministry and insights into official thinking. In any case, the system assures financial security for upper-level bureaucrats and keeps them attached to their old ministries.

Specialization

In nearly all ministries, generalist officials (usually law graduates) are ranked higher than specialists, and vice-ministers are always generalists (except in the Ministry of Construction, where an engineer serves in that post on an alternating basis with a generalist). Specialists in some ministries, such as physicians in the Ministry of Health and Welfare, are formally regarded as equal in status to generalist higher civil servants, but they can rise only to a few designated bureau-chief slots. Most often, professionals are relegated to the category of middle-ranked civil servants, who can aspire no higher than a minor section-chief post before retirement.

The generalist official on the elite track will serve in several bureaus during his career so that if he becomes vice-minister or chief of the ministerial secretariat he will have hands-on experience across the range of ministerial functions. Inevitably, though, some specialization emerges—no Welfare official can master the intricacies of public pensions, health-care delivery, administration of the pharmaceutical industry, and public assistance all at once, and no more can a Finance bureaucrat simultaneously be an expert in budgeting, taxation, international monetary affairs, the stock market, and the banking industry. At the mid-career level most officials therefore put extra effort into studying one or two substantive fields. The selection might be by personal inclination or simply an accident of timing, but the most ambitious will concentrate on the subjects they see as most crucial to the ministry, or which will be most crucial ten years hence when their final position will be determined. In some ministries such specializations become the basis for enduring conflicts. The best known was between the "heavy industry" and "international" groups in the Ministry of International Trade and Industry (MITI) in the 1950s. However, the principle of rotation among bureaus generally prevents the complete institutionalization of such functional conflicts.

Organization for Cohesion

An enduring generalization about Japanese cultural patterns points to the importance of the group and the maintenance of strong *uchi-soto*—"inside-outside," or "we-they"—distinctions.[9] Ministry organization exemplifies this proposition. Ministries are made up only of insiders: mid-career appointments from private industry or academia, so common in the United States, are virtually unheard of; political appointments are limited to the minister plus one or two parliamentary vice-ministers; officials may serve brief tours of duty in other agencies, but typically return to their own ministry and regard it as their home. Recruitment, socialization, and promotion practices encourage each official to internalize the ministry's official and unofficial values as his own. The subordination of professionals and careful strictures against overspecialization are aimed at excluding values and norms other than those of the organization itself. The widespread norm of "permanent employment" makes it difficult to find another job in or out of government, almost forcing bureaucrats to come to terms with their organization. While competition is stiff, it rewards those who best serve the goals of the ministry and thus promotes rather than undercuts organizational cohesiveness.

Total cohesion cannot, of course, be perfectly attained in the real world. Japanese bureaucrats retain some individual preferences, and the imperatives of functional specialization (and the fact that different jobs bring different contacts with outside groups) lead to long-term conflicts among organizational subunits which can be difficult to resolve. The Finance Ministry, for example, has long been known as "all bureaus no ministry" because of the lack of integration among its varied activities; it tries to counter such tendencies toward fragmentation by extra-heavy selling of an organizational ideology of the "Finance Ministry family." MITI, in contrast, holds frequent meetings of officials from all its bureaus to thrash out unified ministry policies. The point is not that all is harmony within a Japanese ministry, but that enormous attention is paid to creating cohesion, both real and psychological, and that these efforts have led to rather more organizational unity within the Japanese ministry than is often found elsewhere.

Cohesiveness and Democracy

The pattern described here could be seen as tending toward democracy or in the opposite direction, depending on whether one focuses on internal processes or on the role of the ministry in its environment. A frequent observation of Japanese corporations and other organizations is that lower-level members are encouraged to participate in decisions. The leader's role is to help move the group toward consensus rather than imposing his own views on subordinates in the top-down manner favored by Americans. There is also less emphasis in Japan on elaborate control mechanisms, such as maintaining a large staff so leaders can keep tabs on what lower-level units are doing. While oversimplified, this characterization of organizational culture captures a real difference between Japanese and American organizations, including public bureaucracies: it is legitimate to infer that allowing lower-level officials more freedom for action and more influence over organizational policy is essentially more democratic.

Not as often noticed is the extent to which these democratic internal practices critically depend on first building an organization which can sustain them. The emphasis in the Japanese personnel practices described above on organizational norms produces subordinates who can be trusted because they are likely to think and act the same way their superiors would in a given situation. Such practices would not be possible in a more heterogeneous organization because, to the extent that subordinates have different goals and interests, strong top-down management becomes the only mechanism that can assure some minimal level of coherent behavior. For example, in an American bureaucratic agency, allowing more internal democracy might well destroy, rather than enhance, the cohesiveness and effectiveness of the organization.

In any case, this question of *internal* democracy is secondary to our analysis of bureaucracy and democracy. The key issue is not how responsive the organization is to its own employees, but to the interests of those outside the organization—in the broadest sense, "the people." Here it must be emphasized that the Japanese ministry's dedication to commitment and cohesiveness tends— in fact, is precisely designed—to protect the organization's autonomy from external forces. The ministry wants to establish its own goals and to devise and control its own means for attaining them. Its ideal of bureaucratic dominance may be quite "rational" and effective, but it is hardly democratic.

Bureaucracies and their Environments

It should be immediately stated that the bureaucrat's ideal has never been achieved in postwar Japan, because the ministry's ability to control its environment is limited. To understand these limitations and their implications for democracy, we must analyze the relationships between the individual ministry and other important actors and see how these have been affected by certain broad trends: the increased conplexity and interdependence of the problems facing government, the emergence of new goals and attitudes among the public, the increased power and confidence of majority party politicians, and—since the early 1980s—resource scarcity. These trends are all interrelated, and they have brought new difficulties and challenges to the lives of Japanese bureaucrats.

Interdependence

If the organizational patterns described above applied to the Japanese bureaucracy as a whole, it would indeed constitute a monolithic power structure allowing very little space for anyone on the outside to influence policy. In fact, the patterns pertain only to individual ministries, and the autonomy of each of these means that no single organization is able to dominate the decision-making system. Interministerial conflict is actually on the rise in Japan. In the past it had been somewhat easier to block off spheres of influence for each ministry, in which others would usually not trespass. Today everything seems connected to everything else: agricultural policy has an international dimension because of pressure from foreign exporters; promoting industrial growth runs the risk of polluting local environments; the emergence of new technologies opens struggles for control, such as between the Postal Ministry and MITI over telecommunications;

expanding pension and health care costs threaten the Finance Ministry's budgetary framework. There is more and more interdependence among organizations, and when responsibilities overlap, conflict necessarily results.

Such trends are at work in all industrial nations, and the response of nearly all of them in the decades since the war has been to reorganize their bureaucratic structures and to strengthen the mechanisms for central coordination and control—the office of the chief executive, the budgeting authority, or organs within the civil service itself. This has not happened to the same extent in Japan: the government's organization chart today is far more similar to that of twenty or thirty years ago than in any other advanced nation, and the Japanese prime ministership in particular still lacks an adequate staff and remains much weaker than its counterparts elsewhere. The trend toward organizational interdependence therefore did not lead to as much real integration and coordination as can be found elsewhere; it tended instead to intensify conflict and accentuate the pattern of fragmented authority (the Japanese call it *tatewari gyōsei*, "slivered administration") which has long been characteristic of the bureaucracy in Japan.

There are some indications of change in the 1980s. The mechanisms for centralized control of the bureaucracy were strengthened by combining the Administrative Management Agency and part of the Prime Minister's Office into a new Management and Coordination Agency (Sōmuchō). Less formally, there have been more examples of "comprehensive policymaking": large-scale plans drawn up by advisory committees, to be implemented on a top-down basis, in such areas as trade liberalization, education policy, and administrative reform. New patterns of conflict emerged as the ministries and their allies resisted these initiatives and attempted to maintain their own jurisdictional authority.[10] These centralizing trends were closely associated with Prime Minister Nakasone, who for many years had explicitly called for a more "presidential" style of government in Japan, but they were also responses to increased needs for coordination within the governmental system, and thus might well continue.

Citizen Assertiveness

The second trend which has limited the autonomy and influence of Japanese bureaucrats is the growing willingness of Japanese citizens to speak up on their own behalf. This is a complicated phenomenon covered more adequately in other chapters in this book, so I will discuss it only from the bureaucrats' point of view. Traditionally, the Japanese notion of appropriate behavior toward authority was the "petition group" (chinjōdan), less a popular demand than a hat-in-hand supplication for a favor. Such deferential behavior has certainly not disappeared today.[11] However, since the 1960s, people have also been more willing to stand up for their own interests. Citizens' movements against pollution and other unpleasant intrusions on local areas have complicated the task of implementing many policies—building industrial parks, extending the shinkansen ("bullet train") system, opening new airports, establishing garbage treatment facilities and hospitals, and so forth.[12] Where bureaucrats could once count on local enthusiasm or at least acquiescence toward any project they dreamed up, today they often encounter active resistance.

The officials' initial reaction to this sea-change in attitudes was confusion and resentment, leading to tirades about "egoism" opposed to the general welfare and heavy-handed attempts to impose their plans by administrative fiat. Over time, bureaucrats have learned to be more cautious. Sites for new projects are selected with careful attention to local views, and a long process of "consultation" with residents precedes construction. Often enough this amounts to deliberate manipulation, including buying-off or otherwise coopting opposition leaders, but unquestionably local interests are now being taken more fully into account in the decision-making process.

The significance of attitude changes among the general public goes beyond public works projects and local areas. The 1960s and 1970s saw a more general broadening of interest from narrowly defined goals of economic growth to a greater concern with quality of life—not just of the environment, but in Japanese society as well. Although citizen-movement activity as such has quieted down, and no large grass-roots social movements beyond those against pollution have appeared, there has been more public attention to such issues as urban overcrowding, pension and health programs for the elderly and the handicapped, and to some extent the problems of minority groups and even women. Bureaucrats must now take such concerns into account to a greater extent than in earlier years, and thus, even if unconsciously, they have become responsive to a greater variety of interests.

Party Power

The most direct impact of changing public preferences has been a shift in policies pursued by the ruling conservative party, which in earlier years had mainly served as the representative of rural and business interests. LDP politicians now get involved in a greater variety of policy areas. Their influence has also become stronger over the years. In an ultimate sense, this trend is the result of the Occupation reforms that firmly established the Diet and cabinet at the pinnacle of government. Under the new constitution, the ministries lost their claims to autonomy and could exert control only to the extent it was explicitly or implicitly permitted to them by elected politicians. And once the LDP was organized in 1955, this single majority party became responsible for Japanese public policy.[13]

Japan's most basic policies—such fundamental orientations as the maintenance of the mixed-capitalist economy and the alliance with the United States—should be seen primarily as the will of the LDP. Moreover, such major policy changes as the transition around 1960 from rolling back Occupation reforms (the "reverse course") to economic growth (the "income doubling plan"), or the move toward active environmental and social policies in the early 1970s, were mainly instigated by an individual prime minister or by the majority party as a whole. Bureaucrats have generally played a supporting role at this grand policy level, throughout the postwar period.

Most of the work of government is more mundane, however, and it is at the lower levels of decision making that the main trend toward increased party power may be observed. The relevant actors are less the prime minister, the cabinet, or the LDP as a whole than groups of rank-and-file party politicians interested in a particular policy area. Over time, many LDP Diet members have learned a good deal about details of policy matters, and a pattern has developed of rather stable relationships among each group of politicians and the interest groups and bureaucratic agencies that inhabit a given policy space. The terms *iron triangle* and *subgovernment* have been coined to describe similar alliances in the United States among specialized interest groups, administrative agencies, and congressional committees, implying durable subsystems within which each participant—despite possible disagreements—shares an interest in preventing disruption by outsiders.

In Japanese iron triangles, the political role is typically taken not by a legislative committee (which would include all parties) but by the specialized committees of the LDP's Policy Affairs Research Council, made up of majority party Diet members only. These committees can be seen as having a veto power over ministry policy decisions—or, more often, decisions can be seen as the product of joint consulta-

tions among the bureaucrats, politicians, and interest group representatives who are most directly concerned. LDP Diet members who
have specialized in a given policy area have been called "families" or
"tribes" (*zoku*), and they can bring intense pressure to bear on bureaucratic agencies to ensure that their constituencies' interests are fully
reflected in governmental decisions.

These subgovernmental phenomena became apparent in the early
1960s, and they have continued to develop. In a recent article that has
attracted much attention, one of Japan's leading political scientists,
working with a young LDP staffer, observed that in earlier years,
"bureaucrats would draft bills and brief the Policy Affairs Research
Council and other organs, whereupon LDP Diet members would
lobby to ministries and agencies involved for changes in the bills to
meet the needs of their constituencies and support groups. Now close
consultations take place between the responsible bureaucrats and the
various divisions of the Policy Affairs Research Council . . . right
from the earliest stages of legislative and bureaucratic drafting."[14]

This pattern might be seen as democratic in the sense that administrative agencies are forced to work closely with politicians and interest groups rather than making policy on their own. On the other
hand, only conservative politicians and what might be seen as "establishment" interest groups are represented; others—such as opposition
politicians and labor or other left-of-center groups—are generally excluded from the system.[15] Moreover, particularistic or "special" interests are better represented than the general interest of the nation as a
whole. In fact, to the extent such subgovernments control decision
making, the power of the central leadership and the coherence of
policy across the entire government are necessarily weakened. This
sort of LDP influence on policy thus reinforces the tendency toward
bureaucratic fragmentation noted above.

Some observers of Japanese politics have argued that despite its
rather fragmented structure and the evident weakness of the chief
executive, the Japanese government is actually better integrated than
most, and well equipped for comprehensive policymaking. They
point to higher-level bodies like the Executive Council in the LDP, to
the "old school tie" from Tokyo University and other informal bonds
among bureaucrats, and to a norm that problems should be solved by
consensual methods.[16]

My own view is that these mechanisms serve more often to avoid
or paper over problems than to resolve them.[17] The impression of

consensus was in large measure created by a particular condition: the extraordinary economic growth that lasted for nearly two decades from the 1950s into the 1970s. Rapid growth produced large surpluses in government revenues every year, so that each agency (or subgovernment) could be given enough funds to work out its own problems and conflict among them was muted. More generally, with such generous resources available, the government was able to respond to demands from various sectors of society with little difficulty.

Resource Scarcity

This comfortable state of affairs was brought to an end with the "oil shocks" of 1973 and 1979 and the economic difficulties which followed. The high-growth economy became a moderate-growth economy, and the upshot in the early 1980s was a major campaign for "administrative reform" (*gyōsei kaikaku*).

In past years, administrative reform efforts had centered on constraining the overall size of the bureaucracy by imposing tight ceilings on the numbers of personnel and agencies. These had been quite successful on their own terms, in that the number of national-level civil servants and public corporation employees was held roughly constant since 1967, and the organizational census actually declined.[18] However, the government's policy responsibilities and certainly its budget continued to expand; since easy spending habits are not easily broken, when growth slowed in the 1970s, yearly budget surpluses became enormous deficits. The Ministry of Finance attempted to hold down spending through the annual budget process, and old-fashioned administrative reform efforts at trimming personnel were intensified, but these traditional mechanisms proved to be ineffective in halting the political momentum which had accumulated behind high public spending.

The result was a new kind of administrative reform, a campaign from 1981 lasting into the mid-1980s which comprised the largest-scale attempt at top-down comprehensive policymaking since the Occupation period. It was led by an alliance of top LDP politicians—particularly Yasuhiro Nakasone, first as chief of the Administrative Management Agency and then as prime minister—with big business leaders worried about higher taxes if budgetary expansion could not be halted.[19] The campaign had three impacts. First, it imposed tight controls on ministerial spending, mainly through governmentwide expenditure ceilings. The growth rate of the budget was sharply reduced, and the size of the deficit dropped. Second, it privatized some government enterprises, most importantly the deficit-ridden National Railways, and made some progress toward deregulation the economy more generally. Third, largely by creating a mood favorable to austerity and policy change, it provided the opportunity for substantial reforms in such major programs as health insurance and social security.

The administrative reform campaign was portrayed by its sponsors as an attack on a "bloated bureaucracy" seen as bent on mindless expansion of government. Even though the Japanese national bureaucracy is quite small compared with most other nations, and its size had long been tightly constrained, such slogans tapped long-held public resentments against the bureaucratic elite and helped make the campaign quite popular, particularly in its earlier years. In a deeper sense, however, administrative reform can be seen as a real if partial victory for the bureaucratic virtues of efficient and rational administration, as opposed to the politicians' inherent tendency to offer more and more benefits to both "special interests" and the general public.

If a "bureaucratic paradise," to use a common Japanese phrase, ever existed in postwar Japan, it had long since dissolved. The trends of increased complexity and interdependence of policy problems, more varied and assertive attitudes among the public, and the expansion of majority party power have all constrained the ability of bureaucrats to define problems and devise solutions autonomously; each ministry has increasingly had to consult with, and not infrequently defer to, party politicians, officials in other agencies, interest groups, and sometimes social movements or public opinion. Resource scarcity has had a more ambiguous impact. On the one hand, bureaucrats have been deprived of money to spend, but on the other hand, they may actually have gained—relative to other participants—in their influence over how those limited funds should be apportioned.

Bureaucratic Influence on Public Policy

Identifying the direction of change, toward more democracy in the sense of decreasing bureaucratic autonomy, is relatively easy to do. Determining the extent of that change is more difficult. One problem is that different policy areas have greatly different configurations of power; general statements about the relative strength of the bureaucracy vis-à-vis the majority party, interest groups, or some other actor are hazardous unless they can be based on detailed evidence across the entire range of public policy.

While a detailed treatment is beyond the scope of this essay, a few examples will indicate how varied these configurations can be. At one extreme, a few policy areas have long been dominated by political considerations. Alliances of conservative-oriented interest groups and LDP Diet members produced cash payoffs to landlords (both in Japan and in the overseas colonies) who had been "expropriated" during the Occupation, and to veterans and the war-bereaved, in the long-drawn-out process called the "post-war settlement."[20] Public works allocations are also greatly influenced by politicians, as the tons of concrete poured into Tanaka Kakuei's election district in Niigata Prefecture well indicate. Americans are most familiar with the power of agricultural interest groups lined with LDP Diet members in preserving protectionist barriers against beef, citrus, and forest products. Bureaucrats have had relatively little influence over such matters.

In highly ideological policy areas as well, LDP politicians tend to be most active and bureaucrats and interest groups less so. Several government policies toward education, including "ethics" teaching, the political contents of textbooks, and administrative control of public school teaching, have been substantially influenced by right-wing LDP Diet members. Japanese defense policy mostly results from the interplay between "hawks" and the more moderate mainstream in the LDP, with more bureaucratic concerns like force levels, strategic planning, and so forth playing a lesser role, at least until recently. With issues relating to the constitution, the position of the emperor, and the government's relationship to religion, officials tend to keep hands off and leave policy to the politicians.

Other sectors are marked by conflict between alliances of LDP backbenchers and interest groups on the one hand and government agencies on the other, usually based on votes versus "rationality," with the prime minister and party leaders mediating. The interactions can be quite complicated. Examples include the Agriculture Ministry's attempts to impose a "comprehensive agricultural policy," the Welfare Ministry's efforts to rationalize the National Health Insurance system, and the Finance Ministry's repeated attempts to enforce tougher tax regulations on interest income. In all these cases the majority party tempered, delayed, or halted the bureaucrats' efforts to make policy more tidy and rational.

Where do bureaucrats dominate? Of course, as in all modern governments, they control most routine and detailed decision making in all policy areas. They will also prevail at the policymaking level wherever concentrated LDP pressure is lacking: foreign aid policy, labor standards, broadcasting regulation, most diplomacy, community education, and programs for the handicapped come to mind as areas where most initiative has usually been taken by the responsible government agencies.

Industrial Policy

We have not yet discussed, however, one policy area that is extremely prominent but in which LDP politicians have generally deferred to the bureaucrats. This is the way the government is said to have structured the Japanese economy by "targeting" specific industries for accelerated development, "picking the winners" itself rather than relying on market mechanisms.

There has been considerable controversy among specialists about the extent to which the postwar economic miracle was due to government direction, and indeed about the fundamental nature of the government-business relationship in Japan. Some see the Ministry of International Trade and Industry as having planned and executed most important economic developments in Japan, with big business generally falling into line; others give more credit to entrepreneurship, hard work, and the private market, and point to the many disputes between MITI officials and businessmen that indicate more conflict than cooperation in their relationships.[21] Two facts are clear, however: that the Japanese government has had a broader and more intensive interaction with big business than Americans are used to; and that the majority party has not played a major role in these interactions. For our purposes a most interesting question is why this policy area has apparently been so insulated from politics, unpenetrated by the party politicians who are the mechanisms of democratic responsiveness. Given that rapid industrial development has been postwar Japan's central achievement, this question is crucial to understanding the relationship between bureaucracy and democracy. Two general lines of explanation may be suggested.

First, Chalmers Johnson argues that precisely because industrial policy was so crucial, it was given over to a small elite bureaucracy "staffed by the best managerial talent available in the system," which was then protected from political interventions into its policy planning and implementation. This was "to fend off the numerous interest groups in the society, which if catered to would distort the priorities of the developmental state." An American analogy is the Manhattan Project to develop the atomic bomb in World War II, which was created by politicians but then left alone simply because it was so important. Johnson asserts that the key task of the political authorities is to "create space for bureaucratic initiative unconstrained by political power."[22]

What then do politicians find to do all day? Johnson says that protests will occur from time to time, and politicians must respond (or better, anticipate) by compelling the bureaucracy "to serve or manipulate" at least the noisiest or most important groups. However, "as long as the developmental projects are succeeding and their benefits are being equitably distributed, the political leaders should be able to deal with these problems symptomatically," and indeed even some political corruption will be tolerated. Agricultural subsidies, rural public works, and perhaps social security programs are part of either the equitable distribution of benefits or the selective appeasement of group interests that permits the true business of the state to proceed.[23]

This is a provocative and insightful general interpretation of postwar Japanese politics. Its assumption that industrial policy is somehow more fundamental and "real" than other policy areas is perhaps questionable, but plausible in the context of the widespread consensus about the priority of economic growth at least in the late 1950s and 1960s. Another basic assumption is more troublesome, however, in terms of both empirical evidence and some normative implications. That is the implied but necessary condition that somebody in Japan has the authority and power to tell elected politicians to keep their hands off MITI and industrial policy. Johnson refers to "the political leadership" without being very precise about who he means—the prime minister plus senior LDP politicians (and perhaps some powerful behind-the-scenes manipulators) would seem the most likely candidates.

There are at least two empirical problems here. First, this leadership group has often seemed too riven by factionalism to unify around any goal. Second, Johnson himself observes that, "as for MITI, over the years since its creation in 1949, prime ministers and ministers have attempted to gain control and use it for political purposes. MITI bureaucrats have been implacable in their resistance."[24] The very leadership that was supposed to protect the bureaucrats has sometimes tried to interfere. In short, there is not much positive evidence to support a view that the political leadership in Japan has been united, powerful, or even motivated enough to protect industrial policy and MITI as a privileged sanctuary by fending off interventions by rank-and-file politicians and the interest groups they represent.

An alternative explanation for why it is that industrial policy has been left to MITI bureaucrats and big businessmen, with rather little political interference, rests on more pluralist assumptions. That is, as the policy patterns described above suggest, politicians are primarily interested in getting reelected, which requires votes, and secondarily interested in pursuing certain ideological goals. The first interest draws them to concentrate on public works, aid to farmers, health care (doctors are influential local opinion leaders), and budgetary allocations in general; the second toward interventions into education, defense, and policy toward China and Korea. Industrial policy appears not so directly related to either votes or ideology, and so was less interesting to rank-and-file LDP Diet members, who were likely to visit MITI mainly to promote programs for small business (a major LDP constituency but not a central concern for the officials). This situation changed somewhat when the economic dislocations of the later 1970s led to pressure on certain "sunset industries," threatening jobs and entire local economies. At that point politicians did begin to intervene more frequently and systematically in industrial policy, with the same goal of protecting declining industries that has been often observed in the United States and Europe. In fact, activity related to industrial policy within the LDP's Policy Affairs Research Council has been more significant since the mid-1970s than earlier, and apparently MITI has had to be more responsive to political demands.

This interpretation does not rquire us to posit a unified and powerful leadership acting to fend off demands from politicians and interest groups; it explains MITI's relative autonomy primarily by the lack of strong attempts at political intervention. Of course, there were some such attempts even in the earlier period, but these were weak and sporadic enough to be handled by MITI itself—as already noted, Japanese ministry organizations can be quite powerful in their own right, sufficiently so to protect themselves against occasional inroads by politicians, though not against sustained attacks.

I might add that a glance at the budgetary system lends support to the latter interpretation. The Ministry of Finance is certainly at least as powerful and as central to the bureaucratic establishment as MITI, and its doctrine of "sound public finance"—earlier expressed as the principle of always balancing budgets (given up in 1965), and later as limiting government spending and deficits—was as important to Finance bureaucrats as the doctrine of rational industrial structuring was to MITI bureaucrats. However, over a twenty-year period from 1955, constant pressure from LDP Diet members (allied with interest groups and bureaucrats from the spending ministries) gradually dismantled the Finance Ministry's control over budget decisions. In effect, the ministry gave up its voice in many substantive policy decisions in order to protect its organizational integrity, particularly in personnel matters.[25] By the late 1970s, when nearly everyone perceived a fiscal crisis, the Finance Ministry was almost powerless to act.

I would suggest that the key difference between industrial policy and fiscal policy is not that the political leadership saw the former as more important and thus worked to "create space for bureaucratic initiative unconstrained by political power," while seeing the latter as trivial and thus available for the appeasement of interest group demands. It is rather that the interest groups and politicians saw public finance as more crucial to their own well-being than industrial policy, and so directed their attacks at the Finance Ministry rather than MITI.

Bureaucracy, Democracy, and Public Policy

I have discussed these conflicting explanations of the autonomy of industrial policy making at some length because they have important implications for our central question, "how democratic is the Japanese bureaucracy?" Johnson's activist and powerful state, able to insulate the most vital sector of public policy from pressures from the people and their representatives, would be a profoundly undemocratic institution. The fact that citizens might be kept quiescent by a relatively equitable distribution of the fruits of economic growth is irrelevant to this point. At best, this interpretation qualifies as democratic only under the most limited and conservative definition, which is that so long as free elections are held in which the populace has the opportunity to replace one governing elite with another, that elite can be free to make policy as it wishes between elections.[26]

The more pluralist explanation I have suggested is far from perfectly democratic. The LDP hardly represents all social groups equally, and its interventions are often behind-the-scenes and devoid of real grass-roots participation. Nonetheless, members of the Diet are primarily oriented toward votes, and most of their policy interventions are directed toward attracting the support of constituents. More importantly, under this interpretation it is the individual representatives of the people who decide where and when they will intervene in public policy decisions, which means they can also—democratically—decide to leave a particular area like industrial policy alone so long as it is performing satisfactorily. That is much more democratic than a conscious state strategy to impose such restrictions from above.

Conclusions

I have explored several aspects of the relationship between democracy and bureaucracy, between responsiveness and efficiency, in postwar Japanese government. Japanese bureaucrats look rather "elitist" in terms of social position and attitudes. Moreover, while Japanese organizational practices can be seen as providing a degree of internal democracy, in the sense of allowing more participation by lower-level officials, these practices are mainly designed to protect bureaucratic dominance within the policy domain of each ministry. Still, that dominance has been increasingly threatened by such trends as the interdependence of policy problems, changing public attitudes, and especially the growth of majority party influence. Given Japan's prewar heritage, a crucial indicator of democratic politics is simply the extent to which bureaucratic autonomy has been penetrated by outside forces, and substantial change has occurred along this dimension in most policy areas. Even industrial policy, where bureaucrats have been most in charge, is now seeing more political intervention than earlier.

Trends are one thing and absolute levels another. The Japanese policy process is less bureaucratic and more democratic than before, but how does it compare with other advanced nations? The easiest comparison is with the United States, where except for matters of defense policies (a large exception indeed) governmental bureaucracies are poorly regarded and often weak and ineffectual, while the opportunities for popular influence over policymaking are plentiful. Americans pay a substantial cost, incidentally, for their lack of ordinary administrative virtues—where else in the advanced world is the requirement of preparing regular budgets so blithely ignored, or are citizens left so in doubt about what programs will be in existence a year or two later? In this as in many other cases, comparing Japan solely with the United States is dangerously misleading because the United States is so extreme an "outlier," so different from usual ideas of normality.

But even from a European viewpoint, Japan's bureaucracy looks rather impressive. To a greater extent than elsewhere, Japanese officials seem to have enough confidence and skill to identify the problems of most significance, come up with plausible solutions, and participate effectively in political struggles to chart the nation's future course. Bureaucratic rationality, the bureaucratic style, and no doubt bureaucratic self-interest as well, have been unusually influential in Japan. Responsiveness to the ups and downs of the popular mood has perhaps been somewhat less evident than in other advanced democracies.

But it must be kept in mind that Japanese policy has been remarkably successful—what other government has done as well in delivering peace and prosperity to its citizens? Were it less so, and dissatisfaction more widespread, one might well find less deference to official pronouncements and more popular intervention into bureaucratic affairs. Every country in every era must find its own balance between democratic responsiveness and technical effectiveness, and its own patterns of accommodation between the dominating institutions of the political party and the administrative bureaucracy. Japan's choice, tilted a bit to the bureaucratic side, in this sense perhaps reflects the preferences of its people.

NOTES

1. Joel D. Aberbach, Robert D. Putnam, and Bert A. Rockman, *Bureaucrats and Politicians in Western Democracies* (Cambridge, Mass.: Harvard University Press, 1981), p. 3.

2. Tsuji Kiyoaki, the dean of studies of public administration in Japan, is best known for this view, best expressed in his *Shinban Nihon no Kanryōsei no Kenkyū* (Tokyo: Tokyo Daigaku no Shuppankai, 1969).

3. Ronald P. Dore, "The 'Learn From Japan' Boom," *Speaking of Japan,* November 1984, pp. 16–24. Dore is ambivalent about this phenomenon; for clearly positive evaluations, see Ezra F. Vogel, *Japan as Number One: Lessons for America* (Cambridge, Mass.: Harvard University Press, 1979), chap. 4, and Chalmers Johnson, *MITI and the Japanese Miracle* (Stanford, Calif.: Stanford University Press, 1982).

4. This paragraph drastically oversimplifies a complex bureaucratic strategy for maintaining dominance. See Bernard S. Silberman, "The Bureaucratic State

in Japan: The Problem of Authority and Legitimacy," in *Conflict in Modern Japanese History,* ed. Tetsuo Najita and J. Victor Koschmann (Princeton, N.J.: Princeton University Press, 1982), pp. 226–37.

5. See T. J. Pempel, "The Tar Baby Target: 'Reform' of the Japanese Bureaucracy," in *Democratizing Japan: The Allied Occupation,* ed. Robert E. Ward and Sakamoto Yoshikazu (Honolulu: University of Hawaii Press, 1987), pp. 157–87. Chalmers Johnson finds the roots of today's officials' behavior back in the 1930s: *MITI,* esp. chap. 3 and pp. 262–80.

6. See Aberbach, Putnam, and Rockman, *Bureaucrats,* chap. 3; Michio Muramatsu and Ellis S. Krauss, "Bureaucrats and Politicians in Policy Making: The Case of Japan," *American Political Science Review* 78 (1974): 126–46; and Thomas P. Rohlen, *Japan's High Schools* (Berkeley and Los Angeles: University of California Press, 1983), chap. 4.

7. For example, 80 percent of Japanese bureaucrats in one survey agreed that the "civil service guarantees reasonable public policy," compared with 21 and 16 percent in Britain and Germany. Muramatsu and Krauss, "Bureaucrats," p. 132.

8. A useful English summary of the more formal aspects of the Japanese bureaucracy is Kiyoaki Tsuji, ed., *Public Administration in Japan* (Tokyo: University of Tokyo Press, 1984).

9. Takeshi Ishida, "Conflict and Its Accommodation: *Omote-Ura* and *Uchi-Soto* Relations," in *Conflict in Japan,* ed. Ellis S. Krauss, Thomas P. Rohlen, and Patricia G. Steinhoff (Honolulu: University of Hawaii Press, 1984), pp. 18–38.

10. These developments are analyzed in T. J. Pempel, "The Unbundling of 'Japan, Inc.': The Changing Dynamics of Japanese Policy Formation," and Michio Muramatsu, "In Search of National Identity: The Politics and Policy of the Nakasone Administration," both in a special issue of the *Journal of Japanese Studies* 13 (Summer 1987): 271–342.

11. For an engaging account of the contemporary rural idea of politics, see Ronald P. Dore, *Shinohata* (New York: Pantheon, 1978), pp. 228–49.

12. The most extreme case is described in David E. Apter and Nagayo Sawa, *Against the State: Politics and Social Protest in Japan* (Cambridge, Mass.: Harvard University Press, 1984).

13. Two good recent accounts are Gerald L. Curtis, *The Japanese Way of Politics* (New York: Columbia University Press, 1988); and Michio Muramatsu and Ellis S. Krauss, "The Conservative Policy Line and the Development of Patterned Pluralism," in *The Political Economy of Japan,* vol. 1, *The Domestic Transformation,* ed. Kozo Yamamura and Yasukichi Yasuba (Stanford, Calif.: Stanford University Press, 1987), pp. 516–54.

14. Seizaburo Sato and Tetsuhisa Matsuzaki, "Policy Leadership by the Liberal Democrats," *Economic Eye* 5 (December 1984): 25–32. The article originally appeared in *Chūō Kōron,* Japan's leading serious magazine.

15. There are exceptions to this pattern, such as union representation in certain ministry advisory committees, and more generally, opposition views have been more influential in periods when the LDP majority in the Diet has been weak. See Ellis S. Krauss, "Conflict in the Diet: Toward Conflict Management in Parliamentary Politics," in *Conflict in Japan,* pp. 243–93.

16. A recent and sophisticated interpretation is T. J. Pempel, "Organizing for Efficiency: The Higher Civil Service in Japan," in *Bureaucrats and Policy-Making,* ed. Ezra Suleiman (New York: Holmes and Meier, 1984), pp. 72–106.

17. See my "Policy Conflict and Its Resolution Within the Governmental System," in *Conflict in Japan,* pp. 294–334.

18. T. J. Pempel, "Administrative Reform: Scrap and Build," in *Policy and Politics in Japan: Creative Conservatism* (Philadelphia: Temple University Press, 1982), pp. 255–95.

19. See the symposium on "Government Responses to Budget Scarcity" in the Spring 1985 issue of *Policy Studies Journal.*

20. See Haruhiro Fukui, *Party in Power* (Berkeley and Los Angeles: University of California Press, 1970), pp. 173–97; and my "Compensation for Repatriates," in *Policymaking in Contemporary Japan,* ed. T. J. Pempel (Ithaca, N.Y.: Cornell University Press, 1977), pp. 103–42.

21. Classic statements of these viewpoints are, respectively, Johnson, *MITI,* and Philip H. Tresize with Yukio Suzuki, "Politics, Government and Economic Growth in Japan," in *Asia's New Giant,* ed. Hugh Patrick and Henry Rosovsky (Washington, D.C.: The Brookings Institution, 1976), pp. 753–811. A recent conflict-oriented view is Richard J. Samuels, *The Business of the Japanese State: Energy Markets in Comparative and Historical Perspective* (Ithaca, N.Y.: Cornell University Press, 1987).

22. Johnson, *MITI,* pp. 315–16.

23. Ibid., pp. 316–17, and also see pp. 46–55.

24. Ibid., p. 54.

25. See chap. 9 of my *Contemporary Japanese Budget Politics* (Berkeley and Los Angeles: University of California Press, 1976).

26. See Joseph Schumpeter's discussion of "Another Theory of Democracy" in *Capitalism, Socialism, and Democracy* (New York: Harper and Row, 1950), pp. 269–83.

7

Democracy and Local Government in Postwar Japan

●

TERRY E. MACDOUGALL

Is strong local government an essential element of democracy? Most theories of democracy provide little enlightenment on this question. Indeed, if local government is mentioned at all in theoretical discussions of democracy, it is usually as an afterthought. Democratic theorists, with some important exceptions, have concentrated instead on national political institutions and processes and on the character of political society more generally. Among those few theorists who have paid more than passing attention to the linkage between local government and democracy are several of considerable consequence, including John Stuart Mill, Alexis de Tocqueville, and James Bryce.[1] These and several others have variously seen strong local government as either an essential or a particularly useful means of realizing central democratic principles, including liberty (personal rights), political equality (collective preference through broad participation in public affairs), and human welfare.[2] In the specific circumstances of post-surrender Japan, SCAP (Supreme Command for the Allied Powers), overriding some internal dissention, made an explicit linkage between the two and, in fact, came to view the decentralization of political authority and the strengthening of local governmental bodies under enhanced citizen control as critical to its overall goal of democratizing Japan.

The purpose of this chapter is to analyze the changing relationship between citizens and local government in Japan since the Occupation and to determine how that relationship influences the character and quality of postwar Japanese democracy.[3] The central thesis is that,

139

despite a disappointing start when Allied Occupation expectations for strong, responsive, and relatively autonomous local governments went largely unrealized, there emerged by the 1970s, through a surprisingly conflictual process, a new "social contract" binding citizens to local governments. By then, local authorities had been forced to carefully consider the interests of residents and to provide opportunities for them to be aired in the course of planning and implementing local public policy.

Take, for example, the siting of public works, a frequently controversial issue common to local governments around the world. Typically, in the years before 1970, Japanese municipal governments would plan such capital construction projects as sewer systems, roads, and waste management facilities in consultation with prefectural and national offices from which partial subsidies would be sought. Local assemblies normally applauded the acquisition of such funding, while local residents benefited, or suffered, as the case might be, without much, if any, opportunity to influence the siting and details of the projects. In the 1969 revision of the country's City Planning Law, jurisdiction for such planning was transferred from national to prefectural and municipal government offices and included some nominal provisions for citizen consultation. This reform, however, fell short of the increasing demand by residents, particularly in urban areas, for a greater say on matters affecting their living environment. The result of this disparity in established top-down patterns of deciding local public policy and increased citizen concern with the quality of community life resulted in significant protests in the early 1970s, including a so-called garbage war in Tokyo. In that particular struggle, housewives and other ordinary citizens literally sat down in front of garbage trucks and bulldozers until government authorities responded constructively to their concerns. The upshot was that Japanese local authorities learned that they must consult residents and consider their welfare if they were to win their trust and compliance in the conduct of public policy.

It is instructive to recall that American cities at the same time experienced a major crisis in waste management policy with the implementation of the Clean Air Act, which brought the construction of incinerators to a virtual halt. In the seventeen years since then, for example, New York City has not built a single new incinerator and has not solved the problem of waste disposal. In the same period, however, Tokyo has built thirteen resource recovery plants in its inner twenty-three wards, as well as several more in suburban communities. Local authorities now engage residents in a thorough discussion of the siting of plants, their designs, what facilities to include, and what public amenities (from heated pools to recreation facilities for the elderly) will go along with them. One can discern in this type of behavior, which cuts across a wide range of local public policy and is prevalent (although not universal) in Japanese localities, the emergence of a new "social contract" between citizens and local government. It is a social contract that places a high priority on the welfare of citizens and provides increased, although some would argue still inadequate, opportunities for collective preferences to be reflected in public policy. In this respect, any discussion of democracy in postwar Japan would be incomplete without consideration of the role of local government.

This chapter begins with an examination of how SCAP sought to use local government reform as a means of democratizing Japan. It then analyzes the evolution of Japanese local government over the past four decades, tracing the fate of several of the principal SCAP reforms and suggesting how changing issue agendas have affected the role of local government in the political system. This is followed by an assessment of the manner and degree to which local government has furthered democratic principles. The chapter concludes by suggesting an interpretation of how and why postwar local governmental institutions and practices have been transformed to serve Japanese conceptions of the goals of political democracy.

Local Governmental Reform Under the Allied Occupation
Assuring the Peoples' Liberty

There is no doubt that the Allied Occupation viewed the strengthening of local government as a critical element in its overall program for the democratization of Japan. Nor can there be much doubt as to why it made this link between local government and democracy. Democratization, in the predominant view within SCAP, required a breakup of prewar authoritarian structures. According to this view, best represented by the Government Section of SCAP, decentralization of governmental authority and strengthening of local governmental bodies under the control of local residents would limit the obtrusive control of centralized authorities over the personal lives and rights of the people.[4] In other words, the chief goal of reforming local government was to better assure the liberty of the people. There were other goals as well, but the essential motivation for undertaking such wide-ranging measures as the dismantling and abolition of the Home Ministry, the decentralization of the police and educational systems, and the separation of the prefectural and municipal civil services from the national level was the belief that the highly centralized character and concentration of power of these institutions in the prewar years had facilitated authoritarian government and the trampling of the rights of the people.

Antiauthoritarianism, not the belief that local government could perform these functions better on their own, was the vital reason for linking local governmental reform to the democratization process and for emphasizing most particularly those measures that might help guarantee the people's liberty. The Government Section of SCAP summed up this viewpoint in its official history of political reform published in 1949: 'Representative government reaches its fullest expression when the citizens of a local community, through officials elected by and responsible to them, determine the policies and manage the affairs of that community. *Under such conditions, authoritarian encroachments on the lives and rights of the people are difficult to impose or perpetuate,* and government retains its proper character as an instrument and servant of the people."[5]

Similarly, General Douglas MacArthur's statement on the Diet's passage of the local governmental reforms of September 1946 also emphasized the goal of assuring the people's liberty. Commenting on the expanded opportunities for local participation, he noted that "such direct participation in local government will profoundly influence the shaping of national policies—will *provide a check rein against arbitrary governmental controls and a safeguard to individual freedom.*"[6]

Democratization Through Participation in Local Affairs

To SCAP's local governmental reformers, limiting the potential abuses of the peoples' rights by central authorities was not simply a matter of shifting the focus of governmental authority to the local level but also one of enhancing the capacity of citizens to protect their rights and resolve their differences for themselves through the training afforded by participation in local government under their control. Hence, along with the goal of liberty, political equality (understood in terms of determining collective preference through broad participation in public affairs) became a major democratic value to be furthered by local governmental reform. Among the means chosen to further this end were the direct election of chief executives (governors and mayors) and local school boards as well as provisions for the recall of local officials and direct demand for both the enactment of by-laws and inspection of local administration.

If decentralization represented the negative aspect of preventing central government abuses, expanded citizen participation in and control of local government represented a positive attempt to use local institutions for democratization more generally. In articulating this view of the value of citizen participation in local government, SCAP reformers were echoing de Tocqueville's theme that town meetings are to liberty what primary schools are to democracy. Participation in local governance was to serve at least two ends: training in democratic citizenship and the development of democratic leadership. Both the Government Section and MacArthur argued this in the same breath as they hailed local government's role in assuring people's rights. The Government Section's report noted above continues: "The local arena thus becomes a training ground for leadership in national affairs." And MacArthur added in a similar vein, "It is axiomatic that such experience in government will develop the dynamic and enlightened leadership and initiative essential to the vigorous and progressive building of a democratic nation."

Contending Views

It was not a foregone conclusion that SCAP would use local government as a major means to try to democratize Japan. After all, economic and social conditions in Japan following the war were chaotic. Weakening the central government's ability to establish economic and social controls through decentralization of authority was opposed by some within SCAP, especially those most responsible for surmounting the early economic crisis. Those responsible for programs of public health, public safety, social security, and resource extraction also tended to favor strong centralized control. Many Japanese reformers as well were more inclined to pursue Japan's democratization through national institutions rather than risk the possibility of having the intent of national reforms obscured or diverted at the local level where traditional attitudes of obedience to authority and the control of entrenched elites were more likely to endure. And, needless to say, national bureaucrats and politicians, enamored with the achievements that centralized authority had brought to Japan during its period of modernization, tended to be skeptical of local administrative capacity detached from national leadership. Nevertheless, SCAP persisted in its effort to use local government as an avenue for achieving political democracy in postwar Japan. But this division within SCAP foreshadowed later political struggles among contending Japanese forces over the fate of the reforms.

Prewar Japanese Local Government

In making their recommendations for local governmental reform, members of the Government Section of SCAP were not imposing a wholly new and alien conception of democracy on Japan. The period of Taisho Democracy in the 1920s had witnessed important advances for local government, including the loosening of hierarchical controls over the selection of mayors, a weakening of the home minister's authority to intervene in local budget-making, a strengthening of the prerogatives of prefectural assemblies at the expense of the centrally appointed governors, and enhanced authority for the big cities.[7] Moreover, Japanese reformers at the time called for a further curtailment of central bureaucratic controls over local governments, the direct election of governors, and a strengthening of local assemblies.

What preceded this period of reform was a local governmental system controlled by the Home Ministry at the center and the ministry's appointed prefectural governors. The governors, at least in theory, could not be constrained by their popularly elected assemblies; they had the final say in selecting local mayors and the authority to intervene in municipal affairs. The work of local government was largely the implementation of national policy with little scope for autonomous local decision making or control by local citizens of their elected representatives.

The local governmental reforms of the 1920s were only partially a result of long smoldering conflicts between representatives of local interests in the assemblies with the centrally appointed or controlled executives. They were also a product of a more general liberalizing trend accompanying strong pressures for incorporating larger segments of the population into fuller political citizenship. This pressure was a result of the increased economic modernization, urbanization, and literacy of the nation. Although the reformed system carried with it more "democratic potential" than what had preceded it, it was neither intended to serve explicitly democratic goals nor was it financially strong enough to support significant local initiative. By the mid-1930s, the central government tried to improve local finance by providing "temporary financial relief" for the poorer municipalities and prefectures. This system became institutionalized by 1940; but, while helping to redress some inequalities among localities, it also tended to increase central government scrutiny of the financial affairs of local governments.

SCAP's commitment to a significant overhaul of Japanese local government was conditioned to a great extent by wartime developments that had reversed earlier liberalizing trends and strengthened the central government's ability to use local units for national mobilization. The Home Ministry had created community associations (*chōnaikai*) in city neighborhoods and in the towns and villages and placed them and their communal property under mayoral leadership to better mobilize resources for the war effort. *Chōnaikai,* and their constituent *tonarigumi* (groupings of around ten households), took on major responsibilities for police and welfare work, as well as food rationing and promoting a national spirit in their areas. By 1943 centralization had proceeded further by the strengthening of executive heads at the expense of prefectural and municipal assemblies and the reimposition of hierarchical controls over the selection of mayors and the conduct of local affairs. Finally, in 1943 nine newly created Regional Administrative Councils were given the authority to control almost everything in their areas. Hence, SCAP officials could argue with considerable justification that "the system of local government in operation in Japan at the beginning of the Occupation was the antithesis of local self-government. Its character was rigidly authoritarian and local governments were but arms of the central government."[8]

Local Governmental Reforms of the Allied Occupation

SCAP's local governmental reforms may be briefly summarized under three broad headings: (1) decentralization or abolition of authoritarian structures that had limited basic liberties in the prewar years; (2) expansion of citizens' participation in and control of local government; and (3) deconcentration and restraint of executive authority by local assemblies.

Decentralization began with a dismantling of what SCAP saw as a monolithic and authoritarian administrative structure with the Home Ministry at its pinnacle and the community associations at its base. Immediate prewar and wartime innovations, like the community associations and regional administrative councils, were abolished. The Home Ministry was stripped successively of its police, fire, election management, public works, and supervisory functions and was finally abolished on December 27, 1947.

SCAP's goal of decentralization was most notably achieved (at least in the short run) in respect to the police and educational systems. Reforms in these areas were motivated by a desire to dismantle structures believed to have contributed to prewar indoctrination and thought control, rather than by a judgment that these functions would be handled best at the local level or that local control was absolutely necessary for their "democratic conduct." SCAP established municipal police forces under the control of local public safety commissions, and, for communities with a population of less than 5,000, a national rural police. Similarly, SCAP sought to free education from the direct control of the Ministry of Education while keeping it independent of local administration by the creation of popularly elected prefectural and municipal boards of education that were put in charge of all public schools and invested with significant budgetary authority.

While the decentralization of educational and police functions was a matter of legal reform subject to later revision, decentralization of the administrative structure per se was guaranteed in a more fundamental sense by the constitution of 1947. Chapter 8 (articles 92–95) guaranteed the "principle of local autonomy" and such basic features of the new system as the separation of local from national administration and the direct popular election of chief executives, as well as assembly representatives.

Despite the ambiguity of the phrase "the principle of local autonomy," the fact remains that for the first time in Japanese history the continued existence of a local governmental system separate from the national administrative structure was established in the fundamental law of the land. Moreover, a new political dynamic was introduced into local government by the constitutional provision for the direct popular election of governors and mayors. This extension of popular sovereignty gave the people for the first time the ability to control the executive and hence the incentive for mayors and governors to address the demands and needs of the electorate and not only the priorities of higher authorities.

Further provisions for the organization and operation of local government were consolidated in the Local Autonomy Law of April 17,

1947, which has undergone yearly revisions as the functions of local governments have expanded, and in a variety of other laws. Some of these provisions further extended the scope of citizen participation and control. For example, citizens were invested with the right to recall public officeholders and to make direct demands for the enactment of by-laws and inspection of local administration.

The new system of local government was intended also to break up and check executive control of local government. Executive authority was deconcentrated by the creation of prefecturual and municipal commissions in charge of public safety, election management, and inspection of local administration. The representative assemblies were strengthened vis-à-vis the chief executive by having the right to approve his appointments to the commissions and certain other offices, to override his veto with a two-thirds majority, and to seek his resignation through a vote of no confidence. (The chief executive, in turn, could choose to dissolve the assembly and take a dispute directly to the people.)

Early Difficulties of the New System

These reforms did not provide as solid a base for local autonomy as intended by Occupation authorities; in practice, the new system more closely resembled prewar antecedents, derived largely from the continental European models of administration, than American-style decentralized local government. Among the reasons for this result were strong bureaucratic resistance to administrative and financial decentralization, skepticism on the part of conservative governments concerning the capacity of local authorities, and failure by SCAP to tackle early and strongly enough problems of local finance. For example, SCAP's attempt to provide a kind of local home rule was unsuccessful as a result of rewording by Japanese bureaucrats of constitutional provisions for local government.[9] Also, much of the national work previously assigned to appointed governors was directly transferred to the popularly elected governors who, in carrying it out, acted as agents of the national ministries and remained subject to their guidance. In fact, this practice, known as agency delegation (*kikan inin jimu*), was extended to the municipalities as well.[10] Belatedly, in a report issued in 1949 by the Shoup Commission, SCAP acknowledged that the new administrative system lacked an adequate tax structure and division of authority, which might have facilitated local control of local affairs and democratic responsibility.

Post-Occupation Evolution of Local Government

The legacy of the Occupation's local governmental reforms was a mixed system combining aspects of prewar centralized administration with postwar norms of local autonomy, a measure of institutional separation between levels of government, and an intensified need for local governmental responsiveness to popular constituencies. It has proved to be a flexible and dynamic system, adjusted constantly over the past three and a half decades to changing issue agendas generated by the nation's social and economic transformation and contending political forces. Local government issue agendas in postwar Japan have evolved through four overlapping phases, each with rather distinct central themes. During the first postwar decade, controversy centered on the relative merits and demerits of the Occupation reforms and on the efforts of the conservative parties nationally to recentralize the administrative system. From the mid-1950s through the mid-1960s, local governments became deeply enmeshed in the national drive for economic growth, which they hoped to harness for local prosperity and for a solution to their financial problems. By the late 1960s or early 1970s local governments throughout the country had to contend with citizen activism spawned by severe environmental deterioration and mounting urban and social problems. From the mid-1970s they have emerged gradually into a pivotal role in defining a new Japanese democratic synthesis quite different from, but not necessarily less democratic than, that anticipated by the Allied Occupation.

Administrative Recentralization

Even before the end of the Occupation, Japan's conservative national politicians, who have dominated the government since 1948, began to assess the utility of the newly decentralized institutions. In general, they were skeptical about local administrative skills, concerned that autonomous local institutions might be unduly influenced by opposition groups, and convinced that Japan's economic recovery depended on establishing greater central administrative controls. Although the most politically explosive aspects of administrative recentralization were legislated by the mid-1950s, the process continued in other respects during the next two decades.

Recentralization of the police and education systems stirred strong opposition from the socialists, labor unionists, and intellectuals fearful of reversion to prewar authoritarianism. Fundamental reform of the police system was delayed by political protest until 1954, when a new Police Law established a single "autonomous" prefectural-level police system coordinated by a National Police Agency under the guidance of the National Public Safety Commission. Similarly, in 1956 the Board of Education Law was replaced by a new educational administration law, which provided for the appointment of regular members of educational commissions by the governors and mayors, with the approval of their local assemblies, and appointment of superintendents of education by higher-level authorities. The commissions' role in budgetary matters was reduced to that of consultation with local authorities, while the Ministry of Education's guidance of curriculum was strengthened.

Recentralization also resulted from the efforts of central government bureaucrats and conservative politicians to achieve administrative efficiency and to facilitate economic recovery and development. Administrative efficiency was pursued through the time-honored practice of encouraging amalgamations of municipalities through a variety of financial incentives. Amalgamations were seen as a means to avoid waste of scarce resources, to upgrade the overall quality of public administration, and to speed the implementation of economic plans and national functions delegated to localities. Opponents, however, argued that amalgamations weakened citizens' control of local authorities and their sense of political efficacy.

Additional plans for replacing the prefectures with broader administrative regions were never realized because of entrenched prefectural interests and the opposition's concern over excessive centralization. But regional blocs were created for the implementation of economic development policies; and cooperation among localities in the delivery of various services, including fire prevention, sanitation, and welfare, was encouraged by national legislation. Financial incentives were also provided for coordinated development among neighboring municipalities.

By the 1960s administrative recentralization was proceeding at a rapid pace, although with less political confrontation than earlier. Revision of certain laws, like that concerning waterways, resulted in effective jurisdiction being reabsorbed by the national ministries, from which local authorities would now have to seek permission for related projects. Branch offices of the central ministries were newly established or strengthened in their role of guiding and checking on local government. By 1975 the number of tasks performed by local governments under central ministerial guidance had doubled for municipalities and increased by nearly two and a half times for prefectures since 1952. Moreover, with the creation of a wide range of centrally funded public corporations, like the Japan Housing Corporation and the Japan Highway Public Corporation, local authorities often lost the initiative and control over public investment and development in their areas. To make matters worse, in many areas of the country private development far outpaced the ability of local authorities to plan or guide the long-term destinies of their cities.

Economic Development

By the mid-1950s, Japan's principal private industries had established a variety of sectional and industrywide national organizations that facilitated close cooperation with the still powerful central bureaucracy and the newly unified Liberal Democratic party (LDP) for the economic expansion of the country. National planning by this time had turned from resource extraction and the redevelopment of light industry to the establishment of various central and regional development laws and banks. These provided mechanisms for public financing and investment in new industrial sites, water resources, transportation, roads, harbors, and other industrial infrastructure. Local authorities joined this effort at industrial expansion by passing ordinances to attract industry. The number of these ordinances, which provided tax incentives, public services to industries, and even subsidies, grew rapidly. In 1955 there were 9 at the prefectural level and 102 among the municipalities; by 1969 there were 41 and 1,303, respectively. However, during the first half of this period major industries continued to concentrate in the large metropolitan areas around Tokyo, Osaka, and Nagoya with their skilled labor forces and relatively high stock of industrial infrastructure.

Significant regional development in other areas was spurred by a series of new laws in the early 1960s that partially reversed the tendency of central government planners to concentrate development in the Pacific industrial belt between Tokyo and Osaka-Kobe. These new laws were largely a response to pressure exerted by local authorities, through LDP representatives in the Diet, who sought national government assistance in luring industries to less developed regions. Local authorities now competed fiercely with each other in so-called petition wars to receive national government designation as target areas, and industries such as petroleum refining, petrochemicals, steel, nonferrous metals, machinery, and other heavy and chemical products spread throughout the country.

In effect, by the late 1960s the process of administrative recentralization and the drive for economic development had forced localities to look toward prefectural offices of the central government for policy leadership, detailed administrative guidance, and financial assistance. The ideal of relatively autonomous localities managing their own affairs was far from the reality. Yet little friction was evident between center and localities, although a great deal of competition emerged among localities in their respective efforts to win central support. At the local level, the new institutional arrangements also did not seem to be working quite as the Occupation had planned. Executive dominance continued, with local assemblies showing little policy ability or initiative. And citizens made sparse use of their new rights of recall and direct demand. Politically, virtually all prefectural and municipal assemblies were dominated by Liberal Democrats or independent conservatives, as were the vast majority of mayoral and gubernatorial posts. This political cohesiveness between the center and local governments undoubtedly facilitated smooth relations.[11] Moreover, the bureaucratic sectionalism of the pivotal prefectural governments, which came to act more and more as liaison offices between the central ministries and the municipalities, perpetuated long-standing practices of seeking support from higher authorities before coordinating policies locally. Hence, when prominent foreign analysts reassessed the legacy of the Occupation in the mid to late 1960s, they generally agreed that much of SCAP's efforts in regard to local government had come to naught, although the extremes of prewar centralization had not returned.[12]

Local Initiative

By the late 1960s and early 1970s many local governments had begun to rethink their priorities. Most had not invested sufficiently in roads, sewers, parks, housing, and other expensive social infrastructure. Instead, they had been absorbed in providing the minimum required educational, sanitation, and welfare facilities and services and in promoting the local economy. Although Japan's rapid economic growth had enriched the country and elevated the standard of living of its people, it had also brought about social changes that generated even greater demands upon local services. Rapid growth had led to a depopulation of the countryside and excessive urban crowding. One result was the spiraling of urban land prices that made the provision of an adequate social infrastructure all the more difficult. Another was the proliferation of new urban problems, like pollution, traffic congestion and accidents, and uncontrolled urban sprawl. Social change also lessened the solidarity of the local community and family, traditional social buffers, and created new needs for social services—particularly for the old, the very young, and the handicapped. The intensity of such problems in many areas led to social unrest and efforts by ordinary citizens to seek help from local government.

Under these circumstances, many localities undertook significant policy initiatives. Efforts were made to improve communications with local residents through public hearings, consultations, and public relations programs. This included the establishment of legal consultation windows, little city halls, and citizens' committees to monitor various local governmental functions. Some cities developed elaborate mechanisms for citizens to participate in local planning. Public relations programs included periodic newsletters, generally distributed through local newspaper delivery circuits, and tours of local social service facilities for specially targeted groups, particularly the elderly.[13]

In addition to these efforts to reorient themselves to their constituencies, local governments pioneered in a wide array of pollution control and social welfare programs.[14] The former were particularly important in reestablishing the credibility of local authorities in the eyes of residents. Pollution had reached such severe levels that it was no longer possible to simply plead lack of jurisdiction and pass the blame for doing nothing on to industry or the central government. Many an incumbent mayor or governor found his political career on the line over this issue, and for the first time, a significant number of them lost to opposition candidates—normally backed by the Socialists and one or more of the other parties in opposition nationally—who promised to do more. That frequently included agreements between local governments and private industry to limit pollution levels, or pollution control ordinances that set stricter standards than in national law. Although such arrangements had dubious legal bases and were strongly challenged by central ministries, the pollution issue took on such salience at the national level that the ruling Liberal Democrats and central ministries were forced not only to give ex post facto sanction to them but also to use the local initiatives as models for national policies.

There was far less popular pressure for new social policies, but local governments began to respond creatively to the increased needs for social services as well. Most notably in terms of the costs involved, over two hundred fifty localities established free medical care for the elderly and childhood allowance programs while the central government was still unwilling to commit itself to such measures. As in the case of pollution control, these local initiatives, combined with pressure from opposition parties and bureaucratic lobbying, forced the central government to implement similar programs in the early 1970s. A wide range of other social welfare policies, generally geared to the weak and those who had earlier been left out of the nation's headlong leap into prosperity, were begun by localities; most of these had no counterpart on the national level.

At least as important as these developments was the tremendous upgrading of local planning skills that took place between the mid-1960s and mid-1970s. In a sense, this was the achievement of central efforts to improve local administrative competence through amalgamations, strict examination requirements for the local civil service, special training programs, and the like. It also marked the turning point in the ability of local governments, particularly the prefectures and larger cities, to undertake relatively autonomous comprehensive planning, to aggregate diverse interests locally, and to argue persuasively with central authorities for funding based on local priorities. By this time, local governments had closed the salary gap between themselves and the national bureaucracy, and in many cases exceeded the latter, enabling them to recruit highly competent people, both technical and generalist. Local civil service employment offered the additional attraction of permanent residency, as opposed to the frequent transfers that employees of the national government and large corporations must go through. At the same time technical specialists at the local level developed their own professional associations which served as a significant avenue for learning from each other.[15] An important symbolic and practical breakthrough occurred in 1969 when, for the first time in modern Japanese history, city planning was devolved from the central government to the prefectural level, and in some respects to the municipalities, giving them greater leeway for responding to local demand and for controlling their developmental destinies.

"The Age of Localism"

Several things made the great activism of local governments from the mid-1960s through the mid-1970s possible: an accumulation of critical public issues that spurred strong citizen pressure on local authorities, the growth of opposition parties that coalesced around the new issues and challenged the conservatives' traditional political hegemony at the local level, a maturation of the administrative capacity of local governments, and the availability of ever-growing resources generated by rapid economic growth—although, of course, these conditions were distributed very unevenly throughout the country. This situation was ironic in that rapid economic growth, which was condemned by many citizens' movements and opposition parties for causing severe pollution and social dislocations, also made possible dramatic ameliorative policies, for which progressive local administrations received a disproportionate share of the credit.

The situation changed abruptly in the mid-1970s. The most salient local programs, such as pollution control and free medical care for the aged, spread rapidly among conservative local administrations as well as progressive·ones and, before long, to the conservative national government. The result was a loss of distinctiveness between conservatives and progressives locally and, after a decade's lapse, a refocusing of the political spotlight from the local to the national level. Electoral and leadership problems within the LDP nationally also precipitated a movement to the political center by most opposition parties, which then jockeyed for position in their efforts to define the political character of post-LDP hegemony. This development moderated the intensity of partisanship in local politics, while it further whetted the appetite of the political parties to share in local power.

Attention also shifted to the national level because of the increased salience of international issues after the first oil crisis of 1973–74 and the second of 1979. These same international economic difficulties resulted in a slowdown of the economy that adversely affected public finance at all levels of government and made dramatic new policy breakthroughs by local authorities less possible. Indeed, in the name of administrative reform and fiscal responsibility, national ministries once again tried to reassert their leadership over local governments.

After some heated political struggles in the mid-1970s, there emerged a new realization of the importance of the local arena for the creation of the open, affluent, and humane society that bureaucrat and politician, government and opposition, businessman and worker alike hoped for. The predominant agenda, in effect, became one of giving substantive content to the slogan, the "age of localism," originated by the governor of Kanagawa, Nagasu Kazuji. As to be expected, a disparity of motives and visions could be found behind the common use of this slogan, although the contending sides tended to be far less polarized than in the preceding decade.

What is most important for our purposes is not the details of these contending views but the common recognition by those who held them that "localism" (*jimoto shugi*), identification with locality and local interests, is a free-floating resource that can be mobilized for policy innovation and may in fact be necessary for its successful implementation.[16] For the most part, it is no longer possible to simply impose outside wishes, whether by national authorities, private developers, or others, upon localities. Persuasion, taking into account the views of local residents and local authorities, not the type of inadequate consultation and coercion symbolized by the central government's development of Narita Airport or haphazard land development by private firms, has become necessary. Moreover, policy initiative is far more often than in the past coming from localities, seeking to carry out projects either on their own or in cooperation with central authorities. There has developed a broad recognition of the administrative competence of local governments and of the necessity for those governments to be responsive to their constituents. In effect, local government has become much more a partner than a client in building a Japanese-style democracy—one, as suggested below, that emphasizes equality in human welfare as well as in participation.

Democratic Values and Local Government in Japan

Liberty

SCAP's use of local government as an instrument of democratization in postwar Japan stemmed, as suggested above, from a reaction to prewar and wartime authoritarianism and a belief that decentralizing state authority could help safeguard the rights of the people. (Given SCAP's tendency to equate authoritarianism with expansionism, it seemed that both the world and the Japanese people would be safer with a weakened Japanese state.) Others, from Montesquieu to Maass, have also pointed out the potential for mitigating the power of the sovereign (or state) by the geographical division of power.[17] This point has not gone unnoticed by Japanese scholars of local government. Most notably, Hoshino Mitsuo, director of research at the Tokyo Institute for Municipal Research, develops the argument that such a division of power is not only essential but also, in most cases, more effective than the traditional three-fold division of power (executive, legislative, and judicial) in safeguarding basic human rights in modern society.[18] Hence, he argues for "an inherent right of local self-government."

As pointed out by Maass, such arguments can be developed on two levels: that of governmental processes and that of the individual or group. In regard to the former, local government might be considered as part of a system of countervailing power among governmental levels. In a sense, it could function as a systemic (or institutional) opposition to central authorities.[19] It might, for example, be a safeguard in protecting a diversity of local values against the impulse toward uniformity in the administration of the modern state. For the individual or the group, the value of local government in assuring the people's rights is its ability to provide points of pressure and control that are more readily accessible than those at the national level. Presumably, by keeping governmental power close to its masters, it should be more responsive and less arbitrary. In addition, minority groups or viewpoints that have a hard time acquiring representation at the center may avail themselves of governmental positions and power locally. A third view, combining both these arguments, might also be suggested. Local governments could be conceived as powerful institutional actors advocating somewhat different societal interests than those that are influential at the center. This will be developed below in elaborating the role of local governments as advocates of consumer interests and rights.

What has been the experience of postwar Japanese local government in the protection of the people's liberty? Overall, it has probably not played as central a role as that anticipated by the Occupation. Other institutions, such as the courts, a free press, and parliamentary opposition, which has stood in defense of the constitution, have been more important. Moreover, the autonomous local police, created for this purpose by SCAP, have been recentralized without any noticeable loss of liberty. The assumption that centralized authority is liable to be arbitrary and trample on human rights is too simple a formulation. Because civil liberties were not well respected by governmental authorities in prewar Japan, a broad range of actors in Japanese society has steadfastly defended them in the postwar years.

Japan today is once again a "strong state," although not as centralized as before the war. That margin of difference appears to have made some significant—if small, in the overall scheme of things— contribution to the defense of liberty:

1. It has acted to some extent as a cushion against bureaucratic arbitrariness. This is not insignificant, since a great deal of the work of national government is performed by local authorities in the form of agency delegation. The tendency of national agencies and ministries is to issue detailed directives (*tsūtatsu*), with generally uniform prescriptions as to how the work should be performed. The danger of this is that the directives might go beyond the intent of the original law in which a particular task was established. Tanaka Jirō, a scholar of administrative law and justice of the Supreme Court, refers to this as "administration by directive" (*tsūtatsu ni yoru gyōsei*) as opposed to what should rightly be "administration by law" (*hōritsu ni yoru gyōsei*).[20] In a wide variety of cases, some publicized, like that involving the nationality rights of Korean residents of Japan, and some not, like the rights of welfare recipients, local governments have openly resisted or ignored central directives that seemed to stretch the laws beyond their intent.

2. Local government has provided additional points of access and influence for minority groups. Since Japan is a relatively homogeneous society, this role has not been particularly prominent. Nonetheless, Japan's largest minority group, the Burakumin, numbering close to three million, have found some assistance from local authorities in realizing their full rights as citizens of Japan. The prefecture and city of Kyoto, for example, have provided special scholarships for Burakumin to further their education and thereby to take better advantage of the opportunities afforded by the open, democratic system.

3. Local governments have furthered the defense of liberties through their efforts to increase citizens' consciousness of their rights. Among many progressive local governments, for example, this takes the form of public observances of Constitution Day. Similarly, some mayors and governors have used constitutional guarantees of basic rights, such as the right to a healthful and cultured living, to justify a variety of innovative public welfare policies.

The point should be reiterated, however, that although considerable administrative recentralization has once again made Japan a "strong state," this has not directly threatened civil liberties. SCAP's equation of state centralization with the endangerment of liberty should be seen in the context of Japan's "dark valley" of crisis immediately preceding and during the war. Still, its separation of local

administration from the national level has provided a supplementary
guarantee of basic rights, in addition to the more critical ones noted
above.

Participation

SCAP attempted to broaden participation in public affairs in several ways: giving full political citizenship to women, lowering the
voting age, lifting restrictions on the freedom of speech and of association, increasing the range of electoral offices, and providing mechanisms for citizen initiative and recall. The most critical reform in
regard to local government was the direct election of mayors and
governors. SCAP's goals at the local level were (1) to facilitate training in democratic citizenship by increasing the people's ability to
control local affairs and hold their representatives responsible; and (2)
to provide additional opportunities for potential national leaders to
learn the art of governance in democracy.

Local government as a site for broad citizen participation that
would in turn have systemwide repercussions for democratic development has drawn far more attention than its potential contribution to
liberty.[21] In brief, four general theses have been suggested: (1) Local
participation can help mitigate the participatory inadequacies of the
large nation-state. The argument here is that local government, being
closer to the citizen, is easier to understand and influence than more
distant national authorities. "Direct democracy" is, in some measure,
possible at the local level. (2) Local government is also a useful site for
citizenship training. SCAP joined a distinguished list of theorists in
articulating this point, including de Tocqueville, Mill, Bryce, Laski,
and Dahl. (3) Also, as suggested by SCAP, local politics can be a
training ground for national political leadership. This point has been
elaborated by Dahl in regard to the role of somewhat autonomous
local institutions in providing controlled conditions under which political oppositions might learn the art of compromise and make the
transition toward power in the grand arena of national politics.[22] (4)
Participation in local public affairs may also provide opportunities for
strengthening fraternity among diverse classes, religions, sectors, or
groups. The argument is that in local communities people must to
some degree adjust their ideas and feelings in order to live together
and that the practice of that locally may have a stabilizing effect
nationwide.

Postwar Japanese local government has contributed significantly to furthering the democratic value of political equality, in the sense of providing broad opportunities for citizens to participate in public affairs, but it has not necessarily done this in ways anticipated by SCAP. Let us consider the four arguments noted above.

Mitigating Participatory Inadequacies of the Large State

Although we do not have comparative data from before the war, it is clear from postwar public opinion surveys that the Japanese people have a greater sense of efficacy in regard to local government than they do at the national level.[23] They feel closer to local government and believe that they can influence it. This is particularly true for women, who are less confident of their ability to influence political processes beyond the local level. Although postwar amalgamations of municipalities and massive urbanization may have made even local government somewhat less tangible for most Japanese, the creative efforts by local authorities in the 1960s and 1970s to establish new modes of two-way communication between themselves and local residents seem to have had a positive impact. The role of Yokohama in the mid-1960s, under Mayor Asukata Ichio, is particularly noteworthy for providing participatory models.[24]

Citizenship Training

SCAP was concerned that Japanese citizens be better able to control or hold their representatives responsible for their actions and, if need be, to take initiative on their own. Although sparse use has been made of the Local Autonomy Law's provision for citizen initiative, by the 1960s instances of recall began to increase—usually to protest political corruption or to change policy directions, particularly regarding the balance between economic growth and the environment. More often than earlier, residents were able to change the policy priorities of local government by rallying around an alternative candidate for mayor or governor. In many cases, this occurred as a result of pressure from groups concerned with environmental issues. Margaret McKean has argued persuasively, based on interviews with participants in a wide variety of such movements, that their involvement was a powerful force for political socialization in a democratic direction.[25] Their object of pressure in most cases was local government; and, in this sense, the new opportunities for controlling the local political process can be said to have contributed directly to citizenship training.

Training for Future National Leaders

Japanese political parties have always drawn on the reservoir of local politicians for national candidates, and they continue to do so today. In addition, what is particularly noteworthy in the Japanese experience is the role of local governmental experience in integrating opposition parties into national political affairs. Before it emerged as a force at the national level, for example, Kōmeitō became a significant force in urban local assemblies, where it often held the deciding votes, and in chief executive elections, where its support could decide the outcome of a contest between a conservative and a progressive candidate. Effective participation in local office also tended to whet the opposition's appetite for national power and generally contributed to its development of moderate and realistic policies. Progressive local governments became a kind of pressure group within the Socialist party, for example, turning its attention toward practical issues and away from a preoccupation with ideology.

Fraternity

Japan has not been plagued with the sharp linguistic, religious, class, and regional differences that trouble many other countries. Nonetheless, the need to adjust ideas and feelings about others with whom one lives in close proximity remains. SCAP, of course, did a great deal to defuse possible explosive relations among people by such measures as land reform. Yet because of its preoccupation with wartime authoritarianism, it also dissolved one important mechanism for achieving fraternity in Japanese communities—the community association. Community associations reappeared, without official recognition, within a few years after their abolition. They have assumed wide-ranging administrative, as well as sone social, economic, and religious functions at the neighborhood level. Although they were frequently criticized as an element of "grass-roots conservatism" because of their supposedly coercive character and dominance by traditional elite groups, by the 1970s their role in fostering community identity and friendly relations among neighbors was recognized, reflecting the importance Japanese place on harmonious relations with those who are close at hand (mijika). Moreover, by that time, women had become leaders in urban community associations, while white-collar workers and others from the "new middle class" also assumed greater leadership than earlier. Although not officially a part of local government, community associations are important in building a sense of community identity and establishing policy priorities based on local interests.

In sum, the contribution of local government to furthering the democratic value of participation has been considerable. Whereas political parties and interest groups are important institutions promoting mass political participation in most Western democracies, these institutions are less effective channels of participation for the Japanese people, thereby enlarging the relative importance of local government in promoting democratic participation. A relatively small percentage of the Japanese electorate belongs to a party or closely identifies with one. Rank-and-file members of interest groups generally leave decision making to the leaders. And even citizens' groups, which have clearly made an important contribution to promoting participation, are transitory. Hence, the role of local government in promoting participation constitutes an important contribution to postwar democracy.

Welfare

SCAP did not emphasize the welfare function of local government; but it is in this area that Japanese local government has probably made its greatest contribution to democracy, particularly if we interpret *welfare* to mean the general well-being of the individual as well as specific services for the needy. There are at least three important ways in which local governments might make such a contribution: (1) as coordinators of development and services; (2) as reconcilers of community opinion; and (3) as advocates of consumer interests and agents for responding to rising demands. Let us consider these in general and in the Japanese case.

Coordinators of Development and Services

The welfare functions of the industrial democracies have grown enormously in the postwar years. For the most part, policymaking in this area is dominated by central authorities which create minimum standards for the nation as a whole. Similarly, national governments have become deeply involved in regional development and urban renewal, often with the goal of lessening regional inequalities in living standards or improving the environment. Yet it is not always easy to adjust such policies to local conditions. And people simply do not live in the ordered categories set at the center. One of the most important functions of local government in the industrialized democracies is mediating between policymaking at the center and application of that policy to the peculiarities of local conditions.

In the case of Japan, most services are not delivered directly through field offices of the national government. Instead, they are channeled through local government, normally in the form of agency delegation. And many other national governmental programs are available on a voluntary or competitive basis, usually with residual supervisory authority vested in the relevant national office. Local governments may choose from a "menu" of national programs. The problem that arises in this system of diffuse responsibility among different levels of government for a particular policy area is known in Japan as "vertical administration" (*tatewari gyōsei*), which implies an inability to coordinate horizontally the public policy involvement of national authorities at the local level. The result, it is often argued, is that local governments favor projects and services sponsored by the better funded national ministries, agencies, or public corporations, without regard for balanced or coordinated development.

Over the years, however, local authorities in Japan have become more independent in determining the particular mix of programs appropriate to their communities and have adjusted them to fit local needs. Perhaps the single most important development in this regard was the growth of local governmental planning departments in the 1960s and 1970s, staffed by experts capable of coordinating public policy at the local level. By the early 1970s, many of these departments became concerned to integrate human welfare needs into city planning. Several of them, including Tokyo and Kobe, developed a process of projecting so-called civil minima for both the hardware, like community centers, and software, such as specific programs for the elderly, of human welfare services and of incorporating these into local plans.

Reconcilers of Community Opinion

Communities not only differ from each other but they also differ internally over which programs and services they need. For the most part, national authorities have neither the time nor the inclination to get involved in local conflicts over such issues. First, local authorities, being closer to the dispute than national officials, can reasonably be expected to be more cognizant of the interests at stake and, because of on-going contact, to be in a more advantageous position to make arrangements that will preserve local harmony. Second and more important, local authorities have the political legitimacy to choose among policy alternatives because they can be held responsible for those choices through election or recall. This may be the most fundamental reason for strong local government in a democratic society.

Japanese localities are probably no less conflict-prone than their counterparts in other industrial democracies. Although the lack of ethnic diversity or sharp class distinctions minimizes these sources of potential conflict, extremely rapid social and economic change has brought numerous problems and the necessity for choices that could be very divisive. National authorities are well aware of this in many cases, from the setting of bathhouse fees to the enforcement of pollution control laws, have chosen to relinquish supervisory authority rather than become involved in local disputes. Even more fundamentally, the ballot box has become a critical means of reconciling local disputes, as citizens have recalled or rejected incumbent mayors, governors, and assembly members and elected others with alternative policy priorities. Moreover, through the proliferation of public hearings and other public relations mechanisms in the 1960s and 1970s, local governments have attempted to incorporate community opinion into policymaking processes. Similarly, the growth of local planning departments noted above provided local government with an important tool for reconciling community opinion in settling priorities. As the case of the siting of incinerators noted at the beginning of this chapter suggests, local authorities now go to great lengths to talk out and reconcile differences of opinion among residents on policy issues.

Advocates of Consumer Interests

Local governments often function as "consumer pressure groups." This is particularly important in the industrialized democracies where "producer pressure groups" of employers and employees are well organized and have good access to the policy process at the national level. Although all producers are also consumers, difficulties arise in consumer advocacy in at least two respects. First, some consumers, like young people, housewives, the handicapped, and the elderly, may be nonproducers or only marginal ones. Second, even those well represented as producers may find that their interests as consumers of, say, a healthful living environment or public safety are not well represented.

In most industrial democracies local governments are the best organized and most influential representatives of consumer interests. Associations of local governments in general, of particular types of localities, and of specific local officials like mayors or governors lobby actively with central authorities or through elected national representatives from their area for a wide range of "consumer interests": new programs, regulations, and funds to clean up the environment, to correct regional inequalities, to reconstruct the cities, to provide for the weak and poor, and so on. A major reason that local authorities play this advocacy role is that service delivery and consumption are local and, hence, local authorities are intimately familiar with the inadequacies of existing programs. Similarly, local governments may be more responsive to consumer interest because rising expectations, or rising standards by the service bureaucracies themselves, may appear first or primarily in specific localities, creating pressure for improvements before national authorities become convinced of the need for action. In other words, local governments may become the channel for putting certain consumer issues on the public agenda and for legitimizing them nationally. They thereby contribute to democracy by their capacity to adjust to rising needs or demands and to channel pressure from poorly organized interests upward in the governmental system.

By the late 1960s and early 1970s, Japanese local authorities frequently found themselves as advocates or facilitators of a wide range of consumer interests, from a healthful environment and new social welfare programs to the "right to sunlight." A seriously polluted environment had spawned citizens' movements that pressed local authorities for amelioration. Local innovations in pollution control channeled further pressure for improved public policies to the national level, as much through their demonstration that something could be done as through specific lobbying at the center. Likewise, certain innovative social policies, most particularly free medical care for the aged and childhood allowances, created political pressure for national authorities to more fully develop what had been only a skeletal welfare system. But whereas local initiatives on pollution control had been largely a response to powerful pressure groups—hence, the discipline of the ballot box—most of the new welfare programs were devised within local bureaucracies, by local authorities and medical or other specialists, or by local politicians responding to perceived needs of the weak who were not always capable of well-organized and forceful advocacy of their interests.

Conclusion

Local government has come to play a critical role in Japanese political democracy, albeit one somewhat different from that envisaged by the Allied Occupation. SCAP sought to decentralize political authority and strengthen local government as a means of safeguarding the rights of the people against the threat of an authoritarian state. To some extent, local government has served this purpose by providing a buffer against bureaucratic arbitrariness, creating additional points of access and influence for groups poorly represented nationally, and serving as an arena for more fully realizing certain rights, such as healthful and cultured living, that were more aspirations than reality when the constitution was promulgated. The role of local government in protecting basic rights, however, has been secondary compared to the constitution, the courts, a free press, and the open parliamentary system. Indeed, the experience of postwar Japan suggests that a strong state, one that is relatively centralized and intervenes extensively in society, need not be a threat to basic liberties if a broad range of the population and political institutions are vigilant in their defense.

SCAP also intended local government to serve as an important avenue for citizens to participate in the political process and to control governmental decisions affecting their daily lives. By comparative standards, Japanese citizens have shown a very high interest and participation in local government through voting and various community-based associations. Participation, however, was not easily translated into control, especially in the first two postwar decades when municipal boundaries were changing and central controls were being reimposed over local governmental operations. By the third and fourth postwar decades, however, many of the goals of participation were being widely realized in Japanese localities. Two-way communication between local authorities and residents was facilitated by new mechanisms for public hearings, consultation, monitoring, and so forth. Groups concerned with the environment were having a discernible impact on local public policy through pressure tactics and electoral politics. And political forces in opposition nationally were getting their first taste of power in the cities. The contribution of local government to Japanese political democracy in providing a sense of efficacy through participation should not be underestimated. This is particularly the case because of the failure of Japanese political parties and interest groups to adequately convey grass-roots opinion and influence to political leaders and because of the strong sense of localism that continues to pervade Japan. The implication that should be drawn from this analysis is not that participation is a prominent normative value in postwar Japanese democracy or that the gap between participation and control has been permanently closed at the local level. These are very difficult goals to achieve in a highly urbanized society like Japan where sheer size creates its own barriers to effective participation and strong bureaucracies, both local and national, work aggressively to orchestrate consent for their own programs. But it is a tribute to the Japanese public and their local institutions that it is no longer possible to ignore local opinion and interests in deciding and implementing public policy.

The most distinctive and probably most enduring contribution of local government to postwar Japanese democracy is in human welfare. Ironically, its effectiveness in performing this function, which is absolutely critical for a modern democracy, has been enhanced by those steps toward "recentralization" that at the same time strengthened the expertise and efficiency of local administration. The lesson to be learned is that interdependence between different governmental levels can provide more levers to local authorities for shaping public policy than any ideal notion of local autonomy based only on a strict separation of functions and finance.

As suggested by Sharpe, if local government did not exist, something very much resembling it would have to be created to decide among and efficiently deliver the many services and programs for human welfare of the industrial democracies. Perhaps most important is local government's role as a reconciler of community opinion. The legitimacy attached to local choices for policies affecting everyday life cannot be replaced by the dictates of extralocal actors; and national authorities simply cannot afford to involve themselves in a multitude of local disputes. Welfare programs in modern democracies, however, have necessitated highly centralized decision making to assure minimal standards of well-being throughout the country, to close regional gaps in development, and to coordinate macroeconomic and social policy; these activities ensure that national authorities will be involved in every locality in the country. In the case of Japan, and most likely other industrial democracies, the permeation of localities by national governmental policies and even personnel does not necessarily mean that in aggregate the results will be what was desired by either the center or the periphery. Hence, local government's role as coordinator of development and services can be critical. The strengthening of the personnel and planning systems of Japanese local governments has enabled many of them to play this coordinating role. Finally, local governments have furthered the goal of human welfare by responding relatively early to rising demands, needs, or standards of "consumers" of the country's living environment and governmental services and by transmitting these pressures upward in the intergovernmental system. Local governments in modern democracies are well positioned to fill the political gap brought about by social and economic change between rising expectations at the periphery and policymaking at the center.

What is most distinctive about Japanese political democracy is the focus on equality in human welfare. This is not to say that Japan is a more advanced "welfare state" than those in the West; it is not. Rather, it is to note that to an extraordinary degree political democracy in contemporary Japan emphasizes that all Japanese, no matter where they live and what their station in life and work, should be treated equally by the state, which shares with them a responsibility for their welfare. This emphasis on equality in human welfare exists despite a fine sense of hierarchy and significant inequalities in status within Japanese society. These views, however, are not necessarily contradictory when one realizes that it is in the public domain that equality is demanded, while inequalities in private life are accepted as a natural, and even desirable, principle of social organization. To borrow a term from the Japanese labor movement, there is a pronounced "base-up" (or "bottom-up") character to postwar Japanese political democracy. Japan's "bottom-up society" has been created in large measure by the ability of local authorities to act as brokers between local sentiment, on the one hand, and higher levels of the intergovernmental system, on the other. One of the major challenges for Japanese local government, and Japanese democracy more generally, is the maintenance of this bottom-up quality of the society in the face of changes in the economic structure that are even today more adversely affecting some areas of the country than others. Another is in their capacity to accommodate significant local variations in public policy priorities, rather than trying to fit every locality into a single mold. If the new social contract between Japanese localities and their citizens is indeed one in which the welfare of the latter is the guiding principle and is reflected in public policy based on local collective preferences, then there is reason for optimism.

NOTES

1. John Stuart Mill, *Considerations on Representative Government,* World Classics Edition (Oxford: Oxford University Press, 1912); Alexis de Tocqueville, *Democracy in America,* Borzoi Edition (New York: Knopf, 1945); James Bryce, *Modern Democracies* (New York: Macmillan, 1921).

2. Dilys H. Hill, *Democratic Theory and Local Government* (London: George Allen and Unwin, 1974); W. Hardy Wickwar, *The Political Theory of Local Government* (Columbia: University of South Carolina Press, 1970); L. J. Sharpe, "Theories and Values of Local Government," *Political Studies* 18 (June 1970): 153–74.

3. Japan's governmental system has three layers: national, prefectural, and municipal (cities, towns, and villages). As a result of postwar reforms, both prefectures and municipalities are considered "regular local bodies" which directly elect both executive heads (governors and mayors) and representative assemblies and have a local public service separate from that of the national government. In practice, however, prefectures engage in extensive liaison work between national authorities and municipalities, while still carrying out their local representative functions. Although, in conformity with the legal status of these bodies, I shall use the term "local" to refer to both prefectures and municipalities in Japan, most of the analysis of this chapter is more pertinent to the latter than to the former. Also, greater distinction should be made than I can in the allotted space between towns and villages, on the one hand, and cities, on the other. Again, the analysis is more descriptive of the latter than the former. This is not a serious drawback, however, since the vast majority of Japanese live in cities.

4. The most comprehensive study of Japanese local government is Kurt Steiner, *Local Government in Japan* (Stanford, Calif.: Stanford University Press, 1965). For a brief overview of Japanese local government since the late nineteenth century, see James C. Baxter and Terry E. MacDougall, "Local Government," in *Encyclopedia of Japan* (Tokyo: Kodansha, 1983).

5. Supreme Command for the Allied Powers (SCAP), *The Political Reorientation of Japan* (Washington, D.C.: Government Printing Office, 1949), 1: 117 (emphasis added).

6. Ibid., 2: 758 (emphasis added).

7. Baxter and MacDougall, "Local Government."

8. SCAP, *Political Reorientation,* 1: 260.

9. Steiner, *Local Government in Japan,* pp. 80–86.

10. Terry E. MacDougall, "Political Opposition and Local Government in Japan," Ph.D. diss., Yale University, 1975, analyzes the growth of agency delegation and its implications for local autonomy.

11. Muramatsu Michio, "The Impact of Economic Growth Policies on Local Politics in Japan," *Asian Survey* 15 (1975): 799–816.

12. Steiner, *Local Government in Japan;* and Herbert Passin, *The Legacy of the Occupation of Japan,* Occasional Papers of the East Asian Institute (New York: Columbia University, 1968).

13. Terry E. MacDougall, *Politics and Policy in Urban Japan* (New Haven, Conn.: Yale University Press, 1989), chap. 6.

14. Ibid.

15. Richard Samuels, *The Politics of Regional Policy in Japan* (Princeton, N.J.: Princeton University Press, 1983).

16. For a further development of this conception of localism, see Terry E. MacDougall, "Political Parties and Local Government in Japan," a paper prepared for the planning conference on Local Government and Public Policy in Industrial Nations, Turin, Italy, January 14–16, 1980, and MacDougall, *Politics and Policy,* chaps. 1 and 8.

17. Arthur Maass, "Division of Powers: An Areal Analysis," in *Area and Power: A Theory of Local Government,* ed. Arthur Maass (Glencoe, Ill.: The Free Press, 1959), pp. 9–26.

18. Hoshino Mitsuo, *Chihō Jichi No Riron To Kōzō* (The Theory and Structure of Local Government) (Tokyo: Shinhyoron, 1970), pp. 17–35.

19. For an application of this concept, see MacDougall, "Political Opposition," and Kurt Steiner, "Toward a Framework for the Study of Local Opposition," in *Political Opposition and Local Politics in Japan,* ed. Kurt Steiner, Ellis S. Krauss, and Scott C. Flanagan (Princeton, N.J.: Princeton University Press, 1980), pp. 16–20.

20. Tanaka Jirō, "Hōritsu ni yoru gyōsei to tsūtatsu ni yoru gyōsei," *Jichi kenkyū* 32 (July 1956): 3–6.

21. For excellent surveys of the literature, see Sharpe, "Theories and Values," pp. 158–66; and Hill, *Democratic Theory,* pp. 131–59.

22. Robert Dahl, *Polyarchy* (New Haven, Conn.: Yale University Press, 1970).

23. An extremely useful survey and analysis of Japanese public opinion polls and behavioral research in Scott C. Flanagan and Bradley M. Richardson, *Japanese Electoral Behavior* (Beverly Hills, Calif.: Sage Publications, 1977).

24. MacDougall, *Politics and Policy,* chap. 6.

25. Margaret A. McKean, *Environmental Protest and Citizen Politics in Japan* (Berkeley and Los Angeles: University of California Press, 1981).

8 *Protest and Democracy*

PATRICIA G. STEINHOFF

When fifty thousand people demonstrate peacefully in the streets against a vote taken in the Diet, should we infer that democracy is strong, or that it is weak? When protesters sabotage public transportation or construction projects to register their opposition to administrative decisions of the government, is democracy safe, or is it in trouble?

The dilemma of democracy is to preserve simultaneously several essential institutions whose underlying assumptions conflict. If dissent is stifled, there can be no democracy. Yet the application of majority rule ensures that not all opinions will become policy. What recourse do the losers have? The standard answer is that they have the right to try again next time, following the same institutional rules. The majority is obliged to tolerate the continued dissent of the minority, because the vote may be different next time.

If there are flaws in the democratic institutions themselves—flaws that block the transmission of opinion or distort the way a majority is calculated—the losers may question the legitimacy of the institutions. Then, to what extent may they expand their dissent into protests outside the institutional channels for the translation of opinion into policy? On the one hand, the protections of civil liberties should permit the organized expression of protest. If protest is suppressed too quickly and too harshly, then the entire underpinnings of democracy are called into question. On the other hand, the state has to protect the institutions through which the rights of the majority are translated into policy and action. If *only* the majority's rights are

171

protected, it is not a democracy; but if the majority's rights are not protected *sufficiently,* that is not democracy, either.

Thus, although protest may appear to be marginal or even antithetical to democracy, it is actually quite central. Some degree of protest attests to the healthy exercise of the civil liberties which make possible informed democratic choice, while too much protest calls into question the legitimacy of electoral politics and the policymaking process itself. What is healthy and what is too much? An assessment of the Japanese case must take into consideration both the abstract model of democracy and the country's historical experience of democracy.

The Legitimacy of Protest in Japan

Japan has a long tradition of local protest as a means of expressing popular grievances. Long before anyone in Japan had ever heard of *demokurashii,* peasants in the Tokugawa era (1603–1868) were petitioning local officials and staging protests to call attention to their problems. Such traditional protest usually prompted a quick response from officials. Michael Lewis reports that the grievances usually involved a violation of accepted local norms of behavior by a landlord or rice dealer, which an official could resolve by ordering the violator to make restitution, or by using other available resources to provide relief. The cleverness and violence of these protests suggests that the peasants utilized a calculated strategy of shifting the power balance temporarily in order to obtain a hearing, and then calling upon the moral obligations of officials to resolve the dispute on their behalf.[1]

The combination of petition and active protest was clearly associated with powerlessness and the absence of normal channels of political participation. The peasants were not seen as individuals with rights to personal opinions; rather, petitioning peasants were viewed as dependent subjects who had a right to seek protection from a paternalistic authority figure. While violent protests were not condoned, by Japanese logic the local officials were responsible for controlling the injustices which provoked peasants to protest. Officials were motivated to settle the problem quickly to protect their own reputations. The peasants did not have any substantive rights, however, so they were completely at the mercy of the authorities to whom they appealed. The authorities often acquiesced to the peasants' demand and then killed the leader of the protest just to clarify who was in charge.

This traditional style of protest can be traced through the period of industrialization, and remnants of it can be seen today in many protests at the local level, although heads no longer roll literally as a result. Environmental protest, for example, often utilizes a combination of petition and protest to provoke official response. The method arouses much debate within the environmental movement, however, because of its "feudal" overtones.[2]

After the Meiji Restoration of 1868, Japan began very cautiously to experiment with some of the institutions of democracy. The popular rights movement which swept the country in the 1870s combined the traditional techniques of sending memorials to the government and petitions to officials with innovations such as political associations, political commentary in newspapers, and public lecture tours around the country. These methods were used to criticize official policies, and to press for constitutional government and the creation of a national assembly. The government responded by promising a constitution but sharply increasing its control over political organization and the expression of political opinion.[3]

During the early twentieth century, the modest civil liberties offered by the Meiji constitution of 1889 were severely restricted. The Peace Police Law of 1910 required all political organizations to register with the police, and explicitly prohibited workers from organizing. Political meetings were closely supervised, with women and schoolteachers prohibited from attending them at all. There was considerable press censorship both before and after publication. These restrictions and many other local ordinances made virtually all protest activity illegal. Expressions of dissent in speech and writing were sharply limited.

When the franchise was extended to all adult males in 1925, the Peace Preservation Law that was passed almost concurrently added new layers of control over political activity. The new law made it illegal to participate in or aid any group which advocated the overthrow of the capitalist economic order or overthrow of the *kokutai*, an all-encompassing concept of the Japanese national values. Although the law was initially intended to control the tiny communist movement, it later was applied very broadly against the left, and even against obscure religious groups.

Overall, protest in the prewar era was limited in scope and carried very high stakes for the participants. The most common arrests were for violations of the press law or the Peace Preservation Law. These were crimes of thought and its expression, rather than acts of public protest as we understand the term today. Persons arrested for such activities were processed through a European-inspired judicial system which offered the defendant very few rights, but maintained the traditional Chinese and Japanese legal principle of rewarding the contrite defendant. Applied to crimes of thought, this principle encouraged the defendant to dissociate himself from the offending political ideas, rather than supporting his right to hold them. The line between law and social sanction was not clearly defined, so family and community pressures were also used heavily to eliminate political dissent and protest.

After Japan's surrender in 1945, the Occupation authorities regarded victims of the Peace Preservation Law sympathetically, and the new postwar constitution provided strong guarantees for civil liberties (see chapter 4). In the nearly forty years since the new postwar constitution was enacted in 1946, its civil liberties provisions have generally been reinforced by court decisions. By virtually any measure, Japan is now a very open society in which people are free to think, speak, and write their political views. These freedoms are exercised regularly. A very broad spectrum of political publications is available, including an enormous range of political tracts put out by ideologically committed groups. In the "protest decade" of 1965–75 there were some instances of postpublication censorship of materials which contained explicit instructions for manufacturing incendiary devices or advocated specific, direct acts of violence against the state. More general expressions advocating antistate violence are seen all the time, however, in publications and on signs and banners.

There is also very broad latitude for participation in protest activities. Although local ordinances may require permits for large demonstrations and regulate demonstration routes, the authorities cannot prevent the organized protest activities of a group and can only arrest the participants if they violate some specific law in the course of their activity.[4]

Structural Sources of Protest

While civil liberties protections make protest possible in postwar Japan, the structure of politics has made the government relatively impervious to it. As J. A. A. Stockwin points out (see chapter 5), at the national level Japanese politics has been dominated by one party for thirty years. This has resulted in close ties between the Liberal Democratic party (LDP) and entrenched economic interests. It has also produced a certain complacency among Diet members whose re-election is comfortably assured. The LDP at the national level is not nearly as sensitive as its American counterparts to the impact of a protest movement on voters.

Movements that begin over local issues, such as citizens' environmental movements, frequently turn to protest because the area's LDP representatives are unresponsive. Such protests naturally attract the support of the minority parties, whether or not the local organizers seek it initially. Margaret McKean found that environmental protests occasionally had an impact on local elections, but this rarely translated directly into the defeat of a national Diet member and his replacement by an opposition party member, although the distribution of votes might change to some extent.[5]

This may be explained partly by the nature of Japanese political loyalties, but a more fundamental reason is that the national election districts have been badly distorted by urbanization since they were originally drawn immediately after the war. The LDP's traditional voting strength has been in rural areas where population has been depleted, hence the party has been unwilling to redraw district lines which vastly overrepresent their rural clientele at the expense of urban voters. The LDP's electoral margin has narrowed significantly in the past decade, but the change has not been particularly issue-oriented. In addition to some minimal formal redistricting, much of the decline may be attributed to the spillover of urbanization into formerly rural districts. For much of the postwar era, a single rural vote has been equivalent to a great many urban votes.

Compounding the situation is Japan's rather unique system of multimember districts in which each voter casts a single vote. In districts with two or three LDP incumbents plus a protégé or two waiting in the wings, voters' dissatisfaction may rearrange the LDP vote count, but seldom produces a major change in political party representation.

This peculiar electoral situation causes structural blockage to the democratic process at two levels. First, it means that many individual LDP Diet members have sufficient electoral security that they need not respond to certain issues even when their own constituents press them. Second, it means that when such issues are brought into the Diet by minority party members, they can safely be ignored by the majority. When the translation of public opinion into effective governmental action is blocked, the public becomes disenchanted with the use of institutionalized political channels.

The largest single example of such blockage was certainly the 1960 Security Treaty issue, in which the Diet was unresponsive to massive street demonstrations by a broad spectrum of the population which was opposed to renewing the treaty. The Diet passed the treaty renewal using the snap vote, a parliamentary maneuver which particularly flaunted the majority's power. Although the cabinet subsequently fell over this issue, the LDP was able to ride out the storm without losing electoral strength.[6]

The problem of electoral insensitivity to protest is exacerbated by the centralized, elite, and highly professionalized Japanese government bureaucracy. Protest is often directed at bureaucratic decisions rather than legislative ones, in which case there is no recourse except occasionally to the courts. If the protesters are fortunate, two parts of the bureaucracy may take opposite stands on the issue. This gives them a bureaucratic sponsor and brings the debate into the normal political process. It does not guarantee success, however, because bureaucratic infighting may deadlock the issue.

Easily the most stunning postwar example of bureaucratic intransigence in the face of protest was the construction of Narita Airport. After initially shifting the proposed new Tokyo airport site from another location because of some local protest which was channeled through LDP politicians, the bureaucracy locked its heels and refused to respond to protests from residents in the area of the new site at Sanrizuka, a rural area near the city of Narita. Although the scale and violence of the protests produced extremely costly delays, both bureaucratic and elected officials remained impervious, and the airport was eventually built.[7]

At this writing, more than a decade after the opening of the airport, the government has still been unable to complete a high-speed rail link and a fuel pipeline to the remote site of Japan's primary international airport because of continuing protest activity. Narita Airport remains an astonishingly militarized zone in an otherwise thoroughly civilian society, with barbed wire fortifications, heavily guarded checkpoints for all persons entering the area, and six thousand riot police permanently on duty. The coalition of farmers and students that has protested against the airport for nearly two decades maintains a series of fortified bunkers around the site and can still mobilize several thousand people for key demonstrations.

In short, postwar Japan's peculiar combination of strong protection of civil liberties, an election system which seriously distorts legislative accountability, and a powerful professional government bureaucracy, greatly increases the probability that citizens will engage in extra-institutional protest. Citizens aroused by a particular issue often discover that the normal institutional channels of democratic participation are unresponsive. Their elected representatives either do not convey their concerns or are themselves minority members without access to power. Such interest groups quickly exhaust the traditional and official modes of expression of grievances, and their frustration mounts. A range of protest activities is readily available to them, however, with little danger of reprisal.

Protest Participation and Organization

Protest participants are not a special category of people with a particular ideology. They are ordinary Japanese who have been mobilized through existing networks and affiliations. Their personal interest and commitment to an issue arise out of their immediate social context and existing social roles. When a problem cannot be resolved through the proper official channels, they seek some other way to deal with it. Protest activities are part of the repertoire of available methods.

Consequently, Japanese bring to protest activity the same organizational style and skills that characterize Japanese corporations and community groups. Planning a demonstration is not very different from organizing a school outing or a large tour group, and publishing for a political protest movement requires the same skills as working for an advertising agency or daily newspaper. Student activists in the extreme left Red Army Faction (Sekigunha), for example, researched their hijackings and political bank robberies with the same attention to detail that the Sony Corporation gives to a new product. They also made their political decisions in characteristically Japanese style, with an expectation of consensus and careful acknowledgment of the privileges of rank. Similarly, protest groups engage in the same sort of organizational rivalry and territoriality that are found throughout Japanese society.

Protest activities in Japan are organized both from the top and from the bottom, and the relations between the two levels are complex. The dominant American theory holds that social movements arise spontaneously out of local issues and groups expressing a new interest and then form larger coalitions to create a national social movement.[8] That model fits only a small proportion of Japanese protests. The situation for most issues and most of the postwar era up to the 1970s might better be described as a national protest cartel, formed by a few political *zaibatsu,* that monopolizes a large share of the protest markets and eagerly swallows up new movements whenever possible.[9]

The dominant groups in the protest cartel are the Socialist and Communist parties. These bitter enemies are part of the cluster of political parties that make up the perennial minority opposing the LDP. Their initial postwar leaders were prewar violators of the Peace Preservation Law who had been vindicated by the course of history and given fresh legitimacy by the Occupation. Somewhat inadvertently, the carefully nurtured legacy of prewar political victimization has turned both parties into important champions of civil liberties. Their status as legitimate but perennially ignored voices in Japanese politics leads them to sponsor and encourage protest activities.

Each national organization envisions itself much like the prewar *zaibatsu,* as a holding company for a complete set of interest- and issue-based organizations. The two major parties of the left garner their voting strength primarily from their affiliated national union federations. The union federations, which encompass workers in government as well as private industry, include large numbers of well-educated white collar workers. The union federations define their role broadly to include taking positions on national and international political issues. In fact, the national federations rarely involve themselves in the economic issues of collective bargaining, which are handled at the enterprise level. Their main function is political organization, which involves mobilizing political demonstrations as well as getting out the vote. The two major parties of the left also organize other special interest groups using the same organizational model. College students, the Burakumin minority, and women are the major categories that operate more or less parallel to the union structures, but with considerably less clout.[10]

The Communist and Socialist parties, and all of the unions and other interest groups they have helped to form, have a soviet-style internal organization with ideological authority concentrated at the top. The leadership takes an ideological position on a certain national or international issue and orchestrates a campaign that includes demonstrations of popular support for that position. Lower-level affiliates are expected to follow suit ideologically and provide the manpower for the demonstrations, but individual participation is quite voluntary. The major areas of party interest have been the interrelated issues of the peace movement, opposition to the rearming of Japan, and opposition to the American military presence in Japan. Vast numbers of ordinary working- and middle-class Japanese have participated in union-sponsored protest rallies and marches on these issues with their co-workers.

Aside from the union strength that underlies the major opposition parties, the largest source of protest activities in the postwar era is surely the student movement. The national student movement was closely allied with the Japan Communist party (JCP) in the early 1950s and bore the familiar organizational structure. Disillusioned by a series of sudden shifts in the party line, the national student movement broke with the JCP and then began to split internally. Factioning continued through the 1960s as the movement became involved in a broad range of campus, domestic, and international issues.

By the late 1960s some sects of the student movement were using quite violent protest tactics, but were also expending a great deal of energy fighting one another. Each had its own national organization and worked energetically to extend its ideological influence, both by organizing new groups of students and by attempting to gain influence in independent local protest movements. A typical pattern developed in which a local dispute would develop spontaneously under its own campus leadership and attract a broad range of students. Then the sects would begin to move in, ostensibly to support the local protest. Inevitably, the sects would begin to quarrel over ideological niceties, and the broad campus support would drift away, leaving the sects to battle among themselves.

Similar power struggles can occasionally be found among subunits of the two leftist parties as well. In the early 1970s, violence erupted at a high school in western Japan when the Burakumin organization of the Socialist party attempted to organize Burakumin students at a school controlled by a teacher's union affiliated with the Japan Communist party.[11]

The cartel-like behavior of the leftist parties and student movement sects is clearly rooted in their Marxist ideology and organizational structure. Each of these groups views itself as the true revolutionary party, which is responsible for organizing the masses according to the correct ideological position. Because they share the same basic ideology but differ on exactly how it should be applied to the contemporary situation, they tend to converge on the same political issues and then squabble viciously over the details of policy and tactics. Each group has some established strongholds which the others respect, but they all pounce on any new arena and grab whatever market share they can. Their efforts are aided by the general Japanese tendency for a local group to commit itself as a whole to a particular affiliation. In effect, the union shop principle is applied to the student government body of each department or faculty in a university, as well as to workplace units of unions and the geographic districts of other organizations. Individual affiliation with a particular protest organization is more a matter of local availability than of consumer choice.

Since the late 1960s a number of movements have developed new strategies and new organizational forms in order to avoid being carved up by the organized left. The antiwar group Beheiren, the Zenkyōtō organizations in the student movement, feminist groups, and citizens' movements on a variety of issues have all used the relatively unusual tactic of recruiting individual members independent of their existing group affiliations.[12] These groups have also tried to maintain participatory democracy within the organization, with varying degrees of success.

Sometimes the natural criterion for membership in a particular movement is sufficiently exclusive to maintain the group's independence. During the 1970s, the leftist parties and various factions of the student movement tried on many occasions to link up with environmental movements. The environmental groups, which had a strong local orientation and were often politically conservative initially, generally resisted this intrusion.[13] As a consequence, the environmental movement has been less ideological and factionalized than have other movements. The price of independence, however, has been an inability to link the separate protests together into an effective national movement.[14]

The relation between protest activity and institutionalized political channels is not a simple either–or proposition. Some protest activity is not viable outside established institutions, and some causes attract institutional support. At one extreme, there are occasional protests which do not solidify into a clear movement, let alone an independent organization. The participants may succeed at the local level and thus have their interests incorporated into institutional channels, or they

may simply fail to arouse enough popular response to become organized movements.

A small movement may have an impact, even though it cannot
succeed alone. During the early 1970s, the tiny feminist movement
used a variety of protest tactics to resist efforts by Seichō no Ie, a
religious group with powerful LDP support, to tighten Japan's liberal
abortion law. The target was a provision in the 1946 Eugenic Protection Law which permits abortion for economic reasons. The feminists' major allies were advocates of rights for the handicapped, who
had been thrown into an improbable coalition because the proposed
trade-off for the economic provision was a new clause permitting
abortions to prevent genetic abnormalities. The two small movements were united by their opposition to the wording of the proposed
changes, but their motives were almost diametrically opposed. The
bill to restrict abortions was finally dropped after the medical lobby
intervened.

When the issue arose again in the 1980s, without the genetic
defects clause, a much broader coalition of women's organizations
and female Diet members from various parties joined with the affected medical groups to stop the attempt to restrict availability of
abortion, The abortion issue helped the fledgling feminist movement to develop, but the feminist movement alone could not have
won on the issue in either the 1970s or the 1980s. By the second
time the issue arose, however, women's issues had much more political legitimacy, in part because of the work of the feminist movement. The coalition of the eighties was not only broader, but much
more public, because the feminists had made it possible to discuss
abortion in public. [15]

At the other extreme are protest activities carried out by organized
interest groups as a ritualized prelude to their use of institutionalized
channels. These activities originated as the protests of an underrepresented group, but they persist as collective rituals even after the group
has achieved strong representation in the political arena. For example,
delegations from farmers' groups throughout the country converge
on Tokyo every year for a militant-sounding rally that marks the
opening of the annual negotiations over the official price of rice. [16] The
participants are for the most part well-connected LDP supporters,
and the aim of their protest is to remind both the Diet and bureaucracy of their political importance. Similarly, the major labor unions
have ritualized their protest into an annual spring offensive which

kicks off the beginning of the collective bargaining season.[17] Such ritualized protests are becoming less effective, but they remain symbolic, socially legitimate forms of political participation.

The institutionalization of ritual protest in turn helps to legitimize similar protest activities by new groups that lack access to regular political channels. Although it is very hard to estimate what proportion of the Japanese populace has any direct experience of participation in protest activity, half of the population must at least have a relative or personal friend who has participated in some kind of a public protest. Most farm villages have sent a representative to the ritual protests connected with the annual negotiations on the price of rice. Anyone who is a labor union member has been asked to participate in a demonstration and knows of co-workers who did so. Through this route, most employees of large corporations and most government employees have been exposed to protest as a relatively legitimate social activity.

About one-third of all young people go on to higher education in Japan, and the parents of a substantial minority of those students have been exposed at least to the possibility of their children's involvement in the student movement. The entire generation of Japanese who received their higher education in the 1960s was confronted with the possibility of participation in protest activity. In addition, tens of thousands of women belong to national housewives' organizations that have sponsored their own protest activities. Since the 1970s, local citizens' groups throughout Japan have engaged in environmental protests, further normalizing such activity in villages, towns, and smaller cities.

This of course does not mean that every person who has contact with a protest participant approves of protest activity. Yet the acquaintanceship is so widespread, among such mainstream segments of the population, that approval or disapproval is more likely to hinge upon the specific issue than on the legitimacy of protest itself.

With this wide an exposure to protest, it is not surprising that the map of protest activity in postwar Japan looks much like a map of the political party system itself. The ritual protests of farmers and small shopkeepers are absorbed within the LDP, while some local environmental movements also find a sympathetic hearing there. The ritual protests of labor unions are similarly absorbed within the major opposition parties, the Socialists and the Communists. Many other protest movements, such as the Burakumin liberation movement, are linked to and supported by these parties, but cannot yet be considered insiders engaged in protest primarily as a ritual reminder of their interests.

Beyond the Big Inside of the LDP and the Big Outside of the major opposition parties lie a host of protest movements that have given up on both. In this wilder terrain can be found the New Left student groups that rejected the Old Left, other products of the late 1960s such as the antiwar group Beheiren, the student group Zenkyōtō and the feminist movement that rejected the New Left because it acted too much like the Old Left, and all sorts of environmental and special interest movements that want to preserve local control over their lives and their issues. These outside groups are not necessarily allied with any of the other small opposition parties, but they convey some of the same quality of perennial alienation.[18]

While the protest movements that are allied with political parties can readily be interpreted as becoming more institutionalized and ritualized over time, the same cannot be said of movements that are alienated from all of the major political players. It is not yet clear whether they will remain marginal, or will eventually coalesce into some new political institution or party.

The Range of Protest Activity

There have been many innovations in the repertoire of protest activities used in Japan over the past several decades, but they have been channeled into rather predictable directions by a combination of Japanese organizational style and the political ideologies within which protest issues have been framed.

The peaceful mass demonstration is the most common and available means of protest in postwar Japan, in part because it is seen as a tactic that is used by legitimate interest groups with access to institutionalized channels for political participation. It has developed into a highly organized art form with its own characteristic style and rituals. Normally a large public demonstration involves participation by members of several supporting organizations. Each group wears its own distinctive headband or other identifying mark and maintains a close formation under the leadership of its own whistle-blowing captains. Slogans for signs are usually determined in advance, either for the entire demonstration or by the participating organizations individually. Group chants and rhythmic whistle-blowing by the march captains are used to keep the marchers moving in unison. A variation made famous in the 1960 demonstrations opposing the Security Treaty is the snake dance, in which demonstrators link arms in a long chain and zigzag along the parade route at a fast clip. Although the snake dance has been likened by some to traditional religious parades, it also serves as a powerful moving wedge with which to taunt and drive back police units along the line of march.

During the 1960s the basic demonstration or mass rally was modified in two different directions, one representing an increase in psychological violence, and the other elevating the level of physical violence. At the local level, Japanese protest sometimes takes the form of a confrontational mass meeting at which the emotional stakes are higher than in an ordinary demonstration. These sessions become kangaroo courts at which a large, angry assembly of protesters challenges and harasses one or more officials until they break down emotionally. A variant of this psychologically powerful tactic, called *kyūdan,* has been used with considerable success by the Burakumin movement to coerce attitudinal and behavioral change among officials who are thought to discriminate against Burakumin.[19] It has been used with equal vigor but somewhat less effect by students in campus disputes.[20] Environmental movements have occasionally used it with even less success against the officials of companies responsible for pollution.

This tactic presents an intriguing comparison with the traditional petition and protest strategy of feudal Japan. In both tactics, officials consent to hear the grievance because their position of authority vis-à-vis the protesters more or less obliges them to do so. In both cases the protesters demand that the officials accept their obligation to treat the protesters properly, thus inducing guilt or at least embarrassment and a sense of threat over the officials' performance of their duties.

The tactics differ profoundly, however, in the stance taken by the protesters during the confrontation. Far from presenting themselves as dependent subjects, the contemporary users of the tactic assert an aggressive egalitarianism by addressing high officials linguistically as equals and by rejecting their apologies as insincere. They seek a change in attitude and demeanor, which they coerce by reversing the dominance roles and forcing the degraded official to repent and reform.

The *kyūdan* or denunciation tactic is necessarily limited by two conditions. First, some relationship of authority or responsibility must link the parties already. The protesters may want to alter the nature of that relationship, but they must first call on it in order to oblige the official's attendance. Second, while the protesters' demands may be global and abstract, they must be connected in some way to changes of attitude or action which the official actually has the power to carry out.

The structural requirements for a denunciation do not fit many of the major issues that have aroused protest in contemporary Japan. If the issues are too broad and fundamental to be altered by one person's change of heart, or if there is no direct relationship between the protesters and the object of their anger, there is no basis for psychological coercion. The absence of these conditions generates further alienation and frustration, because there is no clear target for the protestors' appeal for change. This encourages protesters to increase the level of physical violence against symbolic targets which represent the impersonal, unapproachable opposition.

During the late 1960s, student protesters began to use more physically aggressive tactics for noncampus issues on which they could not engage their opponents in direct dialogue. This primarily took the form of escalating the violence in a mass demonstration, often without the consent of the main demonstration organizers. Initially, the constitutional guarantees of civil liberties, backed by the strong support of minority parties in and out of the Diet, limited the police to a carefully calibrated response which minimized the use of counterforce. Still, by the late 1960s student demonstrations resembled mock medieval military skirmishes, with both sides decked out in helmets, shields, and fighting poles. Although vociferous opposition by the parties of the left in the Diet prohibited the use of tear gas except in extreme cases, the riot police were soon outfitted with mobile riot buses, water cannons, and huge nets to deflect thrown rocks.

In the same general range of violence as militant demonstrations are sit-ins and building occupations, physical obstructions of traffic or work activity, and attacks on public buildings and installations. There have been many such events in postwar Japan to protest foreign military presence, government and private construction projects, university administrative policies, private business activity, or government policies. Although students are most clearly associated with the escalation of violence, similar tactics have also been used by farmers, environmentalists, Burakumin, feminists, and the antiwar movement.

The seriousness of confrontations between students and riot police is revealed in the advice to demonstration participants offered in the 1978 version of a widely distributed pamphlet published by the

Kyūen Renraku Sentā, a support group for the student movement. Kyūen advised demonstrators to wear low-heeled shoes that would not fall off easily (to avoid injuries from broken glass and stones), cotton stockings rather than nylon (which if exposed to fire from incendiary devices would stick to the skin and worsen the burns), and a face mask to prevent identifying photographs and protect against tear gas. The pamphlet offered careful instructions to persons providing medical support to demonstrators, including how to evaluate vital signs and treat head injuries, tear gas injuries, shock, burns, cuts, broken bones, and sprains.[21]

Despite the ominous tone of these warnings, the casualty rates from political demonstrations in Japan have been relatively low. Violent protests often produce injuries, but very rarely deaths. Many more students have been killed in faction fights between student movement groups than in direct clashes with the police. The fundamental reason for the low death rate from violent protest is that Japan, unlike other countries, does not use guns against protesters under any circumstances.

The protests of postwar Japan have largely been collective activities undertaken by individuals as members of organized groups. The movement against fingerprinting among foreign residents of Japan is fundamentally different. All foreigners resident in Japan are required to carry a registration booklet which is renewed annually in a procedure that includes fingerprinting. In recent years a movement has developed around resistance to the annual fingerprinting as a demeaning ritual appropriate only for criminals.

Although resistance to fingerprinting is supported by various political groups, participation in the protest requires an individual act taken on the basis of conscience, with serious personal consequences. The act of refusal must be carried out by an individual at the local city office, face to face with a government official. The potential consequences of refusal include arrest, prosecution, deportation from Japan, and denial of any future petition for Japanese citizenship. The great majority of the fingerprint resisters are second and third generation Korean residents of Japan to whom until recently the Japanese government has been very reluctant to grant citizenship.

Thousands of resident Koreans and a small number of persons of other nationalities have refused fingerprinting, but the government has been extremely selective in its arrests. It is a clever bureaucratic policy. The government maintains its right to enforce the law, but simply declines to do so in many cases, without specifying any new policy. The protesters are denied the satisfaction of a victory, the publicity of heavy arrests, and even the strategy of clogging the judicial system. Local officials can gain some credit for being sympathetic and lenient, thus staving off the threat of a sit-in or worse yet, a *kyūdan*.

While the government response in this instance seems quintessentially Japanese, the more interesting question is whether this type of individual civil disobedience is likely to become part of the normal repertoire of Japanese protest tactics. There are undoubtedly issues to which individual civil disobedience might be applied, but the tactic does not fit easily into Japanese protest style. The escalation from mass demonstration to violent demonstration to urban guerrilla warfare can be accomplished in Japan with little alteration of organizational behavior or ideological orientation, but the use of individual civil disobedience would require fundamental changes in both factors.

Government Response to Protest

In general, the Japanese government's response to protest is measured, sophisticated, and constitutional. Through its response to routine types of protest the government reinforces its image as a benign and stable democracy. As protest escalates, however, the government response becomes more significant as a means of setting limits on the amount of protest that will be tolerated. It is thus important to examine both where the limit is set, and how it is enforced.

The government regulates protest demonstrations at the local level through a parade permit system. Police provide security and traffic control for mass demonstrations, which also gives them the opportunity to identify protest organizers, estimate group size, and photograph participants. Demonstrators and police usually regard one another with a certain hostility, but the atmosphere of peaceful demonstrations is often relaxed and occasionally even festive. Difficulties can arise if the demonstration organizers do not have full control over the participating groups, or if symbolic gestures offend the police.

At a demonstration on the abortion issue in 1972, a member of the feminist group Chūpiren was suddenly arrested because she was using a toy rifle as a pole to hold up her banner. The incident provoked a side demonstration, as fifty Chūpiren members decked out in blue jeans, dark glasses, and pink helmets converged angrily on the police station to demand the release of their colleague. She was soon released, since there is no law against carrying a toy gun in a demonstration.[22]

While most demonstrations are peaceful and most demonstrators do not get arrested, the limits of tolerable dissent are set by the way the government responds to the most extreme forms of protest. The government's response to student violence in the late 1960s and early 1970s, its most severe postwar test, is thus a critical case that needs to be examined in more detail.

Participants in violent protests in Japan are routinely arrested. They cannot be indicted and tried without specific evidence of a law violation, however, and they enjoy a moderate amount of judicial protection even in that event.

During the peak period of student protest from 1968 to 1972, thousands of students were arrested for protest-related offenses ranging from illegally pasting handbills on telephone poles to throwing pipe bombs at riot police lines. Until early 1969, when the offenses were just beginning to get genuinely violent, the pattern was for students arrested in a protest to be jailed for up to about two weeks while an indictment was prepared, and then to be released until they were tried and sentenced. There is no provision for bail in Japan, but persons can be released on their own recognizance or with a personal guarantor. Many more students were arrested and released without ever being indicted, primarily because there was insufficient evidence to prosecute them, but sometimes also on the basis of their demeanor.

As the violence grew and public sympathy shrank, judges began to approve longer and longer periods of pre-trial detention, leading to a new pattern in which students were held for up to a year or two until their trials ended and then were released on probation on the grounds that they had already served sufficient time. By early 1970, the leaders of the most violent student protest groups were being arrested for having planned illegal protest activities in which they did not personally participate. They were held incommunicado during months of interrogation, which cut their links with the rest of their organization. After that time they received the normal communications privileges of persons in unconvicted detention, but were not released.

Criminal trials in Japan are not held continuously as in the United States, but rather are scheduled for a few hours at a time at the mutual convenience of the judges and lawyers, with sessions often weeks or months apart. The most serious of the student protest trials, involving major acts of violence, have been strung out for up to ten years before even the first decision is reached and the sentences handed down. The appeal process then keeps the defendants in unconvicted detention for another several years.

Persons in unconvicted detention are kept by law in solitary confinement, but have greater communications and parcel privileges than convicted prisoners. They are permitted daily visitors, with a guard overseeing the visit and taking notes. They are allowed a broad range of reading matter, including ideological material.

Unconvicted prisoners are also allowed to write and receive letters, including correspondence with other inmates so long as it is channeled through the national postal service. Every page of mail coming out of the prison bears the censor's purple stamp in the corner, but direct criticisms of prison conditions and political statements are usually passed through without comment, presumably because the censor stamps without reading. Incoming mail appears to be treated similarly, but some printed matter is censored. While in unconvicted detention many imprisoned students have written and published political pamphlets, and a few have turned out autobiographical best-sellers. In 1985 a group of prisoners in unconvicted detention even published a major study of the prison system itself, complete with questionnaire data collected from other prisoners. This was followed in 1987 by an incredibly detailed book illustrating every step in the Japanese criminal justice system, from arrest up to the convicted criminal's departure to prison. It was based on drawings mailed out by an artist in unconvicted detention and was published while he was still serving his sentence. [23]

The Japanese criminal justice system maintains a very high conviction rate, and most defendants from student movements have argued over the seriousness or purpose of their actions rather than the fact that they performed them. In a number of cases beginning in the 1970s, however, political defendants protested their innocence and contended that they were framed by a police bureaucracy too ready to arrest them for their political beliefs, or too anxious to solve sensational cases. They claimed that false confessions had been coerced from them under inhumane conditions of interrogation. Due to the slow workings of the judicial system, the decisions are only now being handed down, and a few defendants have been found not guilty after spending a decade in unconvicted detention. [24]

In effect, the leaders of the most extreme protest groups have been treated within the letter of the law, but legal maneuvers have been contrived to keep them out of society for long enough to destroy the effectiveness of their leadership. The limits of acceptable dissent have been set primarily by bureaucrats trained in the law, who are clever enough to uphold it and still accomplish their aims. They do not necessarily set great store by civil liberties, but they adhere firmly to the bureaucratic principle of following the rules.[25]

Violence and arrests are important parameters of protest in post-war Japan, precisely because they occur in a larger context of democracy and strong protections for civil liberties. They are emphasized here not because of their frequency, but rather because they test the limits of tolerance of dissent in Japanese democracy. Those limits are broad by virtually any international comparison. Yet it must be emphasized that this broad tolerance reflects the peculiar structural conditions of postwar Japanese democracy rather than a deep commitment to open debate among politicians, bureaucrats, or even the protesters themselves.

The Effects of Protest Activity

The most direct measure of the effect of protest activity is whether it brings about the changes the movement desired. Given the vast range of movements and issues in postwar Japan, the results are necessarily mixed. Movements with very global political goals have generally remained frustrated, but they have probably raised the level of public consciousness. On a smaller scale, there have been some successes. A housewives' boycott altered the pricing of television sets for the domestic market in the 1960s, and numerous local protests have resulted in small changes in business or government organizational policies. The environmental movement has won some hard-fought battles, although its major successes have been obtained through the courts rather than directly by protest activity.

The Burakumin movement may have won the most through protest tactics. Although this physically invisible minority group has been discriminated against for centuries through residential, occupational, and marital segregation, most Japanese were able to ignore the problem until the group began to use direct confrontation during the late 1960s. At that time a new law was passed offering some official recognition of their plight with promises of better housing and educational opportunities, plus closing of the family registration records through which Burakumin ancestry is traced by residence. Although the law itself had very weak enforcement provisions, it offered sufficient legitimacy for the Buraku Liberation League to launch a campaign of direct harassment against officials who persisted in discriminating against Burakumin. The group's use of highly personalized protest tactics has made public and private officials extremely sensitive about the issue, analogous to the effect that litigation threats have on American bureaucrats.

It can be argued that while the major public protests of the postwar era did not necessarily achieve their specific goals, they did serve to temper the ambitions of conservative politicians and thus helped to keep the country on a moderate course. As public officials have become sensitive to the concerns of protesters, or to the potential of an issue to provoke public protest, they have sometimes supported policies which had the effect of resolving or circumventing the problem. This is the essence of the Japanese style of conflict management. It represents neither altruism nor spontaneous consensus, but rather a strong desire to avoid direct conflict. Protest, or the threat of protest, thus may have genuine policy consequences that are very difficult to document.

Contemporary American theory views social movements as a mechanism through which new interest groups can become recognized and incorporated into the political process.[26] That view certainly fits the environmental movement in Japan and might also be applied to the Burakumin movement. While the latter group is not new, its incorporation into politics is. From this perspective, the peace movement has had some modest success, but the student movement has been less successful.

Farmers and labor unions achieved their political incorporation through the 1946 constitution, though they continue to engage in ritualized protest as a symbolic gesture.[27] Women's issues are being taken more seriously in Japan today, and much of the credit must go to a very broad range of pressures brought to bear by women's organizations. Only a fraction of that activity could be called protest, however. The situation is similar to that of the labor and farm interests in that the group's basic rights were established in principle in the 1946 constitution, but have had to be captured in practice through a combination of protest, legal battles, and interest representation within political institutions. This situation blurs the distinction made by Charles Tilly between proactive claims and reactive claims.[28] The labor, farm, and women's movements in postwar Japan were not reacting against efforts to take away rights they already enjoyed, but rather were making proactive claims to rights they held in principle, but did not yet enjoy in actuality.

A second measure of effect is the impact of protest activities on the political attitudes and behavior of the participants. The evidence to date is mixed. Ellis Krauss found that involvement in the 1960 Security Treaty protests was an important arena of political socialization for student movement leaders, whose political beliefs remained reasonably stable ten years later. Susan Pharr found that participation in protest activities changes women's self-perceptions and political attitudes, but that the changes are not always stable.[29]

In an intensive study of one local urban environmental movement, David Groth found that most of the participants were already affiliated with various community and political organizations. The protest movement served as a channel for the expression of existing political beliefs, rather than bringing newcomers into political roles. Jeffrey Broadbent links a similar finding to the observation that successful environmental protest groups are led by persons who are already positioned as local social leaders; persons without such community ties are unable to attract and maintain a following.[30]

A third measure of effect is the impact of protest activity on the political institutions of the society. Above and beyond its effects on the outcomes of issues and on individuals, the high level of protest activity in Japan certainly has had positive effects on the democratic process. The repeated exercise of protest by broad segments of the population reinforces the legitimacy of protest and opposition. Over time, the acceptance of protest as a legitimate activity helps to institutionalize civil liberties in a society without a strong tradition of the right to dissent.

An essential part of this process of legitimization is the involvement of the courts. The environmental movement has been most notable for its recourse to the courts to press its claims, thus strengthening the court itself as a forum for the resolution of societal conflicts. The environmental movement, the Burakumin movement, and most recently the women's movement have succeeded in obtaining new legislation which permits them to use the courts as an ally in subsequent enforcement of their claims.

Yet protest movements have also come up against the courts because their activities produced arrests and criminal charges. Compared to similar cases in the prewar era, postwar political defendants have had far greater protection during the criminal process. They still are often harassed by the application of bureaucratic regulations, and they still may face judges who find their beliefs incomprehensible and personally offensive, but they no longer are tried specifically for their beliefs. Moreover, their right to hold and maintain their political beliefs is generally respected throughout the legal process.

It may be cold comfort for someone who has spent ten years in solitary confinement in unconvicted detention and then been found innocent, but in a small way these extreme cases reinforce the role of the judiciary as a protector of individual rights and not simply as an agency to enforce social control on behalf of the state. While one could argue that the government's aim was harassment of these political activists even if they did not commit a crime, the courts could just as easily have perpetuated the situation and saved face for the prosecution by finding the defendants guilty. Hence the fact that they did not is significant.

This analysis has emphasized the violent protests of a small minority and the government's firm response, because of the implications of that interaction for the institutionalization of civil liberties in postwar Japan. The effect of the peculiar combination of circumstances outlined above has been the establishment of very generous limits of political expression, well beyond what the average citizen can conceive of utilizing.

The major beneficiaries of this process have been the environmentally oriented citizens' movements, which began to emerge just as the student movement was entering its most violent phase of activity in the late 1960s. With the exception of the Narita Airport case, local environmental movements have stayed well within the protest limits the students tested so violently. To the extent that such movements have carefully chosen tactics of nonviolent direct action, they have increased the odds of public sympathy, particularly in the face of strong police reaction.[31] Yet they gain in power from the veiled threat that if there is no satisfactory response to their complaint, they could become more extreme. This middle position between the conservative establishment and the radical left has enabled the independent citizens' movements to utilize a broad range of protest tactics to make their point and still retain legitimacy. And that, after all, is what protest in a democracy is all about.

Yet the picture is not all positive. Much protest in Japan is an expression of dissatisfaction with a government that is entrenched and arrogantly bureaucratic, even if it is basically committed to the rule of law. Protest is a frustrating and alienating experience if it does not occasionally produce some change. To the extent that the government of Japan can tolerate and ignore a very high level of political protest, the potential still exists for protesters to become radicalized and move farther outside the existing democratic institutions.

Protest in the Future

Protest and the institutions of representative democracy stand in an uneasy balance in Japan. The extent of protest is intrinsically related to the openness and effectiveness of the other institutionalized channels for expression of popular sentiment. As demographic changes obliterate some of the old inequities of the election system, more channels of legitimate political participation should open up. If the Diet becomes a more open arena for the expression of minority concerns, some issues may be directed there instead of onto the streets. At the very least, mass expressions of protest should become more ritualized and less violent if they are directed at a potentially sympathetic audience of voting Diet members. As local politics become more varied, more problems should also be resolved at the local level. And as generational turnover moves the products of postwar education into the higher echelons of the government, the gap between the bureaucracy and the populace may shrink somewhat.

Protest has helped to strengthen democratic institutions in postwar Japan by encouraging the expression of diverse opinions and reinforcing the constitutional civil liberties which permit such expression. Yet protest has occasionally reached extremes of violence which could potentially threaten the other, representative, institutions of democracy. Institutions are, after all, simply the continued willingness of individuals to act in predictable ways. And democratic institutions, as we have seen, are a delicate balance of social arrangements based on somewhat contradictory assumptions.

Democracy is still young and experimental in Japan. Its underlying assumptions are not yet fundamental to the personal and cultural values of contemporary Japanese, although they are becoming so for the younger postwar generations. It is still all to easy for both the government and those opposed to it to turn to undemocratic solutions when their goals are thwarted. Yet even as Japanese democracy matures, the dilemma of majority rule and minority rights will persist, because that structural philosophical tension is inherent in the very concept of a working democracy. It is a perpetual problem of balance, but Japan has become very agile in walking the tightrope.[32]

NOTES

1. Michael Lewis, "The Toyama Rice Riots of 1918: The Persistence of Traditional Protest," a paper presented at the meeting of the Association for Asian Studies, March 1984.

2. See Margaret McKean, *Environmental Protest and Citizen Politics in Japan* (Berkeley and Los Angeles: University of California Press, 1981), p. 156.

3. See Richard H. Mitchell, *Censorship in Imperial Japan* (Princeton, N.J.: Princeton University Press, 1983).

4. The 1955 Anti-Subversive Activities Law, which was partly intended as a substitute for the old Peace Preservation Law, provides for certain kinds of protest activities to be prevented in advance if the sponsoring group has previously been convicted of certain law violations. The provision is so hedged in by legal requirements that it has rarely been utilized.

5. McKean, *Environmental Protest,* pp. 94–96, 216–18, 237–65.

6. See George R. Packard, *Protest in Tokyo* (Princeton, N.J.: Princeton University Press, 1966).

7. For further details of the Narita case see David E. Apter and Nagayo Sawa, *Against the State: Politics and Social Protest in Japan* (Cambridge, Mass.: Harvard University Press, 1984).

8. John D. McCarthy and Mayer N. Zald, "Resource Mobilization and Social Movements: A Partial Theory," *American Journal of Sociology* 83 (1978): 1212–41.

9. The *zaibatsu* of prewar and wartime Japan were large groups of companies linked through a single holding company and interlocking directorates. Prior to 1945 each *zaibatsu* had its own bank and trading company, and a full range of heavy and light industrial components. Each group constituted a complete, vertically integrated economic empire, but the several *zaibatsu* competed among themselves for market shares in each industry. The combines were broken up during the Allied Occupation, but have since re-formed to the extent permitted by postwar antitrust laws. These more loosely integrated postwar company groups are known as *zaikai*.

10. The Burakumin are members of a caste-like group that has traditionally been discriminated against in Japanese society. Although Burakumin are ethnically Japanese and thus an "invisible" minority, economic and social discrimination has been maintained by social labeling based largely on the group's traditional areas of residence.

11. Thomas Rohlen, "Violence at Yoka High School: The Implications for Japanese Coalition Politics of the Confrontation Between the Communist Party and the Buraku Liberation League," *Asian Survey* 16 (1976): 682–99.

12. For a fuller description of the Zenkyōtō movement see Donald Wheeler, "Value Politics, Student Politics and the Tokyo University Struggle," Ph.D. diss., Columbia University, 1974.

13. The one striking exception to the exclusion of student activists from the environmental movement was the Narita Airport protest movement, which began as an environmental issue for local farmers. Students were permitted to join the protest even though they interpreted the issue within a more global ideological framework. Eventually several student sects provided the bulk of the manpower for increasingly violent struggles, but they were never allowed to take control away from the farmers. See Apter and Sawa, *Against the State,* pp. 7, 112, 186.

14. See McKean, *Environmental Protest,* p. 162, and Jeffrey Broadbent, "Environmental Movements in Japan: Citizen Versus State Mobilization," a paper presented at the meeting of the American Sociological Association, August 1983.

15. Sachiko Sakamoto, "Japanese Feminists: Their Struggle Against the Revision of the Eugenic Protection Law," M.A. thesis, University of Hawaii, 1987.

16. Michael Donnelly, "Conflict Over Government Authority and Markets: Japan's Rice Economy," in *Conflict in Japan,* ed. E. Krauss, T. Rohlen, and P. Steinhoff (Honolulu: University of Hawaii Press, 1984), pp. 335–74.

17. See Takeshi Ishida, "Conflict and Its Accommodation," in Krauss, Rohlen, and Steinhoff, *Conflict in Japan,* pp. 16–38, and Tadashi Hanami, "Conflict and Its Resolution in Industrial Relations and Labor Law," ibid., pp. 107–35.

18. I am indebted to T. J. Pempel for this observation.

19. See Frank Upham, "Instrumental Violence and Social Change: The Buraku Liberation League and the Tactic of 'Denunciation Struggle,' " *Law in Japan* 17 (1984): 185–205.

20. For a detailed description of a *taishū dankō,* see Yasuyuki Owada, Alan H. Gleason, and Robert W. Avery, "Taishū Dankō: Agency for Change in a Japanese University," in *Japanese Culture and Behavior,* ed. W. Lebra and T. Lebra (Honolulu: University of Hawaii Press, 1977), pp. 443–49. Another analysis of the phenomenon is offered by Takeo Doi, "Higaisha Ishiki: The Psychology of Revolting Youth," ibid., pp. 450–57.

21. Kyūen Renraku Sentā, *Kyūen Nōto* (Relief Notes) (Tokyo: Kyūen Renraku Sentā, 1978). The center itself is an interesting product of the interrelations between protest and democracy in postwar Japan. It emerged in 1968 as a support group of intellectuals and other sympathizers who were concerned about the escalation of police measures used against student activists. It arranges legal aid to arrested students, collects data on abuse of civil liberties, provides a vehicle for contributions to the legal funds of specific groups of students, and offers a wide range of advice and information through its publications. Its bimonthly newspaper reports on alleged violations of civil liberties and police brutality, proposed changes in the criminal law that affect the student movement, and the current state of the hundreds of legal cases stemming from the student movement. Kyūen's concern with civil liberties is reminiscent of the American Civil Liberties Union, with the critical difference that Kyūen supports only the student left. It has unusual breadth in Japan because it supports students regardless of sect, but it remains a product of and for the ideological left.

22. Sakamoto, "Japanese Feminists," p. 90.

23. Kangoku Hō Kaiaku to Tatakau Gokuchūsha no Kai, eds., *Zenkoku Kangoku Jittai* (Nationwide Prison Survey) (Tokyo: Ryokufū Shuppan, 1985); Hiroshi Nonaka, *Irasuto Kangoku Jiten* (Illustrated Prison Dictionary) (Tokyo: Nihon Hyōronsha, 1987).

24. They neither seek nor receive compensation. The defendants regard the not-guilty verdict as vindication, whereas the authorities hold it up as evidence that the system does work fairly. For details of how these false confessions were obtained, see Gavan McCormack, "Crime, Confession, and Control," in *Democracy in Contemporary Japan,* ed. Gavan McCormack and Yoshio Sugimoto (Sydney: Hale & Iremonger, 1986), pp. 186–94, and Futaba Igarashi, "Forced to Confess," ibid., pp. 195–214.

25. A further constraint in the criminal processing of protesters is the fundamental similarity between the jailers and the jailed. The vast majority of persons who have been arrested and tried for serious crimes of violence connected with political protest are college students. Their social backgrounds are identical to those of the Justice Ministry officials who prosecute and try them, and they often attended the same elite universities. Younger government bureaucrats may even have had some personal experience of student movement involvement in the 1950s and early 1960s.

26. For a good statement of this position, see Anthony Oberschall, *Social Conflict and Social Movements* (Englewood Cliffs, N. J.: Prentice-Hall, 1973).

27. The acceptance of labor as a legitimate interest group does not extend, however, to the recognition of every political cause that is championed by the major labor union federations.

28. Charles Tilly, *From Mobilization to Revolution* (Reading, Mass.; Addison-Wesley, 1978).

29. Ellis S. Krauss, *Japanese Radicals Revisited: Student Protest in Postwar Japan* (Berkeley and Los Angeles: University of California Press, 1974), p. 124; and Susan J. Pharr, *Political Women in Japan* (Berkeley and Los Angeles: University of California Press, 1981), pp. 162–69.

30. David E. Groth, "Strategy and Structure of Protest in Contemporary Japan: The Anti-Shinkansen Movement," a paper presented at the annual meeting of the Association for Asian Studies, March 1984.

31. Broadbent, "Environmental Movements."

32. Takeshi Ishida, *Japanese Political Culture* (New Brunswick, N.J.: Transaction Books, 1983), pp. 147–60.

Social Democracy

9

Equality

●

MARGARET A. MCKEAN

We may easily agree that at the very least, democracy is a matter of procedure and constitutional principle. We can, for example, expect the following minimum conditions for democracy: elections must occur at regular intervals, they must be conducted honestly and by secret ballot so that voters are not penalized for expressing their true preferences, they must provide a genuine choice among alternative candidates and parties, and fundamental freedoms of expression and exchange of ideas must be protected to allow citizens to make informed choices. Some of these procedural and structural democratic requisites are discussed in the other chapters in this volume as they apply to Japan. But it is often argued that democracy must be more than this, that it also depends on a modicum of economic equality so that even the poorest members of society have the means and leisure to inform themselves and participate in politics as independent citizens. Thus in assessing Japanese democracy we need to look not only at political structures, procedures, and processes, but also at economic equality.

No nation perfectly fulfills either ideal of political or economic democracy, but it would seem reasonable to expect the different measures or varieties of democracy to develop in tandem. Thus we might expect, for instance, that the more political competition and alternation of leadership we find in a country, then the more likely that we would also encounter an emphasis on achieving economic equality. However, Japan stands as a rather startling and virtually unexamined exception to most of the generalizations that have been advanced about which political and economic characteristics ought to be found together in the advanced industrial democracies. Japan shares most of the economic and political traits of the least egalitarian democracies, but has nonetheless achieved as much economic equality as the most progressive of the European social democracies (see table 1).

This egalitarianism coexists with several factors that are said to contribute to *in*equality in other countries: extraordinarily high levels of capital accumulation, a weak labor movement, conservative governments, low levels of taxation and public spending, and only the most modest public policies aimed at altering income distribution. In effect, Japan has achieved considerable economic equality without political leadership by those who would promote egalitarian policies and outcomes, without the general public making equality an issue, without the political competition that might force conservatives in power to heed demands from nonconservatives—essentially without

TABLE 1
Income Distribution in Ten Selected Industrial Democracies (ca. 1970)

	Before Taxes		After Taxes	
	Gini [rank][a]	Top/Bottom Ratio[b]	Gini [rank]	Top/Bottom Ratio
Sweden (1972)	.346 [4]	6.75	.302 [1]	5.61
Norway (1970)	.354 [5]	8.35	.307 [2]	5.92
Australia (1966–67)	.313 [1]	6.17	.312 [3]	5.88
Japan (1969)	*.335 [2]*	*5.59*	*.316 [4]*	*5.19*
United Kingdom (1973)	.344 [3]	7.46	.318 [5]	6.14
Netherlands (1967)	.385 [7]	7.76	.354 [6]	6.6
Canada (1969)	.382 [6]	10.07	.354 [7]	8.2
United States (1972)	.404 [9]	11.79	.381 [8]	9.53
West Germany (1973)	.396 [8]	7.93	.383 [9]	7.09
France (1970)	.416 [10]	10.93	.414 [10]	10.91

SOURCE: Adapted from tables 3, 4, and 5 in Malcolm Sawyer, *Income Distribution in OECD Countries,* OECD Economic Outlook Occasional Studies, July 1976.

a. The higher the Gini coefficient, the less equal the distribution; the lower the Gini coefficient, the more equal the distribution. The Gini coefficient is a measure of the deviance from perfect equality (which would equal 1.0) and is the area between a nation's Lorenz curve of inequality and the perfectly diagonal line that represents complete equality.

b. The higher the "Top/Bottom Ratio" the less equal the distribution; the lower the ratio, the more equal the distribution. The "Top/Bottom ratio" (or the "Quintile Ratio") is the ratio of the percentage of total income commanded by the richest 20 percent of the population to the percentage of total income commanded by the poorest 20 percent of the population.

really trying: equality without effort. (And as we will see, as soon as the Japanese became concerned with distribution, they began doing *less* well at achieving equality.) This essay will explore what could have caused such high levels of economic equality in Japan in the absence of the factors that seem to have been essential everywhere else, and what this unusual combination of economic equality with other characteristics has contributed to the development of democratic practice in Japan.

Distribution Patterns in Japan

Before 1945

It is widely agreed that income distribution in the prewar period was considerably more inegalitarian than after 1945, becoming quite severe indeed during the depression.[1] World War II compressed the distribution and also impoverished the Japanese people across the board. The formerly wealthy found themselves emerging from the war as poor as everyone else, while farmers who had to sell daughters into prostitution during the depression now found themselves comparatively well-off. The war did create some new fortunes, of course— black marketeers, labor bosses, the most enterprising farmers—but it undid more fortunes than it created.[2]

1945–52

Reforms enacted during the American Occupation, many with the specific objective of economic democracy, almost certainly intensified this sharp decline in inequality. Probably the most important of these, not undone after the American Occupation left Japan in 1952, was land reform which redistributed ownership of all rural arable land. Because the approximately one million thus deprived of their property were paid in postinflation yen, the reform amounted to outright confiscation and therefore had enormous impact on the distributions of wealth and income. Prior to land reform, only 54 percent of the arable land was owner-cultivated, but this proportion increased to 90 percent by 1950.[3] By 1950, 61.8 percent of the farm households owned more than 90 percent of the land they worked.[4] Ronald Dore points out that even though the land reform made some concessions to prewar landlords and allowed a few new ones to emerge, it was very important not only in leveling incomes within rural areas but also in raising the standard of living in rural areas relative to the urban standard. Moreover, because land subsequently skyrocketed in value, this redistribution equalized the ownership of an asset that later became an important part of family wealth.

Another feature of the Occupation's economic democratization program was the revival of labor unions with guaranteed rights to organize, engage in collective bargaining, and strike. The Occupation itself backtracked a bit when it prohibited a general strike in February 1947, and later the Japanese government hindered union power even further with legislation that denied public employees the right to strike (which simply radicalized the public workers' unions and made them a more important political force instead). In comparative terms, the Japanese union movement is still described as relatively weak. But there is no doubt that being allowed to exist, to bargain, and to conduct work stoppages or work-to-rule campaigns that fall short of a strike has strengthened the labor movement in comparison to the prewar period and improved labor's bargaining position during wage negotiations.

The purge was another Occupation measure that probably contributed to social and economic leveling in Japan, even though it was only temporary and its quantitative impact is difficult to estimate. Relatives of the emperor were demoted to ordinary citizenship and deprived of substantial wealth. Members of the peerage lost their titles and privileges. Finally, the purge of two hundred twenty thousand military officers, politicians, government officials, and businessmen deprived these members of the elite from access to official position and large incomes. At the very least the purge removed some members of the elite from power and made room for others to fill the gaps, and thus for a short time promoted the circulation of people into and out of positions of power.[5] Although the people who were purged returned to active political and economic life eventually, they now had to rub shoulders and compete for privilege with a new, broader elite.

Another Occupation reform was the program of trust-busting. Although only a few conglomerates were actually broken apart, the reform did democratize stock ownership, allowing employees in these companies to buy as much as 26 percent of the stock that was resold, and it removed the wealthy *zaibatsu* (prewar family trusts) families from positions of power and deprived them of their fortunes. Although concentration of stock ownership has risen since then, the increased concentration is in holdings by institutions and does not indicate the emergence of new stock market magnates among individuals. Thus this reform, too, contributed to economic democracy and increased equality of distribution in Japan.[6]

Finally, the Occupation's tax policies were designed, at least at the outset, to promote economic democracy. The Occupation created a capital gains tax for the first time, increased corporate taxes to 35 percent of net earnings (up to 42 percent by 1952), and designed an income tax system that was quite progressive.[7] The Occupation retreated from some of these measures later in 1949 in order to speed up Japan's economic recovery and terminate the Occupation as quickly as possible. Nonetheless, the reversals of the late Occupation and beyond never completely undid the initial reforms: the income tax remained progressive and in place, the capital gains tax persisted in some form, and corporate taxes survived. In this sense the idea of economic democratization that underlay the initial reforms survived as a lasting contribution to Japan's relatively high level of equality in distribution.

1952–59

When the Occupation ended, the trend toward considerably increasing equality of distribution changed to a trend of slowly increasing *in*equality of distribution that lasted through the 1950s. The 1950s were also a period of steady recovery and growth, and the government adopted a number of economic policies in pursuit of that aim. Regardless of how much these policies really contributed to the economic growth that followed, they did contribute somewhat to this new trend of backsliding toward inequality.

The newly independent Japanese government continued the shifts in economic policy that had been designed in the late Occupation era to promote capital accumulation and thus growth: it restricted the applicability of the capital gains tax and added new loopholes, reduced the tax on interest income to a flat rate of 10 percent (and abolished this tax altogether in 1955), reduced the progressivity in personal income taxes by dropping rates in the upper brackets still further, and reduced the corporate tax rate. Firms were once again allowed to form cartels in certain situations, industry and trade associations were revived, and labor unions of public-sector employees were seriously restricted in their rights. Kozo Yamamura argues that in opting for growth the Japanese government and its industrial clients were knowingly opting *against* economic democracy.[8]

1959–62

The slide toward inequality came to a halt in 1959–62, when inequality reached its worst in postwar Japan. However measured, the most inegalitarian year measured falls into this three-year period.[9] Thus this brief era seems to be a turning point between the slow slip toward greater inequality of the 1950s and a restoration of a rapid trend toward greater equality in the 1960s.

1962–74

The decade that preceded the first oil crisis saw extraordinary growth in Japan that broke world records; it also saw a return of the trend toward distributional equality. Kozo Yamamura attributes this shift—already visible in data he used—to another round of changes in tax policy. The Liberal Democratic party (LDP), beginning to fear electoral consequences if it continued altering the tax structure to benefit those who were already better off, introduced adjustments to benefit the poor in 1959 (by increasing exemptions for taxpayers in the lower brackets) and continued these adjustments through the 1960s.[10] These changes were not asked for by pressure groups representing the lower classes, but were generated internally by the LDP's own anxieties. By the early 1970s, after-tax income distribution in Japan was essentially as egalitarian as that in the social democracies like Sweden, Norway, and the United Kingdom, which had tried very self-consciously to become welfare states with policies of comparatively drastic redistribution through taxes and transfers.

1975–Present

Worldwide energy and economic crises seem to have brought on a modest degeneration of Japan's accomplishments in reducing economic inequality, though this trend is a more gentle one than that of the 1950s. It is impossible to date its beginning with any precision (since the shift occurs at different times for different subgroups), and it may not continue into the future. In Japan the crisis increased inflation and depressed growth seriously for a couple of years, but recovery was under way by 1976, and the second energy crisis (1979–80) made much less difference in the major economic indicators.

Causes of Distributive Patterns in Japan

Historical Events

Historical or conjunctural factors clearly played an important role in setting the stage for the postwar pattern of substantial (but still vacillating) levels of equality: the importance of World War II as a social leveler is self-evident, not only in Japan but in many of the countries affected by the war. The reforms of the Occupation era that were aimed at establishing economic democracy intensified this effect.

Social and Demographic Change

Social and demographic trends common to all the industrial societies have multiple effects on patterns of distribution. Some of these work to increase distributive equality: the decline in self-employment, the decline in agriculture, and the increase in female participation in the labor force generally work to increase equality in society. This is simply due to the fact that in most societies self-employed people and farmers tend to be poorer than others, so the decline in their number means that those who are now the poorest in such societies are better off than those who were the poorest before. Similarly, as women from working-class families enter the labor force, the households at the bottom end of the income distribution become better off. Finally, the availability of adequate birth control and, more important, the decision on the part of virtually all families to limit family size, keep Japan's poorest families from having to spread their income as thinly as we find elsewhere.[11]

One might think that the diffusion of education would distribute skills more equally, to equalize the initial bargaining positions of all workers somewhat, and thus to contribute to economic equality. The spread of basic literacy certainly has this effect, but apparently in advanced industrial societies that are already beyond this stage the continued spread of higher education does not produce the same effect, because those with high incomes may "capture" more than their "fair" share of educational opportunities.[12] Japan in the postwar era has prided itself on equality in education—the very best universities were the cheapest and accessible strictly on merit without regard to socioeconomic status, as Edward Beauchamp indicates (see chapter 10).[13] But this may be changing now. Competition for the best universities has now extended to competition for the best kindergartens, and only families with money can buy the expensive private education before university, plus private tutoring after school, that are increasingly the key to success in college and career.

One other effect of mass education upon income that we must remember is that basic education and literacy in Japan are the best or nearly so in the world. Japanese children routinely outdo those of other nationalities in mathematics and science, by a considerable margin and with very little deviation about the mean. Japanese society has no significant segment of functional illiterates or unemployables, and even the least skilled members of the work force are probably more flexible, adaptable, and capable of handling fairly demanding work, even in the context of increasingly sophisticated technology, than is the case in the United States and elsewhere.[14] Their basic skills make them employable, keep them employed, and make them worth relatively more to their employers than equivalent workers elsewhere. Thus Japan's lowest-paid workers do better, compared to other Japanese workers, than the lowest-paid workers and the armies of unemployed elsewhere do relative to other workers in those countries.

Other social factors also work to exacerbate inequality. The aging of society as health improves and the decline of average household size as the extended family breaks down both actually mark an increase in the number of relatively poorer households and thus in income inequality as well.

Economic Factors

Historical and social factors in the Japanese case seem to operate the same way they do elsewhere, though perhaps with even greater speed, and therefore cannot account for the unusual findings we have in Japan. Rather, it is the economic and political factors that can explain the anomalous Japanese patterns of egalitarianism.

There is some confusion about the role of economic growth in changing distribution. Over the very long term, substantial increases in per capita income are associated with greater equality of distribution: richer societies are more equal than poorer ones. But in the short term, bursts of economic growth seem to be accompanied by increases in inequality of distribution. Rapid economic growth depends upon high levels of capital accumulation, and Simon Kuznets argued that the latter is unlikely to occur if wealth and income are distributed very equally.[15] Thus it is taken as a virtual truism by scholars who have studied distribution that high economic growth is inconsistent with high levels of distributive equality.

The Japanese case confirms the observation that over the long term economic growth enhances equality, but it clearly challenges the view that rapid growth must be accompanied by a deterioration of income equality. Among the advanced industrial democracies, Japan has both the highest rate of sustained postwar growth and one of the most egalitarian distributions of income.[16] Moreover, as table 2 shows, Japan underwent a distinct increase in the equality of distribution precisely during the period of the most rapid and record-breaking growth, from 1962 to 1974.[17] One cannot argue that economic growth operated to increase inequality in the 1950s, then to decrease inequality in the 1960s, and once again to increase inequality in the 1970s. A satisfactory explanation must account for the shifts that occurred during all three decades. Either the growth rate was completely irrelevant throughout the postwar era, or it functioned consistently but was sometimes overshadowed by more important factors that changed decisively in conjunction with distributive trends.

Two factors in addition to economic growth that have been suggested as important in explaining distributional patterns are conditions in the labor market and technological change.[18] These three seem to have interacted in a complex way to produce the shifts in inequality from decade to decade in Japan.

First, during the 1950s when inequality of distribution increased in

TABLE 2
**Inequality in Japan Over Time: Nonagricultural Households
of Two or More Persons**

	Gini[a]	Income of Bottom 20% of Population	Income of Top 20% of Population	Top/Bottom Ratio[a]
1956	.312	7.9% of total	39.6% of total	5.01
1959	.335	7.1	41.0	5.77
1962	.340	7.4	41.9	5.66
1965	.324	7.9	40.8	5.16
1968	.301	8.2	38.7	4.72
1971	.307	8.2	39.4	4.80
1974	.295	8.6	38.7	4.50
1977	.301	8.1	38.1	4.70

SOURCE: Ishizaki Tadao, *Nihon no shotoku to tomi no bumpai* (Tokyo: Tōyō keizai shimpōsha, 1983), table 19. Ishizaki does not identify whether these are pre- or post-tax figures.

a. See notes to table 1.

Japan, Japan had a labor surplus that reduced the bargaining power of some workers in wage negotiations, thus making the income distribution more inegalitarian. Although both average real wages and labor share (the percentage of earnings distributed to labor rather than paid to shareholders or reinvested) actually increased,[19] the wages of temporary and day workers dropped relative to those of regular workers during the 1950s.[20] Whereas Japan's regular workers had some protection offered by practices like lifetime employment, the more numerous temporary workers and day laborers did not, and their wages were determined exclusively by market conditions. Repatriated soldiers, returnees from the colonies, and increasing numbers of women entering the labor force obviously exacerbated wage differentials among workers. The technological revolution probably operated as a force for inequality at this time by exacerbating wage differentials between the skilled workers who were in high demand and the unskilled workers who were displaced. Similarly, the gap increased between those who were entirely dependent on wages and those who had many other resources in addition to earned income.[21] Indeed, in this situation unemployment and inequality should have been quite severe. However, high economic growth rates—generated in part by the technological revolution itself—created places for the displaced workers to go and blunted the inegalitarian impact of technological change and labor surplus. This adaptability of Japanese workers, who could keep themselves employable, saved Japan from a situation like that in the United States, where there is a perpetual shortage of highly trained workers that the unemployed cannot fill.

Japan's labor surplus of the 1950s turned into a labor shortage by the 1960s, greatly enhancing labor's bargaining power over wages. Most young people were going beyond the nine years of compulsory education to enter high school, so firms were not finding the thousands of eager, hard-working fifteen-year-olds they had previously been able to hire at low wages. Small firms in particular, which constitute the traditional sector of the Japanese "dual economy," found it difficult to recruit and retain workers. As these workers moved to more attractive opportunities in the modern sector of the dual economy, many small firms went bankrupt. Wage differentials between the two sectors (small traditional firms and large modern highly capitalized firms) decreased substantially through the early 1970s.[22] Like the 1950s, the 1970s combined recovery and modest growth with a labor surplus once again, as the children of the baby boom entered the labor force while the economy contracted or ceased to grow as rapidly as before. This growth in the 1970s, though more impressive than in other industrial countries, was insufficient to absorb the entire labor force, and Japan experienced unemployment, though still at the extremely low rate of only 2 percent.

Thus economic growth can promote distributive equality if the capital accumulation that fuels growth is channeled directly by institutions into investment without becoming the personal income of the economic elite, continues to increase opportunities for employment, and thus gives even an expanding labor force an adequate bargaining position. In Japan, most of the profits that are not distributed to labor are not distributed to hopeful shareholders (who are assumed by Kuznets and others to be wealthy people located at the top of the income distribution who promote capital accumulation), but are recycled immediately into investment within the firm. This is because Japanese firms are financed much more by bank loans than by the stock market. Since profits do not become the income of the rich, one can have capital accumulation without the rich getting richer. Indeed, one often encounters evidence of the alleged "frugality" of the rich in Japan—much more modest than their counterparts elsewhere in consumption habits, much more willing to defer current income in favor of allowing assets to appreciate over the long term, though this may be compensated for somewhat by the fact that many of the elite receive perks and benefits in kind rather than in cash.[23]

Thus economic growth maintained high employment in spite of a labor surplus and a technological revolution that could otherwise have produced high unemployment and severe inequality of distribution. Labor surplus and the technological revolution exacerbated inequality (though one depresses average wages and the other reflects a rising average wage), and economic growth and the resulting high levels of employment worked in the opposite direction (and in contradiction to Kuznets' proposition) by guaranteeing that those at the bottom of the income distribution were poorly paid workers rather than impoverished unemployed who would have been even poorer.

I would therefore argue that economic growth operated throughout the postwar period to promote distributive equality in Japan, but that the very different labor market conditions of the three decades were decisive in controlling the direction of the outcome. Labor surplus overcame the role of growth to allow a gentle slide toward increased inequality in the 1950s, labor shortage worked with economic growth and other factors like tax policy in the 1960s to produce a very clear trend toward increased equality, and serious labor surplus and unemployment, along with ironically regressive transfer policies that I will discuss later, overcame the effects of recovery and growth in the 1970s to restore a trend of mildly increasing inequality.

Political Factors

Above and beyond the statistical consequences of social and economic change, additional political factors have been suggested as likely to enhance levels of equality in a society. In fact, some conclude that among the advanced industrial democracies, political factors override others in importance.[24] In particular, low inequality supposedly goes with powerful labor movements that can extract a high labor share in wage negotiations and thus produce greater equalitarianism in pretax income distributions, and with leftist or prolabor governments that can design tax and transfer policies to produce even greater equality in post-tax and post-transfer distributions. Since substantial transfer policies can only come from governments willing to indulge in large or at least rapidly expanding programs of public spending, high levels of equality are thought to be associated with strong labor movements, leftist governments, large government budgets, and extensive transfer policies.[25]

Japan is an exception in having considerable equality without very effective mobilization by labor or the left. The Japanese labor movement is almost always considered weak because actual wage negotiations occur within enterprises and not through peak associations, there is an extremely low level of strikes and lost work time, and because two unions sometimes compete against each other within a single enterprise.[26] Similarly, with the exception of one short-lived cabinet during the Occupation, all postwar governments and all postwar cabinet seats have been held by conservative parties. Finally, although Japan has undergone a radical increase in public spending on welfare and transfer programs, Japan still has by comparative standards only the most rudimentary tax and transfer policies and by far the leanest government budget among the advanced industrial democracies. In fact, Japan is distinct in having high levels of equality in income distribution both before and after taxes, so that the government role in redistribution can be minor without altering Japan's status as a very egalitarian member of the cohort of advanced industrial democracies.

In Japan, economic conditions in the labor market have largely substituted for the missing political activity by the left to produce substantial egalitarianism on a par with the European social democracies. However, it would be incorrect to give the impression that economic factors alone explain the Japanese pattern and that political factors do not matter at all. Two sources of political pressure generate government policies with distributional impacts, and it appears that the source of the pressure is also related to the nature of the impact. If the pressure comes from within the LDP and its usual client groups (groups that are regular sources of financial or electoral support), the resulting policy will be consistent and have the intended impact on distribution. If the pressure comes from outside the LDP—that is, from the leftist opposition or from new politically neutral groups like citizens' movements that lack long-established relationships with the LDP—the results are less controlled, haphazard, even perverse in their distributional effects.

It is easy to overlook the methods by which egalitarian policies can emerge from a government like Japan's that is dominated by a single long-lived political party. During the 1960s, the LDP adopted progressive tax policies that did increase equality, even if less so than in countries with higher levels of taxation and leftist regimes committed to redistribution. These were adopted in anticipation of unspoken threats, without pressure from outside groups. The LDP decided it needed these policies and was therefore free to design them so as to have the intended redistributive effect.

There are also at least three good examples of redistributions enacted to placate enormous pressure groups consisting of conservative voters. These groups are able to frighten LDP politicians with a credible threat to withhold votes from LDP-designated candidates, leverage that voters who already support the opposition cannot use. One is the 1.7 million former landlords and their close relatives who lost property during the Occupation's land reform (mentioned above), who began mobilizing for compensation as soon as the Occupation ended and finally achieved victory with a large award in 1965.[27] Another is the 3.5 million people who were repatriated from colonial territories after World War II; they also mobilized during the 1950s to demand compensation for lost property and received a small initial award in 1957 and a much larger one in 1967.[28] Thus both groups received their largest awards in the 1960s, during the period when overall distribution was becoming more egalitarian. There is no question that these awards had a consistent redistributive impact, but unfortunately without knowledge of where the recipients stood in the aggregate distribution we cannot detect this impact.

The third conservative interest group of this sort—consisting of a large number of voters who worked through the conservative party and won their demands—are Japan's 5–5.7 million farmers, whose impact on aggregate distribution can be traced in the data. Almost all farmers are members of agricultural cooperatives that are part of a national federation (sometimes called an agricultural *zaibatsu* or cartel) that lobbies every year to maintain and improve farmers' advantages under the system of controls on rice prices left intact after the war.[29] By the early 1960s the Japanese farm lobby had become powerful enough to persuade the government to set the producers' guaranteed price for rice at a level higher than the open market would bring, thus incorporating an annual government subsidy to rice farmers. Distribution data show clearly that the annual income of Japan's farmers rose steadily relative to the income of urban households. By 1966 agricultural households earned more than nonagricultural households, and since 1975 agricultural households have been earning 56–66 percent more than nonagricultural households.[30]

In raising the income of farm households the LDP's agricultural subsidies have contributed greatly to compensating for the relatively lower incomes that we usually find in the primary sector of an industrial economy. Until 1966 this compensation served to equalize distribution throughout the economy; since 1966 it has obviously exacerbated inequality somewhat by giving farmers higher-than-average incomes. Farmers were able to force the LDP to continue these subsidies another twenty years—they were phased out in the mid-eighties—because of their value to the LDP as a secure political base in overrepresented electoral districts. But because of the land reform, no Japanese farmer can grow enough rice to exploit the rice price supports as a path to egregious wealth, in contrast to some American farmers who are paid enormous sums to grow nothing on huge expanses of land.

These redistributive policies generated from within the LDP remind us that a conservative regime in an industrial society does not necessarily choose to serve the industrial elite alone. It may also be dependent on support from other groups that are not particularly wealthy but opt to support the conservative party and seek redistribution through it, like Japan's farmers. The leftist opposition is not the only vehicle available to transmit such pressure.

Although labor unions are comparatively weak in Japan and the leftist parties have not captured power, they and other groups not part of the conservative establishment have also begun to make demands for redistributive policies. In the 1970s, programs of social spending and welfare benefits became the subject of political conflict and an important issue in electoral competition for the first time in postwar politics. The Liberal Democrats, feeling the increasing threat in each election that they would lose their legislative majority, responded with public spending on social infrastructure, retirement benefits, medical care, special programs for the elderly, unemployment insurance, consumer protection, environmental cleanup, and so on. For the first time the Liberal Democrats faced an array of interest groups beyond their customary clientele in business and agriculture and felt pressed to buy each group off in return with a specially designed government program in order to prevent the defection of more marginal voters to the centrist or leftist parties.

Sometimes the conservative regime acted late, and then only in response to repeated pressure, as in the case of compensation for pollution damage to health;[31] but after a while the bureaucracy and the LDP began acting early to preempt demands, as in the case of medical care for the elderly.[32] It is important to note, however, that when distributive issues finally became a point of open contention between the left and right, and not just a quiet discussion among conservatives, the resulting policies emerged as a haphazard patchwork. That is, the nonconservative pressure groups in Japan did not restrict their demands to redistributions with egalitarian consequences, a deviation from the findings of comparative studies that groups mobilized on the left usually seek egalitarian redistributions.

We would ordinarily expect increased government spending on social welfare to enhance equality, but Ishizaki's data on the impact of social spending reveal unexpected results for Japan.[33] It was during the 1960s, when the levels of taxation and social spending were still relatively small in international terms, that government policy (the progressive direct income tax) had the greatest impact on distribution. Somehow, the larger programs of the 1970s did less—almost nothing in fact—for redistribution. The pensions and health benefits include programs that pay out equal amounts to all beneficiaries regardless of their other sources of income, and other benefits that depend on income actually give more to the rich than to the poor, rather than the other way around. What the Ministry of Health and Welfare classified as transfer income until 1978 combined wage-dependent benefits like retirement annuities, life insurance benefits, and annuities from employers with true welfare benefits like old age and disability benefits, public assistance, and unemployment insurance.

Ishizaki also compared the distribution of benefits from transfer policies among several industrial countries.[34] After the new social programs were instituted, Japan stood out among these countries in distributing transfer funds utterly without regard to redistributive criteria: the bottom 20 percent and top 20 percent of the population in Japan received approximately equal benefits! As a result, even after creating what by Japanese standards are budget-busting social welfare programs in response to public demand, the government has made very little contribution to distributive equality.

The Japanese case has several important implications for understanding the causes of different patterns in distribution in industrial societies. First, the proposition that rapid growth is incompatible with high levels of equality and rapidly increasing levels of equality must be modified to take account of the Japanese case. Second, labor is as strong as labor market conditions make it, and organizational strength or weakness is a supplement to this base level of influence. Labor movements that have great organizational strengths can conceivably work to exacerbate inequality by negotiating for benefits that accrue only to a small labor elite. Organizationally weak labor movements may allow greater equality among all workers than an elitist labor movement might. Third, conservative governments can be responsible for progressive income taxes and transfer policies, and conversely the left sometimes demands redistributions that are not egalitarian. Indeed, conservative governments may function in some ways as strong leftist governments do by allowing the market to operate fully in order to produce the socially desirable results that social democracies aim for by purposeful engineering.[35] Finally, generous transfer programs are not needed if underlying socioeconomic conditions produce considerable equality anyway; similarly, lavish spending does not guarantee that transfers will redistribute income in an egalitarian manner.

Consequences of Patterns of Distribution in Japan

No study of equality would be complete without mention of Japan's minorities that suffer from economic as well as other kinds of social discrimination. The two most important cultural minorities, as Edward Beauchamp and Ellis Krauss indicate (see chapters 3 and 10), are the Koreans and the Burakumin (outcastes). Government transfer policies have only just begun to address the needs of these minorities, and even though statistical evidence to prove it is lacking, these three million people probably account for a good measure of what poverty and economic inequality remains in Japan.

Despite this pocket of inequality, Japan fares well on overall measures of equality. Yet it is also important to go beyond this finding and its explanation and also ask about the consequences of relative equality in Japan. Studies of income distribution have paid little attention to the *consequences* of the patterns they have found. They have treated patterns of equality or inequality as the end product to be explained, not as a means, an outcome rather than a resource useful in producing other outcomes. I will conclude with some speculation on what the income patterns found in Japan may mean for that nation's democratic political processes.

First, the relatively high level of egalitarianism achieved through the early 1970s may be responsible in part for the relative absence of conflict over distributive issues from Japanese politics until the early 1970s. The much touted cultural aversion of the Japanese to conflict—especially conflict over sordid material issues—is not as important as the fact that nobody perceived a problem worth fighting over. The absence of conflict over distributive issues may have contributed in part to the emergence of much more conspicuous political conflict over ideological issues. Deprived of the distributive issues on which the left usually bases its efforts to acquire power, the left in Japan instead had to concentrate on matters of principle. Hence the appearance of ideological or "cultural" politics,[36] not because such questions matter so much more than distributive issues to the Japanese people—though they certainly matter more to the political elite actually engaged in the conflict—but because ideology was what remained.

For many years this conflict over ideological questions—the emphasis on foreign policy and such fundamental matters affecting the political system itself as constitutional revision—convinced many social commentators in Japan and outside of it that rioting and revolution were not far away. But these nervous predictions were never borne out. Some observers have concluded that ideological conflict was a face-saving front to maintain organizational cohesion and to conceal backroom compromises not known to the public.[37]

If we accept this view that ideological conflict was never as severe as it appeared, then the relatively high level of economic egalitarianism in postwar Japan not only removed distributive issues from the agenda but thereby reduced the total amount of conflict in society. Thus Japan's egalitarian pattern promoted social and political stability. Growth was sufficient to convince most Japanese that they were fairly comfortable in an absolute sense, and distribution was egalitarian enough to convince them that they were also well off relative to the next fellow. Hence the frequently cited survey results revealing that over 90 percent of the population have the statistically impossible notion that they are in the middle class. Even Marxist analysts admit that class conflict is virtually nonexistent and class consciousness is quite blurred.[38] Thus Japan's relatively egalitarian distribution, along with other factors, contributed to political stability during an era of rapid economic change by preventing class from becoming an important basis of mobilization or conflict. Hence Japanese political parties are not class-based parties, and the leftist opposition concentrates on ideological issues other than class conflict.

Similarly, class affiliation and income level have little to do with the level of participation in Japan. Whereas we usually find that high income groups also have the highest participation—because they are moved to action by their high stakes in the system and their activity preserves their own advantages—in Japan, income and participation are uncorrelated.[39] That is, low income is not an obstacle to participation. Farmers and small and medium businesses have been able to win considerable benefits from government through political participation. Ikuo Kabashima argues that Japan is characterized by a virtuous cycle in which economic development (growth) promotes economic equality, which promotes supportive or enthusiastic participation in favor of the dominant party (which happens to be conservative), which in turn increases government stability and provides an encouraging environment for still more economic growth.[40]

Japan's conservatives have benefited from this virtuous cycle and from the egalitarianism so crucial to it at least as much as they have contributed. Whereas a poor economic performance has undermined conservatives and strengthened the left in other countries, Japan's impressive economic performance even after the oil crisis has deprived labor and the left of grievances to convert into political strength and contributed to the perpetual disarray among opposition parties from centrist to communist. Egalitarianism has therefore postponed the emergence of a party or coalition that could take power from the conservatives and prolonged the unbroken rule of the Liberal Democrats.

Political competition that is weak or exclusively symbolic is not good for democracy, but the stability due to the absence of distributive conflict also has benefits. Regardless of who has power, the task of governing is much simpler with an entire category of conflict missing from the political agenda. This reprieve has allowed the conservatives to adjust slowly and constructively (certainly from their own point of view, and possibly for the system's sake as well) to the gradual emergence of more conflict. With time, for instance, the conservatives and the opposition have learned to negotiate and compromise more skillfully in the legislative arena.[41] Similarly, the conservatives have spearheaded the drive for administrative efficiency, something that conservative governments elsewhere talk about but cannot seem to do.[42]

This essay began with a discussion of how anomalous the Japanese combination of political and socioeconomic characteristics is—a conservative regime overseeing social democratic outcomes as if by magic. But perhaps what is really anomalous is simply that the Japanese Liberal Democrats are not purely conservative and are enabled— by having a constituency that is not class-based and by having to contend with a level of political conflict that remains manageable—to be other things as well, or to be "creative" conservatives (in T. J. Pempel's terms).[43]

Finally, we can also argue that in providing stability and governability, economic equality or economic democracy helped to buy Japanese political democracy the time needed to become solidly established. Much of the fascination with Japanese politics in the early postwar period amounted to amazement that democracy could exist in Japan after its leaders and people had allowed the Taishō Democracy to evaporate in the face of militarism and war. Skeptical observers noting the violence of struggles over ideological questions and the lack of civility in parliament worried that perhaps Japan had a political culture utterly unsuited to democratic practice and that the militarists would soon be back in power. But all the while Japan had a comparatively healthy level of economic democracy. Thus in spite of fragile appearances and a noncirculating conservative elite, in at least one fundamental way political democracy was growing sturdier over time. Today one rarely encounters predictions that Japanese democracy is about to collapse; rather the prevailing assumption is that Japanese democracy is here to stay.

The combination or rapid economic growth, relatively egalitarian distribution, low levels of political conflict over distributive issues, high governability, and conservative dominance began to unravel in the 1970s. This is not to say that if conservatives stay in charge all should be well, or that the political complexion of the regime determines all else. Rather, economic conditions changed the nature of political conflict and competition so as to complicate political survival for any dominant party of any political stripe. Japan's rate of growth slowed, the trend of increasing levels of equality began to falter, and distributive issues emerged as a major subject of political debate and government policy. New citizens' groups with rising expectations of government lobbied for public expenditures to benefit their members at the same time that the government felt pressed to reduce its own deficit through administrative reform.

The more concerned people became with distribution as an outcome and the more government intervened to alter distribution patterns, the less egalitarian the results in Japan. As political competition intensifies, politicians and political parties become increasingly concerned over day-to-day survival as opposed to long-term performance (whether their own, the party's, or the economy's). When politicians and parties have shorter time horizons for calculating their own rational strategies, it becomes easy for political lobbies to extract payoffs from governments, and thus for policy to lose any overall cohesion and instead to reflect the particular groups most able to frighten the ruling party.[44] Thus the distribution policies that the LDP adopted during the 1970s, hoping to acquire the image of a party flexible enough to build a cradle-to-grave welfare state while maintaining the conservative image, could assuage the groups the LDP fears without producing egalitarian outcomes.

Thus far, if all of the trends we observe for the 1970s—slower growth, unemployment, more inequality, more conflict, more balanced competition between left and right, less stability, less governability—were to continue, Japan's anomalous status as a nation with a bourgeois government but a social democratic pattern of income distribution would evaporate. In the mid-1970s and again at the end of that decade it seemed that the Japanese miracle was over and that Japan might have to go through the same economic difficulties, cultural malaise, and political upheavals we have seen in the other industrial democracies in recent years.[45] Indeed, some Japanese social commentators have made a living predicting disaster.

But there are other reasons to think that the indicators of change visible in the 1970s will not matter much. They have not yet brought about drastic change: the LDP continues to rule, the left seems incapable of taking advantage of the situation, the new centrist parties are not taking off as expected, the economy remains resilient (Japan still leads the member nations of the Organization for Economic Cooperation and Development in real growth since 1973), nor can we tell yet whether inequality will continue to increase or will eventually be halted by socioeconomic change or altered transfer policies. Japan could remain the exception among advanced industrial democracies or could begin converging toward them.

NOTES

1. According to studies by Shiomi Saburō cited in Takafusa Nakamura, *Economic Growth in Prewar Japan* (New Haven, Conn.: Yale University Press, 1971). See also Martin Schnitzer, *Income Distribution: A Comparative Study of the United States, Sweden, West Germany, East Germany, the United Kingdom, and Japan* (London: Her Majesty's Stationary Office, for the Royal Commission on the Distribution of Income and Wealth, Background Paper 4, 1977).

2. Jerome B. Cohen, *Japan's Economy in War and Reconstruction* (Minneapolis: University of Minnesota, 1949), p. 46; Ronald P. Dore, *Land Reform in Japan* (London: Oxford University Press, 1959).

3. Kozo Yamamura, *Economic Policy in Postwar Japan: Growth Versus Economic Democracy* (Berkeley and Los Angeles: University of California Press, 1967), p. 18.

4. Dore, *Land Reform in Japan*, p. 176.

5. Hans H. Baerwald, *The Purge of Japanese Leaders Under the Occupation*, University of California Publications in Political Science 18 (Berkeley, 1959).

6. Cohen, *Japan's Economy*, pp. 427–36; Yamamura, *Economic Policy in Postwar Japan*; and Eleanor M. Hadley, *Antitrust in Japan* (Princeton, N.J.: Princeton University Press, 1970).

7. Yamamura, *Economic Policy in Postwar Japan*.

8. Ibid.

9. Ishizaki Tadao, *Nihon no shotoku to tomi no bumpai* (Distribution of Income and Wealth in Japan) (Tokyo: Tōyō keizai shimpôsha, 1983), pp. 21–24.

10. Yamamura, *Economic Policy in Postwar Japan*, pp. 136–37.

11. Samuel Coleman points out that the prevalent birth control methods used in Japan are relatively old-fashioned (there is little use of oral contraception or sterilization), and that abortion is widely relied upon as birth control. See *Family Planning in Japanese Society: Traditional Birth Control in a Modern Urban Culture* (Princeton, N.J.: Princeton University Press, 1983).

12. Lester Thurow, *The Zero-Sum Society* (New York: Basic Books, 1980), pp. 155–214; J. Corina Von Arnhem and Guert J. Schotsman, "Do Parties Affect the Distribution of Income?: The Case of Advanced Capitalist Democracies," in *The Impact of Parties: Politics and Policies in Democratic Capitalist States*, ed. Francis G. Castles (Beverly Hills, Calif.: Sage, 1982), pp. 283–364, esp. pp. 305–07.

13. William Cummings also argues that Japanese education fosters social egalitarianism in attitudes, although this is not the same as economic egalitarianism as an actual outcome. See *Education and Equality in Japan* (Princeton, N.J.: Princeton University Press, 1980).

14. Thomas R. Rohlen, *Japan's High Schools* (Berkeley and Los Angeles: University of California Press, 1983), speaks about the capabilities of Japanese schoolchildren and the likely socioeconomic consequences throughout. Compare to Jonathan Kozol, *Illiterate America* (Garden City, N.Y.: Anchor/Doubleday, 1985), which explains how one-third of adult Americans, including many who have graduated from high school, are functionally illiterate.

15. Simon Kuznets, "Economic Growth and Income Inequality," *American Economic Review* 45 (1955): 1–28.

16. Malcolm Sawyer, *Income Distribution in OECD Countries*, OECD Economic Outlook Occasional Studies, July 1976.

17. Ishizaki, *Nihon no shotoku to tomi no bumpai*, pp. 27–42; Mizoguchi Toshiyuki, "Sengo Nihon no shotoku bumpu to shisan bumpu" (The Distribution of Income and Wealth in Postwar Japan), *Keizai kenkyû* 25 (October 1974): 345–66.

18. Ishizaki, *Nihon no shotoku to tomi no bumpai*; Mizoguchi, "Sengo Nihon no shotoku bumpu to shisan bumpu."

19. Yamamura, *Economic Policy in Postwar Japan*, p. 155.

20. Ishizaki, *Nihon no shotoku to tomi no bumpai*, p. 13.

21. Ibid., pp. 8–18.

22. Ibid., pp. 37–48.

23. "Frugality Characterizes Japanese Top Executives' Personal Finance," *Japan Economic Journal*, 18 December 1984, p. 8; Ron Napier, "Japanese Executive Compensation and Performance," lecture at Duke University, 14 April 1986.

24. Von Arnhem and Schotsman, "Do Parties Affect the Distribution of Income?"

25. Ibid. Anthony Barnes Atkinson, *The Economics of Inequality* (London: Oxford University Press, 1975); Sten G. Borg and Francis G. Castles, "The Influence of the Political Right on Public Income Maintenance Expenditures and Equality," *Political Studies* 29 (December 1984): 604–21; David Cameron, "The Expansion of the Public Economy: A Comparative Analysis," *American Political Science Review* 72 (December 1978): 1243–61; J. Dryzek, "Politics, Economics, and Inequality: A Cross-National Analysis," *European Journal of Political Research* 6 (December 1978): 399–410; J. D. Stephens, *The Transition from Capitalism to Socialism* (London: Macmillan, 1979).

26. Tadashi Hanami, "Conflict and Its Resolution in Industrial Relations and Labor Law," in *Conflict in Japan*, ed. Ellis S. Krauss, Thomas P. Rohlen, and Patricia G. Steinhoff (Honolulu: University of Hawaii Press), pp. 107–35; Hiroshi Nishizawa, "Shuntō and Changes of Economic Conditions in Japan," M.A. thesis, Duke University, 1983; and Peter Lange and Geoffrey Garrett, "The Politics of Growth: Strategic Interaction and Economic Performance in the Advanced Industrial Democracies, 1974–1980," *Journal of Politics* 47 (August 1985): 792–827. T. J. Pempel and Keiichi Tsunekawa have called this arrangement "Corporatism Without Labor? The Japanese Anomaly," in *Trends Toward Corporatist Intermediation*, ed. Philippe C. Schmitter and Gerhard Lehmbruch (Beverly Hills, Calif.: Sage, 1979), pp. 231–70.

27. Haruhiro Fukui, *Party in Power: The Japanese Liberal-Democrats and Policymaking* (Berkeley and Los Angeles: University of California Press, 1970), pp. 173–97.

28. John Creighton Campbell, "Compensation for Repatriates: A Case Study of Interest-Group Politics and Party-Government Negotiations in Japan," in *Policymaking in Contemporary Japan*, ed. T. J. Pempel (Ithaca, N.Y.: Cornell University Press, 1977), pp. 103–42.

29. Michael W. Donnelly, "Setting the Price of Rice: A Study in Political Decision-making," ibid., pp. 143–200; and Aurelia D. George, "The Japanese Farm Lobby and Agricultural Policymaking," *Pacific Affairs* 54 (Fall 1981): 409–30.

30. Kokumin seikatsu sentaa, *Kokumin seikatsu tōkei nempō '80* (People's Livelihood Statistical Yearbook, 1980) (Tokyo: Shiseidô, 1980), p. 57.

31. Margaret A. McKean, *Environmental Protest and Citizen Politics in Japan* (Berkeley and Los Angeles: University of California Press, 1981).

32. John Creighton Campbell, "The Old People Boom and Japanese Policymaking," *Journal of Japanese Studies* 5 (Summer 1979): 321–57.

33. Ishizaki, *Nihon no shotoku to tomi no bumpai*, pp. 125–43. Japan's transfer programs might not seem so perverse if we could separate true transfers from

other government programs. The Ministry of Health and Welfare changed accounting procedures in 1978, and better data may soon permit more appropriate international comparisons on this point.

34. Ishizaki, *Nihon no shotoku to tomi no bumpai*, tables 56 and 57.

35. Lange and Garret, "The Politics of Growth."

36. Joji Watanuki, *Politics in Postwar Japanese Society* (Tokyo: University of Tokyo Press, 1977).

37. Hans H. Baerwald, *Japan's Parliament: An Introduction* (London: Cambridge University Press, 1974), pp. 103–20.

38. Rob Steven, *Classes in Contemporary Japan* (Cambridge: Cambridge University Press, 1983).

39. Ikuo Kabashima, "Supportive Participation with Economic Growth," *World Politics* 36 (April 1984): 309–38.

40. Ibid.

41. Ellis S. Krauss, "Conflict in the Diet: Toward Conflict Management in Parliamentary Politics," in Krauss, Rohlen, and Steinhoff, *Conflict in Japan*, pp. 243–93.

42. T. J. Pempel, *Policy and Politics in Japan: Creative Conservatism* (Philadelphia: Temple University Press, 1982), pp. 255–71.

43. Ibid.

44. Mancur Olson, *The Rise and Decline of Nations: Economic Growth, Stagflation, and Social Rigidities* (New Haven, Conn.: Yale University Press, 1982).

45. Suzanne Berger, "Politics and Antipolitics in Western Europe in the Seventies," *Daedalus* 108 (Winter 1979): 27–50.

10 Education

EDWARD BEAUCHAMP

A major problem in discussing education and democracy in Japan or, indeed, in any other country is one of definitions. Although providing a clear and rigorous definition of what is meant by democracy and democratic education is theoretically desirable, this approach often leads to other difficulties. For example, if democratic education is defined in terms of an idealized version of democracy, it becomes nothing more than a paradigm existing only in the minds of political theorists. Under these circumstances it is difficult to suggest that a system of democratic education can exist anywhere in the world. Perhaps democratic education, on the other hand, should be pragmatically evaluated as to how well it compares with the somewhat imperfect and different democratic systems found in places like the United States, England, or France. If a country's educational system contains both democratic as well as undemocratic elements (as many do), should it be classified as democratic or undemocratic? At what point does it become one or the other? Finally, we should recognize that democratic institutions can exist in a variety of configurations resulting from unique historical and cultural circumstances. Democratic institutions are not monolithic, and viable variations can be found in both decentralized and highly centralized societies, as well as in states on all but the extremes of the political spectrum.

In this essay, I assume only that the educational system in Japan, as in all other countries, to some extent reflects and to some extent creates the democratic and undemocratic aspects of the wider society and political system. One of the purposes of this essay, therefore, will be to

225

discuss how the accomplishments and problems of Japanese democracy and society impinge upon education, and another will be to show how education contributes to those strengths and weaknesses.

Two of the most important ways in which education and the wider society are connected is through *access* to education and through the *process* and *content* of education. Access to education in all modern societies is one of the prime means by which social and economic status is distributed in society and therefore is closely related to the problem of equality in democratic society. The process and content of education constitute some of the major means by which societies socialize their young to important shared values and behavior, including political values and behavior. What pupils learn, and how they learn, is therefore crucial for the kind of democratic citizens they will become as adults. This essay will focus on these problems of access and equality, and eduaction and democratic citizenship. In the course of the essay, it should become increasingly apparent that the Japanese, despite the many serious problems facing their educational system, have fundamentally solved the ancient contradiction between democratic access and the maintenance of world-class standards of quality of education.

Prewar Education

There is no doubt that the Occupation of Japan (1945–1952) was a watershed of gigantic proportions in modern Japanese history and that it triggered significant changes in that nation's life. It is important, however, to recognize that democratic elements in the educational system did not emerge only from the seven years of American Occupation. Indeed, despite the overwhelmingly authoritarian character of prewar Japanese education, one can discover some potentially democratic elements at least as early as the Meiji era (1868–1912) when Japan opened herself to the world and consciously set about learning from its more advanced nations, some of whom were themselves in various stages of democratic evolution.

The influence of these Western democracies on Japan was especially strong in the first dozen years of the Meiji period. Japan's new leaders realized that a modern educational system was an essential tool for transforming Japan from a weak, feudal state into a strong modern one. This is not to suggest that the Japanese oligarchs were motivated by democratic principles, but rather to point out that their actions served democratic ends by increasing literacy, expanding the number of people possessing at least a basic education and opening up people's minds to Western learning.

One of the most significant actions taken by the early Meiji authorities was the so-called imperial Charter Oath (1868) which laid down the aims of the new government and insisted that "knowledge shall be sought throughout the world." In response to this clarion call, many Japanese students journeyed, at government expense, to the United States and Western Europe to pursue their studies, and several thousand foreign experts, the so-called *oyatoi gaikokujin,* were brought to Japan to teach, to advise the government, and to promote Japan's rapid development in a wide variety of fields.

Although usually hired to teach such "practical" subjects as science, technology, or English, it was not possible to restrict the foreigner's teaching to narrow channels. One of the earliest and most influential *yatoi,* William Elliot Griffis, for example, spent a year teaching science in the castle town of Fukui, deep in the interior of Japan, and found that some of his most exciting teaching was done during informal evening gatherings in his home with several of his students and local townsmen anxious to learn not only about science and manufactures, but also about life in the United States, its religion, history, and constitution. Griffis' experience was not unusual; other *yatoi* recount similar experiences. Many of his students went on to become political, business, and academic leaders, and it seems reasonable to suggest that Griffis' informal teaching had an influence on at least some of them.

A large percentage of the foreign educators were Americans, many of whom urged their employers to design Japan's new educational system on the American model. In fact, Americans held many responsible positions, including Professor David Murray of Rutgers who served as Japan's National Superintendent of Education (1873–1878), and Marion Scott who established the first teacher training institution in Tokyo in 1872. French and German influences were also present in the creation of Japan's education system, and at least some of them were not hostile to democratic education.

The school system was highly differentiated with elementary school being the common experience providing both a general education and a moral education for all. The amount and kind of education a youngster received after completing elementary school was based on the needs of the state. Admission to post-elementary schools, especially those leading to higher education, was extremely selective and usually based in large measure upon entrance examinations. Although girls as well as boys received the benefits of compulsory education (ultimately extended to six years), public secondary schools catered primarily to boys. The women who went on to secondary and higher education did so mostly at private schools.

From about 1880 a conservative reaction to the earlier liberal decade emerged, and authoritarianism clearly became the dominant characteristic of prewar Japanese education. The educational system became highly centralized, unabashedly elitist, and strongly state-centered. Ideologically the system was driven by Confucian principles, especially the version propounded by the followers of Chu Hsi (1130–1200) and expressed most eloquently in the 1890 Imperial Rescript on Education which, until 1945, was the guiding document for Japanese education. This rescript emphasized the five human relationships considered necessary by Confucians for a good society: loyalty to the emperor (as a symbol of the state), filial piety, affection among siblings, harmony between husband and wife, and trust among friends. Chu Hsi's thought was congenial to Japan's conservative leadership in that it emphasized the need for unswerving loyalty to the state and one's superiors. The educational philosophy expressed in the Imperial Rescript, and the required moral education courses, was hostile to democratic education. It was expected that the individual submerge himself in service to the emperor as symbol of the state.

There is little doubt that Japanese schools generally succeeded in inculcating loyalty, obedience and the technical skills needed to produce efficient workers and loyal, unquestioning citizens. Thus, it is also likely that the educational system established and developed after the 1880s contributed greatly to creating a Japanese public eventually susceptible to the ultranationalism and authoritarianism of the military, once it took power it the 1930s.

The prewar educational system, therefore, presents a mixed picture. In terms of access to education, prewar Japan was in many ways remarkable. Educational opportunity was relatively widespread, especially compared to many European democracies of that era. A universal compulsory education system was quickly developed, leading to almost universal literacy by the turn of the century. Males at least could advance to secondary and higher education based on ability, and there were some private schools and other facilities for women. Financial support for students, and tuition-free education in the case of teacher-training normal schools, decreased the cost of education for many. Upward mobility through education, therefore, was probably greater in Japan than in many other industrialized nations by the first quarter of the twentieth century. By providing universal access to primary education, creating basic literacy, and exposing some Japanese at highter educational levels to rational, secular knowledge, the system contained elements which, if not automatically democratic, nonetheless provided the potential for positive integration with a democratic system after the war.

On the other hand, the system itself was thoroughly undemocratic in its goals (to serve the state), its processes (hierarchical, authoritarian, and centralized), and its content (a curriculum guided by an emperor-centered and nationalist ideology). Ironically, the combination of relative equality in distribution but undemocratic process and content of education probably contributed to nondemocratic politics in prewar Japan. The imperial state ideology was broadly disseminated, and support for the elite inculcated, to a significant extent through a broad-based educational system.

The American Occupation and Education

Almost fifteen years of unbridled military rule at home and aggression overseas culminated in Japan's unconditional surrender following the atomic horrors of Hiroshima and Nagasaki. The experience of the 1930s and the 1940s left Japan devastated physically and spiritually, and the nation searched for an organizing principle that would offer hope for the future.

One of the primary goals of postwar American policy was the democratization of Japan, and democratic education was believed to be vital in this quest. Before Japan could be democratized, however, the American policymakers believed that it was necessary to dismantle those elements of the existing Japanese educational system which were antidemocratic or militaristic in nature, and to replace them with components that would foster the desired democratic tendencies. These initial steps were, of necessity, negative ones—the clearing away of the old to make way for the new.

Democracy Imposed: Occupation Reforms

The negative period consisted of two separate but related stages. One was the steps taken by the Japanese themselves. Even before the

Occupation authorities made any demands upon it, the Ministry of Education abolished the old Wartime Education Law, and on September 15, 1945, promulgated a new "Educational Policy Towards Construction of a New Japan." Although "democracy" was not specifically mentioned, the general thrust of this policy was clearly toward the elimination of militarism and its replacement with a democratic educational system. It is significant that the Japanese not only anticipated the overall direction of American educational policy, but also made an early effort to accommodate themselves to it.

The Americans followed through with the second stage by issuing four basic directives in the autumn and early winter of 1945. These directives cleared away much of the foundation of prewar Japanese education by purging teachers with "militaristic and nationalistic" tendencies, abolished state supported Shinto, and suspended all courses in moral education, history, and geography. These actions essentially completed the negative phase of educational reform and forced American authorities to think seriously about what the new structure they were committed to build would look like. Fortunately, presurrender planning for the Occupation had begun in 1943 and was based on several assumptions which were particularly relevant for the reform of Japanese education. The United States, for example, did not envision the destruction of Japan's cultural heritage and the imposition of American values and institutions. American planners, in fact, believed that rather than destroying Japanese culture, they could "use it, as far as possible, in establishing new attitudes of mind conforming to the basic principles of democracy and fair-dealing." In addition, these same planners assumed that a peaceful postwar Japan "presupposed the existence of those in the country who would be predisposed to accept the [liberal American] vision and carry out the task of reconstruction along liberal lines."[1]

One of the first steps taken by the relatively inexperienced Americans put in charge of reforming Japanese education, most of whom were not professional educators, was to request that a high-level educational mission be sent to Japan to provide advice and, perhaps more important, a legitimation of their plans for reform. A twenty-seven-member mission under the chairmanship of Dr. George Stoddard (former New York State commissioner of education and president-elect of the University of Illinois) arrived in Japan in March 1946. Consisting primarily of school administrators and education professors, the First United States Education Mission to Japan (USEMJ) can be fairly described as representing the mainstream of American progressive educational thought, but it had virtually no knowledge of either Japan of Japanese education. The report which it issued, under the imprimatur of General Douglas MacArthur, was widely viewed as a blueprint for reforming Japan's education. Both its tone and recommendations faithfully articulated the fundamental tenets of America's notion of democratic education. Given the composition of the USEMJ, and the brief time it spent in Japan, this document with its stress on decentralization, demilitarization, and democratization could have been written in New York, Chicago, or San Francisco with less trouble and expense.

Decentralization was viewed by the mission, as well as by the Civil Information and Education Section of MacArthur's headquarters (CI&E), as the key to reforming Japanese education along democratic lines. The centralized power of the ministry of education was, in the mission's words, "the seat of power for those who controlled the minds of Japan." After all, local control of American schools had kept them "close to the people" and out of the hands of the machinations of national government. The Americans, however, failed to consider that their decentralized system was an organic outgrowth of an enormous geographical expanse and the "rugged individualism" which flourished on the frontier. Japan was a small, heavily populated island nation which placed great emphasis on cooperation and harmony. Throughout their modern history the Japanese had had a centralized educational system that reflected the belief that education's function was clearly one of serving the needs of the state, not to fulfill the potential of the individual.

To achieve decentralization, the USEMJ strongly urged that the role of the Ministry of Education be reduced from a controlling organ to one providing only advice and assistance to local educational entities. Although abolishing the Ministry of Education had been seriously considered, the combination of the ministry's political influence and the need of the Occupation authorities to use the ministry's administrative skills to implement Occupation policy made this option impractical.

Given the assumptions inherent in the argument for decentralization, the next logical step was to enhance local decision making by advocating locally elected school boards. In 1948, the required legislation was put in place. It was a very controversial experiment from the outset and did not last long. Four years after the end of the Occupation, the Local Education Administration Act was passed which eliminated the popular election of school board members and their power over the educational budget.

Among its other major recommendations the 1948 legislation urged curriculum and methods of education be expanded beyond the old pattern of a single textbook and teacher's manual. Moreover, it proposed that individualization according to student needs and abilities be instituted, that the content and approach of moral education be overhauled and no longer treated as a separate subject in the curriculum, that a 6-3-3 system be installed and compulsory schooling be extended to nine years, that normal schools be transformed into four-year institutions to better prepare teachers in content and democratic pedagogy, that the educational opportunities of women be expanded, and that guidance be stressed in the schools. For good or ill, all these recommendations spoke to a faith in dominant American educational theory and practice, and almost all were to be adopted by the men and women of the CI&E and eventually imposed.

Meanwhile, the legal foundation of educational reform was being constructed. After much discussion a new constitution came into effect on May 3, 1947. Unlike the American constitution, which fails to mention education, the Japanese document specifically states that "all people shall have the right to receive an equal education correspondent to their ability, as provided by law. All people shall be obliged to have all boys and girls under their protection receive ordinary education as provided by law. Such compulsory education shall be free."

In the spring of 1947 the Diet passed two basic pieces of educational legislation, the School Education Law and the Fundamental Law of Education, which effectively codified the Occupation's educational reforms and set Japan's schools on a democratic course. The former set down detailed administrative regulations, from kindergarten through university education, while the latter was a bold policy statement articulating democratic objectives. "Having established the Constitution of Japan, we have shown our resolution to contribute to the peace of the world and the welfare of humanity by building a democratic and cultural state. The realization of this ideal shall depend fundamentally on the power of education." The several provisions of this law called for the full development of personality, respect for academic freedom, equality of educational opportunity for all without discrimination of any kind, coeducation at all levels, education for citizenship, and the separation of church and state.

When American control was withdrawn in the spring of 1952, the educational reformers had succeeded in clearing away the old undemocratic structures, replacing them with ones more to their liking; they had replaced those individuals identified as ultranationalists or militarists with Japanese who seemed committed to democratic values; they had provided Japanese educators with new curricula, textbooks, and methodologies. In short, they had given their best effort and now, as they withdrew to the sideline, they could only hope that their best effort had been enough.

Democracy Revised: The "Reverse Course"

It should not be surprising that with the return of sovereignty in 1952, the Japanese began a careful examination of the reforms of the previous seven years and modified or changed those things which they believed were not in harmony with the nation's political and cultural traditions. Education did not escape this scrutiny, and by 1956 the government had, for all intents and purposes, scrapped the American-imposed school board system and allowed the Ministry of Education to regain control over the educational system, particularly in the areas of administration, curriculum, and textbook selection.

These changes did not, however, signal a rejection of democracy as a concept and a return to "the bad old days." If the Japanese were to have democracy, they were determined to have a variant that was consistent with their traditions and culture. The Japanese penchant for centralization reasserted itself, but this was not necessarily undemocratic. Local control over education, as the study of American education amply demonstrates, can result in a greater sensitivity to the needs of the area, but can also lead to racial discrimination, religious bigotry, textbook censorship, and other undemocratic acts. One can also argue, and many Japanese did, that a centralized system ensured that every child—from Okinawa to Hokkaidō—enjoyed "equality of educational opportunity" because of the relatively equal physical facilities throughout the country, a uniform curriculum administered by the Ministry of Education, equal access to the same textbooks, teachers of relatively equal competence, and a uniform set of national standards.

Postwar Education: Access

Three decades after the United States relinquished its authority over Japanese life, the results of American efforts to democratize

Japanese education are more clearly visible. There is no question that democratic education exists in contemporary Japan, but it exists in a form quite different from the the model that the United States advocated in the postwar years. In examining its structure, one finds elements that resemble those found in European as well as in American education. This pattern is not unlike that found in Meiji and prewar Japan in which aspects of French, German, English, and American systems were part of a mosaic uniquely Japanese.

A careful examination of several key elements found in any definition of democratic education provides a measure of the fundamental health of Japan's system in terms of access to education and standards of quality. There can be little doubt that postwar Japan has made enormous strides in providing expanded educational opportunities for its young people. In the thirty-five years between the end of World War II and 1980, the number of students attending school in Japan increased by over 80 percent, from 15 million to over 27 million. Virtually all young people now complete the nine years of compulsory education (99.98 percent in 1980), and an impressive 94.2 percent of these graduates go on to the noncompulsory senior secondary school. Perhaps most significantly, the Japanese have demonstrated that mass education does not have to be purchased with diluted standards. Time and time again, international achievement tests have placed the Japanese at, or close to, the top in a variety of subjects. Furthermore, in 1980, 37.4 percent of the senior high school graduates attended some kind of institution of higher education.

The Examination System

Japan's remarkable achievement of accessible, high quality education has not been without its problems and costs. One of the most widely criticized elements of Japanese education is the examination system which not only determines one's educational future, but also one's lifetime career opportunities. Ezra Vogel has commented that "no single event, with the possible exception of marriage, determines the course of a young man's life as much as entrance examinations, and nothing, including marriage, requires as many years of planning and hard work."[2]

Japan is an intensely education-oriented society, and graduation from a university is a prerequisite to success in that society. This, however, tells only part of the story, for university graduation is not enough—the real test is found in the question, "From *which* university did you graduate?" Japanese universities are ranked according to prestige and, while this element is found in other countries, the fine gradations between universities, faculties within universities, and professors studied under is often difficult for outsiders to comprehend. If viewed as a pyramid, the apex of Japanese higher education is firmly occupied by the University of Tokyo, and the most prestigious faculty within that institution is its Faculty of Law (in Japan a combination of political science and public administration). Just beneath Tokyo are a handful of other former imperial universities such as Kyoto, and Kyūshū, closely followed by a gaggle of prestigious private universities such as Keiō and Waseda. The broad base of the pyramid contains hundreds of other institutions, most of which are perceived as second or third rate.

In nearly all Japanese universities success on the entrance examination is, if not the sole criterion, by far the most important one for admission. Those who are able to pass the examination for a prestigious university, preferably Tokyo, can look forward to an assured future, because once the student enters the university, completion of the degree is virtually automatic. Competition for the best universities is, in a word, fierce. It is not uncommon for only one of every fifteen or twenty applicants to be admitted to the best schools. This statistic takes on added meaning when one realizes that only the best students are encouraged by their teachers to aim this high. In other words, a preselected elite take the Tokyo University examination and only a small minority can expect to pass it.

Getting on the escalator to career success is, therefore, dependent upon passing the entrance examination to one of a handful of elite schools. This results not only in high school education being distorted by an undue emphasis on passing examinations, but also in lower education being distorted by these pressures. An important consequence of this preoccupation with passing exminations is a lack of emphasis on creativity or the noncognitive aspects of education. Students desiring to compete in the university examination war know that they must start preparing by the lower secondary level or earlier. It is not uncommon to find weary youngsters riding home on the subway or commuter trains at 10 P.M. after having attended supplementary lessons from late afternoon. Parents, notably, the *kyōiku mama* or "education mama," work very hard to help their children pass entrance examinations, even for preschools or kindergarten. There are many bizarre, but often true stories about the sorting process at this level. For example, one preschool was unable to devise a suitable entrance test for two-year-olds and after much discussion decided that, under the circumstances, they could best determine the children's ability by testing the mothers instead!

This distortion of lower education is also reflected at the high school level. Since the reputation of a school and its teachers is, in large measure, dependent upon the number of its students who go on to prestigious universities, it is not uncommon for teachers to spend a great deal of time drilling their students to pass examinations. Junior high school teachers, taking their cue from the higher level, often become similarly absorbed, and it is not unheard of for some primary school teachers to conduct mock examinations to accustom their charges to the reality of the system.

At least from junior high school, ambitious students are committed to extra study, extra texts, and practice examinations which will rule their lives until they either succeed or admit failure in the university examination competition. Assisting students to prepare for examinations is big business. A visit to virtually any large bookstore in a Japanese city illustrates both the centrality of entrance examinations to student life and the vast profits being made by entrepreneurs. These bookstores are filled with students of all ages. They flock to the shelves appropriate to their interests where they discover books and pamphlets on techniques to help them pass the ubiquitous examinations. Shelves are conspicuously marked with signs such as "For Secondary Entrance Preparation." Provocative titles include *The Complete Study Guide for Passing University Entrance Examinations,* or *English Vocabulary Most Likely to Appear on the Entrance Examination,* and so on. Pamphlets containing past examinations and sample questions fill the shelves.

A few years ago a government *White Paper on School Children and Youth* linked examination pressures with personality changes in children, pointing out that because study takes up virtually all of a youngster's waking hours little time is left for play. As a result, children do not have sufficient opportunity for socializing. The report complained that "gregariousness which used to be a hallmark of school children can no longer be taken for granted." Related to this are increasing reports of health problems in youngsters that are attributable to examination pressures.

Another problem related to the examination system, challenged by some researchers, is the widely perceived causal relationship between examination pressures and teenage suicide. No one doubts,

however, the so-called *rōnin* phenomenon. This term, which originally referred to the "masterless samurai" of feudal days, is now used
to describe students who, having failed to pass the entrance examination to the school of their choice, spend an extra year (and sometimes
much longer) studying to pass the examination. Thus, today's *rōnin*
are "students without a university." In at least one important sense,
Japan's entrance examination system is eminently democratic. Success on these examinations is based on merit, that is, one can succeed
regardless of one's station in life so long as one has the basic intelligence and is willing to work as hard as necessary to master the material that appears on the examinations. Perhaps most important, the
cost of attending the most elite national universities—which are supported by the state—is only a fraction of the tuition of third-rate
private universities. This fact takes on great significance when we
reflect that in the United States the best universities are generally
perceived to be expensive private institutions. In Japan most people
feel that the best education is obtained in the public sector.

One cannot argue, however, that there is no correlation between
success on the examinations and one's social and economic circumstances. As elsewhere, the child from a middle-class home will not
only have greater resources enabling him to attend supplementary
schools, benefit from private lessons, and purchase learning aids, but
also will be the recipient of a much richer cultural experience.

Despite a good if somewhat flawed access record, an increasing
number of scholars are recognizing that a significant area of inequality
in Japanese education is represented by the fact that approximately 75
percent of students attending four-year institutions are in the expensive
private sector. Therefore, although access to relatively inexpensive
national universities is reasonably democratic, the access problem is
much more complicated. In the past several years the children of the
affluent have begun to dominate entry to the public institutions at a
significantly greater rate than two decades ago, and poorer families find
it increasingly difficult to pay the higher costs of private education. In
addition, unlike the United States and other industrial nations, the
Japanese government has not recognized the need to provide financial
aid to deserving students, making their plight even more difficult.

Women

Prior to 1945, Japanese females had very limited access to advanced education. The secondary education alternatives that were

available to them heavily favored domestic education, while university preparatory schools were a male preserve. Today, however, things have changed for the better: girls outnumber boys by 94.5 to 93.1 percent at the senior high school, and one out of every three female graduate advances to some form of higher education. It should be pointed out, however, that the vast majority of these women graduates enroll in junior colleges and most of those who go on to four-year colleges major in fields such as English literature.

While teaching in International Christian University and Keio University in the mid-1970s, I was impressed by the contrast between the numbers of female students attending ICU, a good university, and Keiō, which is among the most prestigious in Japan. It was striking that a seemingly high percentage of the ICU women, daughters of international businessmen and diplomats, had received much of their secondary education in North America, Europe, or Australia, while the few Keiō women had spent their lives in Japan. Upon being asked why they chose ICU rather than applying for more prestigious universities, it was clear that unless one not only attended a rigorous Japanese high school, but also attended so-called cram schools and supplementary schools, there was little chance of passing the requisite entrance examinations to the elite schools. ICU, of course, places much importance on its entrance examination, but also takes into consideration a variety of other factors in making admission decisions.

A second reason, mentioned almost as often by ICU female students, suggests that despite thirty years of democratic education, there still exists a widespread ingrained prejucice against women. It is rare in Japan for a young man to marry a woman graduate of a more prestigious university than the one he attended. Therefore, a young woman graduating from Tokyo University has in effect significantly narrowed her pool of eligible suitors. The other side to this coin, in the ICU case, is its well-deserved reputation for effectively teaching English to Japanese students, and Japanese to foreigners. A female graduate of ICU is, therefore, presumed to have a high level of English-language ability, is accustomed to dealing with foreigners and, therefore, is an attractive potential wife to ambitious young male graduates of elite universities planning careers in international business, diplomacy, or any field in which such an internationally oriented wife is an asset. Educational decisions are still made in the 1980s on such assumptions.

Another example of the widespread attitude toward the education of women is seen in a recent policy implemented by the Kyoto Pharmaceutical University which announced in late 1983 that it would give preferential treatment to *male* applicants for admission. As the number of young men successfully passing the entrance examination declined over the past several years, more women were accepted. School officials felt threatened by what they called the "feminization" of their institution and sought to reverse this trend. Their justification, according to the school's officials, was that Japanese companies overwhelmingly prefer to hire men and that the university saw no point in producing graduates who will not be hired by industry. It is clear that although Japanese women have made important educational progress since the end of World War II, they still have a long way to go to catch up with their brothers.

The important point, however, is that the political process does allow for change to occur within the system. Several examples of this process can be seen in the contemporary media. Japanese families have forced the Ministry of Education to set up a commission to study whether the present regulation making home economics a required secondary school course for girls should be retained, modified, or abolished. In another case, women and teachers' groups are agitating for the elimination of what they consider sexist biases in a number of widely used textbooks. Although change occurs slowly, it does occur. One can present many examples of educational discrimination against Japanese women, but viewing their situation in the broad historical sweep since 1945, it is difficult not to be impressed with the progress made.

Minority Groups

One of the most widely known facts about Japan is that its population is an unusually homogeneous one. On the other hand, relatively few non-Japanese are aware that this homogeneous population contains several relatively small, but significant minority groups, including approximately 3,000,000 former outcastes called Burakumin, more than 1,000,000 Okinawans, and close to a million indigenous Ainu, Koreans, Chinese, *hibakusha* (atomic bomb victims), *konketsuji* (offspring of interracial parents), Indochinese refugees, Southeast Asian "entertainers," and resident foreigners (including several thousand Americans and Europeans). This essay will not deal with this wide range of peoples because of space constraints, but will concentrate on the Burakumin and Korean minorities.

The Burakumin, literally "hamlet people" because they lived in *tokushu buraku,* specially designated hamlets, are descendants of the outcasts of Tokugawa Japan (1603–1868). They are the largest minority group in Japan and are heavily concentrated in the west, with more than half found in the western parts of the main island of Honshū (Kinki and Chūgoku regions). Legally emancipated in 1871, the Burakumin made no significant educational gains until their agitation for governmental attention succeeded in 1969 with the passage of the "Law of Special Actions" for Dōwa Policy, which provided a legal framework for actions promoting the welfare of Burakumin. Although it contained no specific educational provisions, it did require that both national and local officials identify Burakumin educational problems and take the necessary steps to solve them. In the same year the government announced a Long-term Dōwa (Integration) Policy Program effective to March 1979, later extended to March 1982. Upon expiration, this law was replaced, after much debate, by the compromise Area Improvement Measures Law, valid for five years.

The results of these actions have been mixed. On the one hand, whereas only about 30 percent of Burakumin children attended senior high school in 1963 (compared to 64 percent of non-Burakumin children), studies by Nobuo Shimahara of Rutgers University conclude that the situation has significantly improved. The current national high school enrollment is about 95 percent and Shimahara suggests that "the difference in high school enrollment between the eligible minority and majority populations has narrowed to less than 10 percentage points." In fact, Shimahara provides evidence suggesting that important gains have also been made by Burakumin at the college level. He is careful to point out, however, that "there is still a significant difference between Burakumin and majority youths in educational attainment at the postsecondary level," although the gap has diminished somewhat.[3]

Another Japanese student of the Burakumin educational problems, Fumiko Okamura-Bichard, contends that although attending senior high school in increasing numbers, Burakumin youngsters are "deprived of equal *opportunites* within school, requiring compensatory measures."[4] For example, in a country of virtually universal literacy, the rate among Burakumin is only 80 percent. Indeed, the dropout rate for Burakumin students ranged from a high of 5.4 percent in Okayama Prefecture to only 1.6 percent in Nagano Prefecture. Among majority students the *highest* dropout rate was 2.7 percent, in Kōchi.

Japanese reactions to this minority problem vary. Some recognize the need for social justice, others see such demands as a sign of deleterious social change. The majority are disinterested because it has no direct impact on their day-to-day lives. The Burakumin and their supporters have tried mightily to educate the broader public to the problem, but their success has so far been limited. For example, the director of the Justice Bureau, in 1982, was quoted as telling a group of local government officals that "the rather unsavory parallel has been drawn . . . that public servants are as much a fact of life as the Tokushu Buraku. But public servants are, after all, just human beings." It is attitudes of this sort, not only among government officials who should know better, that need to be changed if Burakumin are to overcome their historic disability.

Another group that has traditionally faced discrimination is Japan's approximately 700,000 Korean residents. In discussing the problems of Koreans in Japan, Thomas Rohlen concludes that "it is not a question of barriers existing within the school system itself," but rather obstacles which spring up when Koreans "seek employment in the Japanese labor market."[5] That a Korean problem exists in the school system is, however, widely recognized. There have even been some efforts, in cities with large Korean populations, to inject into the public schools what one might call "ethnic studies" for Korean students.

Although Japanese education is highly centralized, especially by American standards, it is wrong to assume that there is no differentiation among schools. Not all Japanese school boards are the same. For example, Kobe, a city with historic foreign ties and controlled by political progressives, has confronted its discrimination problem. The school board has published various antidiscrimination materials for use in both junior and senior high schools in an attempt to deal with discriminatory attitudes toward both Burakumin and Koreans. Although not entirely successful, because many teachers feel uncomfortable discussing such issues, this is an approach that may lend itself to long-term improvements in the situation.

On the other hand, as in the case of the Burakumin, anti-Korean prejudice is often deep-seated. Some Japanese parents will change their residence or send their children to private schools in order to avoid having them attend school with Korean youngsters. The irony is that these young Koreans have usually been born in Japan, speak Japanese as their native tongue, and have taken on Japanese cultural patterns. Many have even gone to the extreme of hiding their Korean roots by using a Japanese name. Some Koreans, however, remain wedded to their Korean heritage. In September 1983 there was a heated public controversy over an alleged attempt of school officials in Nagoya to pressure Korean parents into enrolling their son under a Japanese name. The school officials claimed that they "suggested" this to the parents for educational reasons, that is, the child was apt to be teased by his classmates because of his "strange" name. Korean organizations and other opponents of discrimination refused to accept this explanation and charged that it was reminiscent of the Japanese occupation of Korea when all Koreans were forced to adopt Japanese names.

Koreans, however, do have the option of sending their children to two sets of Korean schools in Japan, one subsidized by the government of North Korea and the other by South Korea. The major problem with attending a Korean school, however, is that their graduates are not allowed to take entrance examinations for the prestigious national or public colleges and universities. This is a contributing cause to the fact that, according to Rohlen, Koreans in Japan "have statistically half the average chance of going to a university." Despite this, however, Rohlen argues persuasively that there is "little evidence that the difference in outcome stems primarily from discrimination in the education and matriculation process itself."[6] This conclusion is scant comfort for Japanese educators because the Korean minority does have legitimate grievances which, if not satisfied, contain the potential for serious social discontent.

Democracy in the Schools: Process and Content

Access to education is only one part of the issue of democracy in education. Another important aspect is the role that schools play in educating pupils to democratic citizenship, that is, in performing the function of political socialization. Schools may influence beliefs and behavior in several ways, among the most important of which are (1) direct teaching about democracy and politics (that is, the intentional inculcation of beliefs and values); and (2) the authority structure and students' experience in the classroom (that is, providing models and training in democratic decisionmaking and participation).[7]

There is no doubt that democracy as a political doctrine to guide conduct is widely accepted by an overwhelming majority of Japanese youth. The reverse side of this, however, is a widespread acceptance of the thesis that the democratic creed is the only vehicle with which peace and prosperity can be secured. Thus, unlike many other countries, democratic education has a very strong orientation toward peace and world order. As Joseph Massey has concluded, "there is substantial and consistent evidence to indicate that democracy has become established in the attitude structure of young Japanese, and indeed of their elders as well, as the preferred system of government."[8]

The question arising from this is an important one. What caused this widespread faith in democracy among postwar generations? Certainly a large part of the answer can be found in the trauma of defeat in World War II (compounded by the nuclear conflagrations in Hiroshima and Nagasaki) and the subsequent East-West cold war. But the radically reformed postwar educational system is also at least partially responsible. Another significant cause, if one accepts the premise that the political orientation of the nation's teachers does make a difference in the ideological tenor of the classroom, is the emergence of the Japan Teachers Union (Nikkyōso).

One of the major results of the American Occupation of Japan was the creation of a strong teachers' union which, since its birth in the years following World War II, has consistently been politically to the left of center. Less interested than their American counterparts in bread-and-butter issues, the Japan Teachers Union is committed to a socialist model of an egalitarian society as part of a peaceful world order. Inculcating democratic values is, therefore, an important part of the union's ideological commitment.[9] If, indeed, an important part of what a child learns in school is a result of what educators refer to as the "hidden" or "latent" curriculum, then it seems not unreasonable to suggest that teacher attitudes and behaviors have exerted an important influence on the political socialization of young people.

During the "reverse course" of the 1950s the Japan Teachers' Union fiercely resisted the conservative politicians's efforts to undo the democratic educational reforms imposed by the Americans, and during the turbulent 1960s and 1970s, its members were in the forefront of opposition to the Vietnam War, Japanese rearmament, U.S.-Japan security arrangements, and so forth. One knowledgeable and perceptive student of Japanese education, William K. Cummings, in his valuable study of Japanese elementary education, has concluded that there is a close correlation between "the extent to which teachers of a school are unionized" and those schools where "egalitarian educational themes are paramount."[10]

Classroom atmosphere and teacher-student authority relations in
the postwar period also no longer resemble the stiff, rigid, and authoritarian conditions of the earlier period. Although teachers are
respected and clearly in charge, pupils interact relatively freely in an
informal and relaxed atmosphere. Ronald Dore, writing about his
observations of Japanese classrooms in the late 1950s, found an absence of inflexible discipline and widespread free expression by students. He concluded that "what was to be seen in these schools certainly did not suggest the educational system which one associates
with an authoritarian society."[11] This was reaffirmed by Benjamin
Duke in the 1960s when he concluded that "today the Japanese student has greater freedom than students in most countries," and they
"have little inhibition in asking questions, and usually in only some of
the classrooms of the older 'pre-war' teachers does one find an atmosphere of strict obedience."[12]

Perhaps the single most telling characteristic of Japanese teachers is
that they are not only democratic, but they are highly professional in
their approach to their work. The organization of Japanese schools,
with morning and weekly faculty meetings, biweekly research meetings, and quarterly public research seminars, provides strong incentives for teachers not only to systematically discuss classroom
problems with their colleagues, but to actually conduct important
educational research. While it is undoubtedly true that American
teachers also spend a substantial amount of time in faculty meetings,
it is the rare faculty meeting that goes beyong the principal's agenda.[13]
In addition, the concern of many Japanese teachers for their charges
goes far beyond the classroom. It is not uncommon to find teachers
checking up on their students in coffee shops, or spending time in
after-school club activities. More than a formal student-teacher relationship exists in the Japanese educational context; teachers are often
more like older brothers or sisters, as much concerned with the youngster's total development as with classroom performance.

Another important dimension of the democratic changes which
have taken place in postwar Japan is the dramatic increase in parental
and community involvement in school matters. Parent-Teacher Associations are common, but tend to leave pedagogical questions to the
principal and the teachers to address. Most schools have some type of
student government, usually with at least some autonomy, and many
homerooms are democratically organized. Ronald Dore believes that
"it seems safe to say that the products of postwar schools, as com-

pared to their fathers, are more like citizens than subjects, are better capable of forming public opinion . . . and are more certain of their right to hold and express such opinions."[14]

Furthermore, both in the classroom and outside it, the Japanese child is constantly embedded in a network of relationships with adults and peers that emphasize cooperation in a "community." This can best be illustrated through the experiences of my son when he attended a typical Japanese elementary school in the mid-1970s. From the very outset, it was clear that one of the major goals of his teacher was to create a "community" from the fifty children assigned to her second grade class. As a result several interesting things occured. Immediately an open line of communication with the home of each child was established through a class newsletter, a telephone tree, home visits by the teacher and so on. Group activities requiring cooperation and harmony were stressed over individual activities. A sense of belonging and loyalty to the class were encouraged in a myriad of ways. This group orientation may not be the typical American's idea of democracy, but it is very Japanese. The individual in Japan seeks self-fulfillment not as an autonomous individual, but as part of a group. This is not only true in the classroom, but also in the worlds of business, government, sports, and crime.

Stress on cooperative and harmonious behavior is also reflected in nonacademic activities. For example, most elementary schools do not have a cafeteria where the children eat lunch. Rather they eat their noon meal in their classroom *with* their teacher. The food is either prepared at the school or brought from a central location, and each class sends a delegation, complete with white aprons, face masks, and chef's hats, at a specified time, to pick up the food for their classmates. The youngsters then serve the food to each student. The teacher eats with the students to set an example of the correct way of eating and to ensure that things run smoothly. When lunch is completed the class cleans the classroom in preparation for the resumption of formal teaching.

The democratic lessons of this exercise are clear. The class is a group in which everyone shares the food and the work involved in getting it and cleaning up. The implicit lesson demonstrated is one of the dignity of labor and everybody's obligation to do their fair share for the good of the group. This principle is also carried out at other times during the year when teachers and students will embark on clean-up projects to improve the appearance of the school. This also serves to give both teacher and taught a sense of shared pride in their school.

The process of democratic education is, however, only one half of the picture. The content of democratic education, or what is taught about democratic education also needs to be examined. Social studies and moral education are the courses most relevant for inculcating democratic values and what follows is a summary of their content at the elementary, lower secondary, and upper secondary levels.

At the elementary level (grades 1–6) among the overall objectives of the social studies curriculum is the cultivation of "a fundamental awareness of being citizens in a democratic and peaceful nation and society." With this in mind, first graders are taught that the school's physical plant and equipment, as well as surrounding parks, are "owned jointly by the people." The second grader learns that all jobs in his community are important for the community's well-being and worthy of respect. By the third grade, students are taking "geography" with an emphasis on knowing their local area and community. Fifth graders are exposed to more sophisticated democratic concepts such as popular sovereignty, parliamentary and representative government, constitutional guarantees, and the like. The amount of time devoted to social studies begins in grade one with a modest 68 forty-five-minute class periods per year, increasing to 70 periods in grade two and jumping sharply to 105 class periods per year in grades three through six.[15]

Moral education at the elementary school is a constant 35 class periods per year from grades two through six, but only 34 class periods during grade one. The content of moral educaion classes is a far cry from prewar Japan when moral education was a synonym for unrestrained nationalistic propoganda. Today, moral education "is aimed at realizing a spirit of respect for human dignity . . . , endeavoring to create a culture that is rich in individuality and to develop a democratic society and state, training Japanese to be capable of contributing to a peaceful international society, and cultivating their morality as the foundation thereof."[16]

At the lower secondary level (grades 7–9) the social studies curriculum is designed to "develop basic qualities of a civic nature essential to the builders of a democratic and peaceful nation and society." At this level, geography, history, and civics are taught and, although there is democratic content in the former two subjects, the civics course is undoubtedly the single most important vehicle for transmitting democratic values. In this course, usually taught in grade nine, and meeting for 105 class periods per year, a wide variety of relevant topics are treated. These topics include "Respect for man and the constitution of Japan," "The individual and society," "Foreign trade and international cooperation," "Democracy and law," "International society and peace," and so forth.[17]

Moral education classes in the lower secondary school meet for 35 class periods per year in grades 7, 8, and 9 (private schools may substitute religious education for all or part of the moral education courses). The objectives of moral education at this level are identical with those postulated at the elementary level, and the content of the course, although its treatment is more sophisticated than that of the elementary schools, is not significantly different in its nature.[18]

The objectives for upper secondary (grades 10–12) social studies are basically similar to the lower levels, but reflect a greater complexity. The aim remains, however, to develop in the students the "qualities necessary as citizens which are essential for competent builders of a democratic and peaceful nation and society." At this level electives play a greater role than in the earlier years enabling students to choose from courses in contemporary society, Japanese history, world history, ethics, geography, or politics and economy. A student's choice of electives depends upon what kind of program he or she is pursuing in high school (general, vocational) and upon the student's future academic plans. In any event, the objectives and content of all of these possible electives reflect varying degrees of democratic content.[19]

How effective are these classes in instilling democratic values? Political socialization studies find it extremely difficult to separate out the various influences that form a young person's political identity, so it is impossible to say with any precision. Massey did find that Japanese students were very positively oriented toward the symbol of democracy and toward democratic institutions such as the diet and elections.[20] Classroom teaching probably helps to inculcate, or at least reinforces, these attitudes. On the other hand, Massey also found that Japanese school children, even in early grades, were extremely cynical about their national political leaders (much less so toward local leaders) when compared to children in other democratic countries. Whether these cynical attitudes toward politicians derive from school experiences or from the transmission of attitudes in the family or media is difficult to say. It is clear, however, that whatever contribution civics and social studies courses may make toward positive attitudes toward democratic institutions, they are not able to overcome or counteract an early developed cynicism toward politicians and political leaders.

Democratic Education: Recent Problems

Because education performs such a crucial function in modern society—the transmission of values and behavior to the young—educational systems everywhere are subject to constant pressures and problems, some of which are political. Japan is no exception, as some recent controversies show.

One of the universal problems afflicting Japanese education is the increasing bureaucratization of school administration. The enormity of the educational enterprise in Japan can be seen by the facts that there are almost half a million teachers at the primary level and another quarter million each at the middle and high school levels. The relative centralization of education in Japan also adds to bureaucratization: the largest ministry in the Japanese government is the Ministry of Education, employing over 132,000 persons. Even with this large staff, the number of pupils per class is relatively large, in 1983 averaging over thirty-three per class at the primary level and thirty-eight per class at the middle school level.[21] As a result, alienation of both students and teachers is not completely absent from Japanese education.

Despite the "community" aspects of Japanese education, increasing bureaucratization of the school system, alienation, and the fierce pressures for educational attainment through examinations have probably contributed to a recent phenomenon that has caused consternation in Japan: rising incidents of school violence. Police records indicate that incidents of school violence nearly doubled (1,292 to 2,125) in the five years between 1978 and 1983, with those involving violent attacks on teachers showing a nearly fivefold increase (from 191 to 929 cases) during the same time period.[22] Compared to some American urban school systems where violence is endemic, these figures may not seem too disturbing; but in the Japanese context, where education and teachers are so respected and harmonious social relations so valued, these trends have caused tremendous alarm and controversy.

Another recent issue reflecting problems in Japanese education explicitly involved questions of democratic control over educational content and Japan's relations in the international community. In Japan's centralized system, the Ministry of Education must still approve the limited range of textbooks used in the schools. The ministry thus may request authors to make changes in text content prior to approval. In one such case that became a major political issue, the ministry requested that a text describing the Japanese invasion of China in the late 1930s not use the word "invasion" (*shinryaku*) but rather the word "advance." This change was greatly criticized, both at home, where many are concerned about the tendency for the government to want to emphasize national pride in the curriculum, and abroad, where other Asian countries are still very sensitive to Japan's aggression in World War II. This issue caused a major diplomatic controversy with the People's Republic of China.

Conclusion

Japan's postwar record in democratic education is a good one, but by no means perfect. Japan shares the problems of most modern democratic nations of bureaucratization and alienation in the school system with consequent problems of maintaining feelings of purpose and value among teachers and students. Japan also has particular problems of excessive pressures for examination achievement and of preventing education from becoming a political football in the conflicts between left and right. Some problems of discrimination against women and minorities remain. Finally the high degree of centralization of the system, while providing uniform nationwide standards, creates issues of academic freedom, as the recent textbook controversy illustrates.

On the other hand, the successes of Japanese education are undeniable. The prewar authoritarian and ideological system has been thoroughly revamped, although retaining and expanding its relatively egalitarian access and meritocratic standards. Postwar education provides relatively easy access at most levels; it bases competition for the most elite schools not on the accident of birth but on merit; it provides experiences—academic and nonacademic—that reinforce basic democratic principles; it maintains world-class standards, and, for the most part, strives to strengthen democratic elements, but within the context of Japanese culture with its emphasis on educational achievement and "community" norms. It is clear, therefore, that the Japanese have considerably democratized postwar education and, in doing so, have socialized the younger generation to life in a democratic polity. If we set Japan's democratic education next to that of the United

States, England, West Germany, or Switzerland we will find that they have different contours, but contain a common core of democratic values. To have accomplished both relatively egalitarian access to basic education *and* the maintainance of very high academic standards in the context of providing training for democratic citizenship is no mean achievement.

NOTES

1. SWNCC, "Directive—Positive Policy for Re-Orientation of the Japanese," National Archives of the United States, Record Group 319, Records of the Army Staff, ABC 014, Japan (13 April 1944).

2. Ezra F. Vogel, *Japan's New Middle Class* (Berkeley and Los Angeles: University of California Press, 1963), p. 40.

3. Nobuo Shimahara, "Toward the Equality of a Japanese Minority: The Case of Burakumin," *Comparative Education* 20, 3 (1984): 347–48.

4. Fumiko Okamura-Bichard, "Promotion of Equality Through Education: The Cases of Japan's Burakumin and India's Scheduled Castes," paper presented at the 28th Annual Conference of the Comparative and International Education Society, Houston, Texas, March 24, 1984.

5. Thomas P. Rohlen, *Japan's High Schools* (Berkeley and Los Angeles: University of California Press, 1983), p. 133.

6. Ibid.

7. For a discussion of the political socialization process and a case study of the family, school, and adult political socialization of Japanese student activists, see Ellis S. Krauss, *Japanese Radicals Revisted: Student Protest in Postwar Japan* (Berkeley and Los Angeles: University of California Press, 1974).

8. Joseph A. Massey, *Youth and Politics in Japan* (Lexington, Massachusetts: D. C. Heath, 1976), p. 68.

9. On the teachers' union see Donald R. Thurston, *Teachers and Politics in Japan* (Princeton, N.J.: Princeton University Press, 1973); Benjamin C. Duke, *Japan's Militant Teachers: A History of the Left-Wing Teachers Movement* (Honolulu: University of Hawaii Press, 1973).

10. William K. Cummings, *Education and Equality in Japan* (Princeton, N.J.: Princeton University Press, 1980), p. 107.

11. Ronald P. Dore, *City Life in Japan* (Berkeley and Los Angeles: University of California Press, 1958), p. 240.

12. Ben C. Duke, "American Education Reforms in Japan Twelve Years Later," *Harvard Educational Review* 34 (Fall 1964): 534.

13. Cummings, *Education and Equality in Japan,* p. 12.

14. Ronald P. Dore, "Education: Japan," in *Political Modernization in Japan and Turkey,* ed. Robert Ward and Dankwart Rustow (Princeton, N.J.: Princeton University Press, 1964), p. 198.

15. Ministry of Education, *Course of Study for Elementary Schools in Japan* (Tokyo: Ministry of Education, Science, and Culture, 1983), pp. 27–35.

16. Ibid., p. 111.

17. Ministry of Education, *Course of Study for Lower Secondary Schools in Japan* (Tokyo: Ministry of Education, Science, and Culture, 1983), pp. 14–34.

18. Ibid., pp. 121–25.

19. Ministry of Education, *Course of Study for Upper Secondary Schools in Japan* (Tokyo: Ministry of Education, Science, and Culture, 1983), pp. 23–39.

20. Massey, *Youth and Politics in Japan,* p. 185.

21. PHP Research Institute, *The Data File, 1984* (Tokyo: PHP Kenkyujo, 1984), pp. 346–50.

22. Ibid., p. 361.

Economic
Democracy

11 Corporate Power

GLEN S. FUKUSHIMA

> *Corporate discretion poses an increasingly serious threat to popular control as the business enterpise grows in size. The discretionary decision of a single large corporation. . . . can create or destroy a town, pollute the air for an entire city, upset the balance of payments between countries, and wipe out the livelihoods of thousands of employees.*
>
> —Charles E. Lindblom

Corporate power is central to any discussion of democracy in a capitalist state. To the extent that private ownership forms the basis of the economy, the influence of such private interests on the society and polity require careful examination in assessing the extent to which a state is "democratic." The purpose of this chapter is to examine the role of corporations (or "big business") and thereby to evaluate corporate power in Japan.

Most analyses of postwar Japanese politics indicate that a "triad" or "triumvirate" of actors rule the country: big business interests, politicians of the conservative Liberal Democratic party (LDP), and senior government bureaucrats. Many Japanese and some American scholars share one or more versions of this "elitist" view of Japanese politics. An oft-cited statement of this view is the following, attributed to a prominent Japanese politician: "The businessmen have influence over the politicians, the politicians control the bureaucracy, and the bureaucrats keep the businessmen in line. It's a natural system of checks and balances."[1]

Some observers have emphasized differences and conflicts among

255

these groups whereas others have described a harmonious consensus. In its extreme form, the latter opinion has led to the vision of a "Japan Incorporated," a cohesive and monolithic entity that acts in unison domestically and internationally. In this view, the bureaucracy, big business, and the ruling party always act cooperatively to advance the interests of big business, and all other actors have little or no influence in decision making. Some variants further portray acquiescent labor unions in Japan as indirectly making this system possible.

How true are these stereotypes of Japanese policymaking and the power of big business in Japanese government, politics, and society? To answer this question it is necessary to take an objective, realistic, and comprehensive approach to the role of big business in Japan. Only by such an approach can we evaluate the relationship between corporate power and democracy in contemporary Japan.

Historical Background

It is difficult to understand Japan's contemporary economy in general or the role of corporate power in particular without first examining the historical background that led to the present structure of the national economy.

Between the Meiji Restoration of 1868 and 1940, Japan's real national income grew over fifteen times. The last forty years in particular saw a real per annum growth rate of nearly 5 percent, an achievement unmatched by any other country. Although much attention in recent years has focused on the activities of private entrepreneurs, there is little question that the central government played a crucial role in promoting Japan's industrialization, especially in the early to mid-Meiji period. This led in part to the "dualism" which developed in Japan between the large bureaucratic capital-intensive firms which benefited from state sponsorship and the small private firms which did not.

Ronald Dore has argued that many of the differences between British and Japanese industry can be more generally understood as differences between early developers and late developers—as part of a general late capitalist development syndrome. Two of his generalizations are particularly relevant to the discussion of corporate power in Japan:

1. The later industrialization begins, the less likely . . . that it will be dominated by a laissez-faire philosophy, the more likely that the state will play a predominant role.

2. The later industrialization begins, the sharper the dualism between the big firm sector . . . and the small firm sector.

Both of these features can be seen in the prominent role played by *zaibatsu* ("money cliques," referring to family-owned financial and industrial conglomerates) in prewar Japan. The sale of most of the government's properties to private enterprise after 1880 reduced the size of the public sector, and subsequently the government's direct participation in the manufacturing industry by outright ownership was limited to a few enterprises. The four major *zaibatsu*—Mitsui, Mitsubishi, Sumitomo, and Yasuda—played a vital role in the economic rise of Japan, but their importance and influence extended to the political sphere as well.

Close connections were established between *zaibatsu* and government, and the *zaibatsu* acquired state properties at low prices and received valuable government contracts. The two top *zaibatsu* each established close ties to one of the two major political parties that developed in prewar Japan, the Seiyūkai and the Minseitō. Just as World War I saw an extension of their enterprises in heavy industry, the decade after that war saw a marked growth in their commercial and financial interests. By 1929 the *zaibatsu* had reached the zenith of their power and influence. Some *zaibatsu* leaders were even the target of radical right-wing ire and terrorist attacks, as they and their close relationship to political leaders were blamed for economic distress and political corruption.

With defeat in World War II, Japan's economy lay in ruins. The Occupation authorities at first took little interest in promoting the country's economic recovery. The twin goals of democratization and demilitarization were vigorously pursued, with particular attention given to the permanent destruction of Japan's capacity to wage war. After 1947, however, there was a shift to rebuild the economy in accordance with the onset of the cold war. By 1950 price stability had been restored and manufacturing production was not far short of the prewar level. With the outbreak of the Korean War in June 1950, industrial production shot up. By 1954 Japan was able to regain prewar per capita levels of productivity, national income, and personal consumption.

Before World War II the four largest *zaibatsu* controlled a fourth of all paid-in capital in Japanese industry and finance. The U.S. Occupation authorities carried out a *zaibatsu* dissolution program as part of their attempt to bring economic as well as political democracy to

Japan after the war. The family-owned trusts were broken up, and companies were converted to modern forms of public ownership companies with professional management. Antitrust laws were also established to prevent monopolies and reconcentration of ownership in the hands of a few families as in the prewar period. To this extent, the Occupation was successful in permanently destroying the *zaibatsu* in its prewar form.

The original Occupation goal of permanent decentralization of industry was somewhat less successful, however. The old *zaibatsu* companies subsequently regrouped in looser form through intercorporate stockholdings, ties to trading companies and *zaibatsu* successor banks, and regular "club" meetings among their executives. These informal links among Japanese businesses usually center around a major bank. These *keiretsu* ("affiliate") ties represent a cooperative, informal, conglomerate pattern rather than the hierarchical, formal, family trust pattern of the prewar *zaibatsu*. Nevertheless, they do represent a degree of reconcentration in postwar Japanese business. By 1960, the three leading *keiretsu* successors to the *zaibatsu* controlled 7.4 percent of the paid-in capital of all Japanese corporations if only firms with very close interrelations were counted, or 17.3 percent if firms with weak *keiretsu* links were included.

The 10.8 percent real growth rate of Japan's national income between 1946 and 1954 was rapid, although the rate was derived from the extremely low base of the early postwar years. But this growth continued: between 1954 and 1972, Japanese GNP measured in constant prices grew at an average rate of 10.1 percent, almost three times as fast as the growth of the U.S. economy for the same period. This was also the period in which Japan reentered the international economic system through joining such organizations as the United Nations, the International Monetary Fund, the World Bank, the Organization for Economic Development, and the General Agreement on Tariffs and Trade. The oil shock of 1973 brought an abrupt end to the era of double-digit real annual growth. But after two years of stagnation, real growth rates had recovered to a 5 to 6 percent per annum level.

Concentration Compared Internationally

Given the Occupation goals of decentralizing Japanese industry in order to promote economic democracy, how concentrated is the Japanese market today compared to that of other advanced industrialized societies? Given Japan's rapid rise to become the second largest capitalist economic power in the world, how big in comparative terms is "big business" in Japan? Table 1 provides some data for a preliminary assessment of economic concentration.

Japan's aggregate concentration appears lower than for the United States in all three categories (assets of the 100 largest manufacturing corporations, and sales of the 100 largest manufacturing corporations). The unavailability of comparable data makes direct cross-national comparisons with other countries difficult, but the figures suggest that Japan's aggregate concentration is comparatively low among the advanced industrialized countries.

Yet such simple comparisons can be misleading. Relying on some-

TABLE 1
International Comparison of Aggregate Concentration

Country	Concentration (%)
Japan (1980)	
100 Largest nonfinancial corporations Total assets	21.4
100 Largest manufacturing corporations Total assets	33.8
Sales	27.3
USA (1972)	
100 Largest nonfinancial corporations Total assets	30.7
100 Largest manufacturing corporations Total assets	49.0
Sales	41.0
UK (1972)	
100 Largest manufacturing corporations Net output	41.0
West Germany (1972)	
100 Largest nonfinancial corporations Sales	21.7
100 Largest manufacturing corporations Sales	45.4
France (1973)	
500 Largest manufacturing corporations Sales	26.0

SOURCE: Seno Akira, *Gendai Nihon no Sangyō Shūchū* (Tokyo: Nihon Keizai Shimbunsha, 1983).

what older data, the economist F. M. Scherer made the following analysis. The 100 largest manufacturers in Japan generated 29 percent of all manufacturers' sales in 1967, apparently less than the comparable U.S. figure of 33 percent. However, extensive affiliations among separately reporting Japanese firms (especially *keiretsu*) are not consolidated. When Scherer performed the appropriate consolidations, he found that the 100 largest nonfinancial corporations controlled 50 percent of all Japanese nonfinancial corporation assets in 1970. In the United States, the largest 660 nonfinancial corporations accounted for 54.6 percent of all nonfinancial corporation assets in 1972, leading Scherer to conclude that aggregate concentration is probably higher in Japan than in the United States.[2] Caves and Uekusa, the leading economists of comparative market structures in the United States and Japan, caution that it is "impossible to compare overall concentration in manufacturing" with precision because the Japanese data do not take account of affiliates.[3]

Another comparative measurement of industrial size is *Fortune*'s annual list of the world's largest industrial corporations. As table 2 indicates, Japan (with five firms) ranks third in the world after the United States and West Germany in the number of industrial firms in

TABLE 2
Location of Companies Ranked in the
World's Top Fifty Industrial Corporations,
1981 (by sales)

Country	Number of Companies
USA	21
West Germany	7
Japan	5
France	4
UK	3
Italy	2
Holland	1
Other	1

SOURCE: Seno Akira, *Gendai Nihon no Sangyō Shūchū* (Tokyo: Nihon Keizai Shimbunsha, 1983).

Note: Ranking based on consolidated financial statements including subsidiaries (if more than 50 percent shares held by parent company). Companies with two nationalities are included in "Other."

the top 50 based on total sales. However, it ranks second by a comfortable margin in the number of firms in the top 500 based on sales. Table 3 indicates the composition of the top 500, excluding the United States. Japan's 130 firms comprise 26 percent of the top 500, indicating that perhaps additional Japanese entries in the top fifty are forthcoming in the near future.

As one final quantitative measure of corporate size, let us examine some representative large firms in several major industries in the United States and Japan. As table 4 demonstrates, with the exception of the steel industry, where Nippon Steel has greater assets than U.S. Steel, the leading U.S. corporations are still considerably larger in scale than their Japanese counterparts.

Corporate Power and Social Life

Japan demonstrated a single-minded effort in the postwar years to recover economically and regain its place in the community of nations. With military revival prohibited by article 9 of the new constitution and by the postwar domestic and international environment, Japan was able to devote all of its resources to economic reconstruction. To a greater extent than in most Western countries, therefore, national attention has focused on business and economic activity. The Japanese themselves are the first to admit this; the economist Miyamoto Ken'ichi once labeled the United States a "military state," the United Kingdom a "welfare state," and Japan a "business enterprise state."[4] Let us exam-

TABLE 3
Location of the Five Hundred Largest
Industrial Corporations Outside the USA,
1981 (by sales)

Country	Number of Companies
Japan	130
UK	92
West Germany	58
France	38
Canada	33
Other	149

SOURCE: Seno Akira, *Gendai Nihon no Sangyō Shūchū* (Tokyo: Nihon Keizai Shimbunsha, 1983).

TABLE 4
Comparative Data on Large Firms in the USA and Japan, 1979

Industry	Profit Ratio of Total Liabilities and Net Worth	Sales Profit Ratio	Turnover Ratio of Total Liabilities and Net Worth	Ratio of Internal Reserves to Net Profit	Comparison of Assets
Steel					
Nippon Steel	3.14%	3.67%	0.85%	69.17%	1.00
U.S. Steel	2.54	2.12	1.20	146.93	0.72
Chemicals					
Mitsubishi	1.92	2.20	0.80	39.77	1.00
Dupont	11.25	7.16	1.48	55.48	2.50
Oil					
Nisseki	1.80	0.58	3.08	64.30	1.00
Exxon	9.75	5.31	1.84	58.07	9.91
Electrical equipment					
Hitachi	3.43	3.14	1.09	69.94	1.00
GE	9.07	6.40	1.42	54.63	2.23
Communications					
NEC	1.69	1.67	1.01	58.20	1.00
ITT	2.85	2.41	1.18	12.68	4.45
Computers					
Fujitsu	3.37	3.17	1.06	63.96	1.00
IBM	13.29	13.17	1.01	48.82	10.72
Automobiles					
Toyota	7.39	3.62	2.04	81.60	1.00
GM	9.27	4.36	2.12	47.00	4.87

SOURCE: MITI, *Sekai no Kigyō no Keiei Bunseki*, 1981.

ine, then, the role of corporations with reference to several dimensions of social life—employment, consumption, mass media, and education.

Corporations and Employment

Corporations play an important role as employers in Japan, but on an aggregate basis their coverage of the work force is lower than in many other advanced industrialized countries. This can be inferred from table 5. A major reason for the comparatively high figures in Japan for the "self-employed" and "family workers" categories is that 25 percent of the former and 40 percent of the latter are in primary industries such as agriculture, which still employed almost 10 percent of the work force as of 1982, a figure nearly double that in West Germany or Canada, and nearly triple that in the United States or Britain.[5] Another reason is the large proportion of Japanese employees who work for small and medium enterprises, and the large number of small "mom and pop" stores in Japanese urban areas.

Despite this somewhat lower percentage of the work force employed in business organizations, the presence of corporations is felt with perhaps greater intensity than in other countries. This is because for the average Japanese worker in a large enterprise, his corporation plays a central role in his life—providing not only a steady income and long-term job, but a primary source of peer group reference, of social ties for recreation, sports, and other extracompany activities. In addition, the facts that most labor unions are organized on the basis of

TABLE 5
Employment in Major Industrialized Countries, 1984 (in thousands)

	Japan	USA	UK	W. Ger.	France
Total workers	57,660	105,005	23,657	24,822	20,941
	(100.0)	(100.0)	(100.0)	(100.0)	(100.0)
Employed	42,650	95,120	21,162	21,540	17,574
	(74.0)	(90.6)	(89.5)	(86.8)	(83.9)
Self-employed	9,190	9,338	2,494	2,419	3,366[a]
	(15.9)	(8.9)	(10.5)	(9.7)	(16.1)
Family workers	5,820	548		863	
	(10.1)	(0.5)		(3.5)	

SOURCE: Yano Hisashi Kinenkai, ed., *Nihon kokusei zuei, 1988* (Tokyo: Kokuseisha, 1988), p. 93.

Note: Figures in parentheses are percentage of total workers.
a. Includes "Family workers" and "Self-employed."

enterprise rather than industry or trade and that workers in large enterprises tend to identify more with their corporate employer than with their profession tend to strengthen the sense of corporate affiliation. Japan's relatively low rate of labor unionization compared with Western European countries can be seen in table 6.

Whether one welcomes or abhors the all-encompassing nature of Japanese corporate employers is a subject of lively debate among foreign observers of Japan. On the one hand are the "learn from Japan" advocates who stress, mainly from a management perspective, the apparently harmonious, efficient, and loyal character of Japanese workers. On the other hand are those who point out the regimented, authoritarian, and harsh conditions in the workplace that confront Japanese employees and the "exploitive" nature of Japanese corporations.

Only a minority of Japanese workers are subject to the security and paternalistic benefits the large corporation confers. The vaunted "lifetime employment" system of Japanese companies applies primarily to employees of large corporations, not the numerous employees of small enterprises. The insecure life of the small enterprise employee, compared to his large enterprise counterpart, is graphically illustrated in Christena Turner's article in this volume (chap. 13). But not even all large enterprise employees are guaranteed "lifetime employment." It applies primarily to white-collar, permanent employees, less to blue-collar, and not at all to the many temporary and part-time employees of large enterprises or their affiliated small subcontractors. It is the latter, of whom a large percentage are women, who do not receive many of the company benefits and who may be laid off in hard economic times, thus giving the company labor force flexibility without disturbing the security of its permanent employees. "Lifetime" employment, even

TABLE 6
Unionization in Major Industrialized Countries

Country	Number of Union Members (thousands)	Unionization Rate (%)
Japan (1987)	12,272	27.6
USA (1985)	16,996	18.0
UK (1984)	11,086	52.0
W. Germany (1985)	9,081	40.8

SOURCE: Yano Hisashi Kinenkai, ed., *Nihon kokusei zuei, 1988* (Tokyo: Kokuseisha, 1988), p. 104.

for permanent employees only means until the age of fifty-five, which is the common retirement age in Japan.

We should note too the potential political abuses that can result from the large Japanese corporation's encompassing attitude toward its employees. The *Asahi,* a leading newspaper, featured a series on "corporate society" in July and August 1983. The lead article cited the following true story about the family of Mr. A, a "salaried man" (white-collar employee, comprising 77 percent of the male work force in 1981). Mr. A was a manager in a large corporation. On orders from his employer, Mr. A had five years earlier registered himself and his wife, without her knowledge, as members of the LDP. In November 1982 two envelopes were delivered to Mr. A's home mailbox containing ballots for the party primaries for prime minister. As instructed by his company, Mr. A sent his blank ballot to his company. Mrs. A told her husband that she would send in her ballot separately but did not do so. Several days later, Mr. A's boss called him into his office to ask why Mr. A's wife had not returned her blank ballot to insure that the family would not have to make "a move." She came to realize that sending her blank ballot to the company constituted a test of loyalty in the eyes of the company. She was quoted in the *Asahi* article as asking, "Is the wife of a salaried man not even allowed to have her own thoughts or opinions?"[6]

Nakamura Takatoshi cites this as an example of how corporations in Japan not only affect the economic well-being of their employees but intrude into even the psychological and ideological makeup of the society, demanding unquestioned loyalty not only by the employees themselves but by their family members as well.[7] Thus to the extent that corporate power is conceived in its broadest sense to include the penetration of an individual citizen's totality of values, orientations, and behavior, Japanese corporations appear to have the potential to wield considerable power indeed.[8]

Corporations and Consumers

Japan's high rate of economic growth in the postwar period has resulted in increases in incomes and purchasing power and the elevation of the quality of life for most consumers. Ownership of homes, automobiles, and electric appliances has equaled or surpassed that of Western industrialized countries. Innovations in technology, engineering, and produce application have been transformed into increased gadgetry and home conveniences for consumers.

At the same time, however, the power of consumers as a group has remained curiously weak. Except for certain points in the post-war period—most notably the late 1960s through the mid-1970s—consumers have had only limited impact on shaping the conduct of corporations. The late 1960s saw major uprisings by Japanese students, consumers, and other groups against established power in general. This was a period during which big business was under attack both domestically (for example, by victims of environmental pollution) and internationally (among others, by Southeast Asians protesting the invasion by "Ugly Japanese"). As the purely economic goals of postwar Japan were met, the nation was wracked by self-doubts about its sense of identity. The assistance given to the U.S. military effort in Vietnam by the Japanese business and government and their continued adherence to the U.S. anti–mainland China policy were additional targets of widespread protest in Japan.

The oil shock that hit Japan in 1973 saw a further excoriation of big business behavior. Most notable were the trading companies and oil companies, criticized for allegedly taking advantage of the panic that followed the shock to corner the market on certain paper and petroleum-related products. Among the most celebrated incidents to emerge from this were the Fair Trade Commission's investigation of trading companies and consumer group lawsuits against oil companies for price-fixing and production limitations.

Out of this critical phase of the mid-1970s emerged new restrictions on the activities of trading companies, courtroom victories by consumer and environmental protection groups, and a strengthened antimonopoly law. Some of these represented only partial victories, however. For instance, even though the Tokyo High Court in September 1980 ruled largely in favor of the consumer plaintiffs in the oil cartel case, and the Supreme Court of Japan upheld this ruling in February 1984, some women activists were forced to sever their involvement in similar cases in which consumer groups pursued legal remedies against corporate defendants. The pressures reportedly came from their husbands, who in turn had been "persuaded" by the corporations in which they were employed that their own future in the corporation might be jeopardized by such "antisocial" behavior by their spouses. Some of these women submitted to the pressures, whereas others obtained divorces in order to continue their activity.

As in the earlier case of forced LDP membership and submission to corporate demands of loyalty, here again corporations apparently intruded into the lives of employees and their families in a way that went far beyond what one might expect of an employer-employee relationship in Western societies. On the other hand, this concern (or meddling, depending on one's point of view) with an employee's private life appears to be expected by many Japanese workers. Public opinion polls taken on the subject every five years since 1953 indicate a consistently stronger preference by Japanese respondents for managers who involve themselves in the after-work life of their subordinates. The separation between one's work life and one's "private" life, including one's political views and activity, seems less strict in the "total community" context of Japanese large enterprise.

The revision and strengthening of the antimonopoly law in 1977 was a major achievement for those concerned about excessive corporate power in Japanese society. Yet this too did not lead directly to an increased role for consumers; it was instead a government agency, the Fair Trade Commission (FTC), that was strengthened. Although legal scholars and consumer activists had urged that the antitrust statutes be revised to allow for treble damage actions by private parties, as is allowed in the United States, this option was not pursued vigorously. Unlike the United States, where plaintiffs, acting as private attorneys-general can bring antitrust suits without first going through the Department of Justice or the Federal Trade Commission, in Japan the FTC must issue an initial determination before private plaintiffs can pursue such actions in court. This continues to be a significant difference between antitrust law in the United States and Japan and, according to legal scholars and attorneys, a major reason antitrust has not played a greater role in economic regulation in Japan.

Corporations and the Mass Media

The above consumer activities in the late 1960s through the mid-1970s were aided by the mass media, in particular such newspapers as the *Asahi* and *Mainichi*. The anti–big business "mood" of the period was in part reflected, and in part encouraged, by the proconsumer articles and editorials carried in these national newspapers. The pollution issue, antitrust revision, and incidents of corporate irresponsibility both at home and abroad were prominently reported by these newspapers and certain weekly and monthly magazines. Of the major dailies, the *Yomiuri* (with over 8 million circulation daily, the largest newspaper in Japan) and *Nihon Keizai* (the *Wall Street Journal* of Japan) tended to be less critical and more favorable to big business.

Differences existed within each newspaper. For instance, the political and economic news bureaus of the dailies tended, on the whole, to be more conservative and pro-business than the social news bureaus, staffed by reporters who were in some cases personally sympathetic to the goals and methods of the consumer activists and citizen protest leaders. And editorial writers tended to be more critical of the staus quo and establishment interests than the reporters actually in the field covering political or economic affairs on a day-to-day basis.

While certain mass media organs have at times been critical of corporate conduct, there is no denying that they themselves constitute big business. As such, they are careful not to go too far in criticizing representatives of big business, particularly of financial institutions, or of the political world. It is often pointed out, for instance, that Japan lacks a tradition of investigative journalism, at least within the establishment press, and that as a result such controversial stories as former Prime Minister Tanaka Kakuei's business activities and connections, and his involvement with the Lockheed scandal, were picked up by the major media organs only after they had been pursued and exposed elsewhere and given prominent play by the foreign media.

Although the mass media are generally not included within the triad of elite actors who are seen as ruling Japan, many Japanese politicians and bureaucrats consider the press to be a major influence in Japanese society. Furthermore, although part of the press may take a critical view of the Japanese conservative political elite, a delicate process of interaction and mutual influence exists between the mass media on the one hand and big business interests, government bureaucrats, and LDP politicians on the other. In particular, the close personal ties often established between Japanese journalists and their subjects encourage the development of symbiotic relationships. Thus in addition to their function as reporters of the news, journalists in Japan have sometimes performed the function of intermediaries or messengers between and among high-level decision makers.

Corporations and Education

The most obvious link between corporations and education is the use of universities as "sorting devices" to screen potential company recruits. The "examination hell" syndrome in Japanese education, described by Edward Beauchamp (see chap. 12), is closely related to this practice of Japanese corporations. Many Japanese corporations employ a policy of "designated schools," whereby students at only certain universities are considered for employment. Thus the pressure to pass the exams to enter a good university is very much a function of corporate recruitment practices. Often ties have been established between certain professors in universitites (especially in departments of economics or business), who will recommend their students in their senior-year seminars to favored corporations. Through such networks, corporations are able to establish a fairly assured quantity and quality of new recruits each year.

A recent phenomenon has been for corporations to establish schools of their own. The most prominent example is the Matsushita Juku, founded by Matsushita Konosuke for the purpose of producing "future leaders" of Japanese society. Another is the Nomura School of Business, established by the Nomura Securities Company and Nomura Research Institute and modeled on American graduate schools of business administration.

In addition to forming links with new and existing educational institutions to recruit and train personnel, corporations have formed ties with government agencies and certain universities for the purpose of advancing research and development. An especially prominent role has been played by the Agency of Industrial Science and Technology in the Ministry of International Trade and Industry (MITI), which in 1981 allocated over 300 million yen (about 1.5 million dollars at current exchange rates) for research projects, 73 percent of this amount to companies in the form of subsidies and research expenses. Although the amount of money involved in these subsidies and grants is not large compared to American government aid to higher education or defense industry research, the bureaucracy also plays a major role in informally encouraging and coordinating high technology research in other ways. Especially noteworthy in recent years is the *sangaku fukugōtai* ("industrial-academic complex") that has developed between certain universities and corporations to further research in such areas as high-energy physics, biotechnology, and artificial intelligence.[9]

Corporate Power and Policymaking

Business and Politicians

The relationship between business and politicians in Japan is probably not significantly different from that in other advanced industrialized countries: business wants politicans to provide legislation and governmental assistance favorable to its interests, while politicans in exchange seek the financial resources business commands. What is distinctive about the Japanese case is the extent to which the relationship is openly acknowledged and commented upon, the methods by which the funds are collected and distributed, and the large amounts contributed by business intersts not only to the LDP but to other political parties as well.

The Japanese public tends to take a rather cynical, pessimistic, and distrustful view of politics and the political process. This is in part a reflection of the less active role citizens have played in national politics compared to the United States. Cross-national surveys consistently show that Japanese respondents have a much lower evaluation of their political efficacy and competence than American responsents, regardless of levels of education.

The low expectation of what political leaders can do is perhaps a reason that "money politics" is tolerated or even expected of politicians. Japanese critics of the political system are fond of listing the string of periodic scandals that have rocked the political world in the postwar period. Among the most prominent was the Lockheed scandal, in which Tanaka Kakuei was convicted of receiving 500 million yen to influence an aircraft contract. Even after his conviction, the LDP refused to consider a resolution sponsored by opposition parties to force Tanaka's resignation from the Diet. And although national public opinion polls showed that the majority of the Japanese people wanted him to resign his Diet seat and retire from politics, Tanaka won an overwhelming reelection victory to represent his district in Niigata Prefecture, demonstrating that his district's voters were more impressed by Tanaka's power to direct national funds to his home constituency than by his conviction in a court of law.

The close relationship in Japan between the political and corporate world attracted renewed attention in 1988 as a result of the so-called Recruit scandal. The Recruit Corporation, a data services and real estate company, courted top politicians, bureaucrats, businessmen, and journalists from 1984 to 1986 by offering them unlisted shares of stock in a rapidly growing subsidiary, Recruit Cosmos. Inside information allowed the buyers to reap millions of dollars in profits when the stock was later offered to the public and the shares tripled in value.

Although the stock deals were not illegal under Japan's lax securities laws, the transactions raised serious questions about ethics, fundraising, and influence-peddling. The government of Prime Minister

Takeshita Noboru was weakened by a decline in public confidence, resulting in the successive resignations of Minister of Finance Miyazawa Kiichi on 9 December 1988, Minister of Justice Hasegawa Takashi on 30 December, and Economic Planning Agency chief Harada Ken on 24 January 1989. Also forced to resign were Morita Koh, president of the prominent daily newspaper *Nihon Keizai Shimbun* and Shinto Hisashi, chairman of Nippon Telegraph and Telephone Corporation.

One interesting aspect of this scandal was the role of the mass media. In contrast to the Lockheed scandal of the mid-1970s, which became news in Japan only after it was uncovered and initially pursued by the foreign press, the Recruit case was exposed by the domestic media—although, it is said, only because the newspaper that broke the story had conducted an internal review and determined that none of its own employees was implicated in the wide-ranging scandal. Many observers welcomed this new assertiveness by the media as proof that investigative journalism could help root out egregious cases of political corruption in Japan.[10]

It is difficult to find accurate data on the amounts and sources of campaign contributions to political parties; much of the money is unreported, and estimates vary widely. Table 7 summarizes one recent estimate of the income of political parties and factions and the

TABLE 7
Income and Contributions to Political Parties and Factions, 1982

Party	Total Income (1000 yen)	Percent from Business and Other Organizations' Contributions
Liberal Democratic (LDP)	12,692,480	66.2
Japan Socialist (JSP)	5,033,930	2.1
Clean Government (CGP)	8,853,090	0.0
Democratic socialist (DSP)	1,596,520	42.6
Japan Communist (JCP)	21,671,070	0.0
LDP Factions		
Tanaka	696,460	
Suzuki	569,720	
Fukuda	1,083,630	
Nakasone	2,004,360	
Komoto	1,239,780	

SOURCE: PHP Kenkyūjo, ed., *The Data File, 1984* (Tokyo: PHP Kenkyūjo, 1984), p. 32.

Note: Majority of remaining funds is from party activities and/or dues.

percent derived from organizations' contributions. Contributions to the LDP are typically made by corporations and industry associations. Although the Political Contribution Control Law of 1948 was strengthened during the Miki administration (1974–1976), effective January 1976, it has resulted in little change in the amount of money contributed. Figure 1 shows the channels by which funds typically flow from business interests to the LDP, factions, and individual politicians.

It should be noted that many of these contributions are not necessarily for the purpose of influencing a particular piece of legislation. Big business in Japan also contributes to the LDP in order to ensure that a party that supports the capitalist system and helps create a pro-business climate in general stays in power.

Business may also have influence on conservative leaders and politicians through informal social contacts and "old school ties." The extent to which these translate into real political power, however, is unclear, and some observers believe that the importance of these informal connections reached its peak in the 1960s and has been declining since.[11]

FIGURE 1
The Flow of Political Contributions to the LDP, Factions, and Politicians

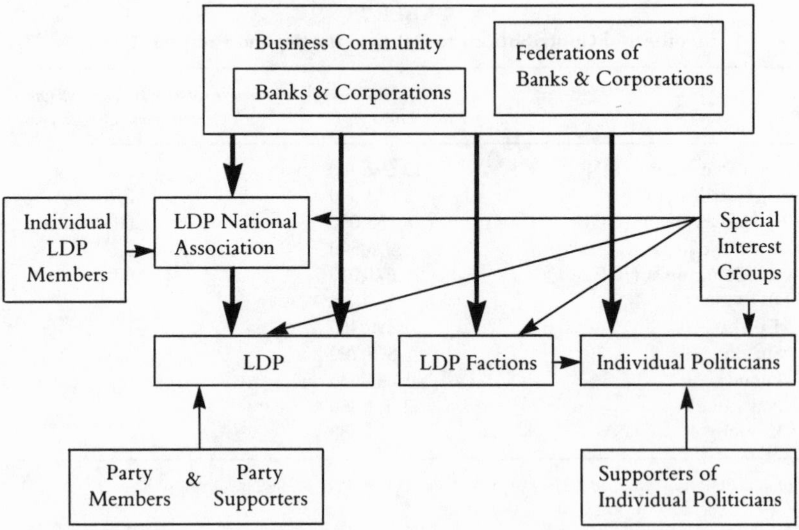

SOURCE: Gendai Seiji Mondai Kenkyukai, *Jiminto Gigoku Shi* (Tokyo: Gendai Hyoronsha, 1979), p. 285.

Big business, despite its influence on conservative politicians dependent on its financial support, also does not always get its way. An interesting example of this is the failed attempt in 1983 to revise and weaken the antimonopoly law. The impetus for this attempt came, on the one hand, from certain LDP politicians, who felt that the FTC was growing too active, especially in its prosecution of construction companies in bid-rigging cases, the construction industry being one of the largest financial contributors to the LDP. Certain business interests also were receptive to weakening the law. In particular, leaders in Keidanren (Federation of Economic Organizations), some of whom had been defendants in antitrust proceedings, especially in the steel industry, welcomed the opportunity to weaken both the law and the power of the FTC.

After holding seventeen hearings in early 1983, and after conducting a research tour of the United States and Europe in August 1983, the LDP's special investigation committee on the antimonopoly law submitted a report on its findings. The attempt to revise the law made little headway, however. This can be attributed to: (1) vigorous opposition by the FTC, consumer groups, and certain scholars and journalists; (2) unenthusiastic response by MITI; (3) lukewarm response by most sectors of the business community; (4) losses suffered by the LDP in the December 18, 1983, general election; and (5) concern expressed by Japan's trading partners, already critical of what they perceived as lax enforcement of antitrust laws, with detrimental consequences for the importation into Japan of foreign products. The case demonstrates the close interaction and coordination that can and often does go on between LDP politicians and certain big business interests on issues of shared concern, but also the fact that big business cannot unilaterally dictate policy when other political interests are mobilized against its desires.

Business and Government Bureaucracy

Although it is in many ways an oversimplification to speak of a "Japan Incorporated," it is also undeniable that business interests in Japan have a closer relationship to the government bureaucracy than is the case in many other advanced industrialized societies. This is in part a historical byproduct of the "late development effect" discussed earlier. The interaction is especially noticeable between bureaucrats and businessmen in industries under the jurisdiction of certain government ministries—for example, Finance, International Trade and Industry, Construction, and Transportation.

In addition to frequent meetings on specific issues of government policy or industry concerns, ongoing consultation is routinized in such forums as advisory councils and study groups initiated at times by ministries and at other times by big business, usually on the trade association or federation level. As of 1979 there were 162 advisory councils connected with various ministries and agencies of the Japanese government. This figure greatly underestimates the actual level of regular contact between representatives of business and government, however, inasmuch as these comprise only "official" advisory councils. Countless other informal groups exist, either formed on the level of ministry bureau or divisions or attached to external organizations affiliated with ministries. In advisory councils for such ministries as Finance, International Trade and Industry, Construction, and Transportation, business interests are numerically well represented, although their influence varies from group to group and from issue to issue.

One of the best-known mechanisms by which business interests and government bureaucrats interact is *amakudari* ("descent from heaven"). Typically, a bureaucrat at or near the end of his career in a government ministry will "descend" to another organization, usually a public corporation, trade association, or private corporation, often in that order. In 1982, there were 266 higher level civil servants who "descended" after retirement from their ministries. The largest number came from Finance (52), followed by International Trade and Industry (32), Construction (30), Agriculture and Forestry (28), Transportation (22), and Post and Telecommunications (19). Although there are several varieties of *amakudari,* each with distinctive characteristics, motivations, and purposes, most attention is usually given to those in which the former bureaucrat enters a trade association or corporation in a business over which he exercised jurisdiction while in government service. It is widely understood that these former government bureaucrats function as intermediaries between their former agency and their new employer or, more frequently, represent the new employer's interests to the regulatory agency. This is sometimes cited as a mechanism by which big business interests attempt to influence government industrial policy.

Organized Representation of Big Business

Business influence on Japanese politics and society at the level of individuals and corporations is in many ways similar to that found in all advanced industrialized societies. But the aggregation and articulation of business interests in Japan evince some distinctive features, one of which is the prominent role played by the four main national economic organizations: Keidanren, Nisshō (Japan Chamber of Commerce and Industry), Nikkeiren (Japan Federation of Employers' Associations), and Keizai Dōyūkai (Japan Committee for Economic Development).

Keidanren, undoubtedly the most important of the four, represents large business interests. Founded in 1946, it comprises both company groups (associations and federations) and large individual companies. Thus among its members are the Japan Iron and Steel Federation, Japan Automobile Manufacturers Association, Petroleum Association of Japan, Federation of Electric Power Companies, trading companies, banks, insurance companies, and securities firms. Each of Keidanren's five presidents has played an important role in the postwar business community and in relations between business and government. In recognition of this role, the nickname "Prime Minister of *zaikai* [business community]" has been given to the person occupying the Keidanren presidency. Keidanren strives to mobilize consensus within the business community and influence the government to adopt policies that are responsive to industry's wishes. Keidanren is also an important source of funds for the LDP. It assesses each constituent trade or industrial association a specified amount for transmission to the Kokumin Kyokai (National Association), an organization established to channel funds to the LDP.

Each of the other three organizations also has influence within a particular sphere of business activity. Nisshō is the forum mainly for smaller and medium-sized enterprises, but probably the least influential of the four major business organizations. Nikkeiren represents big business as employers. Thus although its membership is similar to that of Keidanren, its focus is primarily on management-labor relations. Comprised of both regional and industry-based groups, one of its major functions is to develop countermeasures to labor union demands in the areas of employment, wages and work conditions, labor legislation, and welfare issues. It plays a prominent role each year in coordinating management response toward the annual spring offensives launched by trade union federations. Nicknamed the "*zaikai's* 'anti-labor' headquarters,'" it has mobilized support for management in several major strikes.

The Keizai Dōyūkai is a small group of policy-oriented business leaders. In recent years it has payed particular attention to cooperation between government and business and to the social responsibility of business. It differs from the other three organizations in that individuals, rather than corporations or associations, comprise its membership.

Although disagreements at times have erupted among these four business organizations, differences have been attributed more to the personalities of the organizations' leaders than to fundamental divergences in organizational goals. The four major business organizations share a commitment to develop consensus (both within the business community and between business and government) in ways that will benefit the entire business community in the long run. This has at times led to differences between the views of individual industries and what is perceived by, for instance, Keidanren to be in the best long-term interest of Japan's industry and economy. Keidanren and Nisshō in particular have vigorously promoted Japan's foreign economic relations with a wide variety of countries and regional blocks, but especially with such countries as China and the Soviet Union where governmental relations with Japan had been seriously constrained in the four decades following the end of World War II.

Although some outside observers have ascribed more power to these four organizations than might be warranted, it is nonetheless true that the business community has benefited enormously by their domestic and foreign activities. The influence of Keidanren alone in the Japanese business context probably outweighs the combined efforts in the United States of the Business Roundtable, Conference Board, National Association of Manufacturers, Committee for Economic Development, and the Chamber of Commerce. Japan is not unusual in having a business community active in politics and policy-making issues. It, however, is somewhat unusual in the extent to which that community is well organized and so close to one political party, the only party to have governed Japan since 1955.

Conclusions

Having briefly surveyed the role of corporations and big business in the history, society, and polity of Japan, what conclusions can we draw about corporate power and democracy?

Our answer depends in part, of course, on our definitions of "corporate," "power," and "democracy." It also depends on our criteria for the measurement of power, how findings based on such measurements compare cross-nationally, and whether we wish to "explain," draw implications, or make judgments about Japan derived from such comparative results. The difficulty of measuring "corporate power" is exacerbated by the fact that much of that influence, in any country, is exercised indirectly. Before we can truly evaluate the power of big business in Japanese democracy we will need many more systematic studies of business influence in various areas of Japanese life. These studies must go beyond simply assuming big business runs the nation, as many Marxist studies do, or citing a few selected counterexamples to prove that it doesn't, as many anti–"power elite" studies do.

Based on the evidence presented here, it is safe to conclude that the role of big business in Japanese society and politics is considerably more complex than that imparted by any of the ideal types hitherto applied to it. Business *is* a major and extremely well organized actor in politics, with close connections and influence in the ruling party. Employees in large firms *are* more embedded in a total community within the workplace than is customary in the West, and business influence on the media and education *is* pervasive. Business concentration *is* greater than the Occupation intended, and antitrust *is* less vigorously enforced than might be inferred from the statutory language. And competition between firms appears to be more structured, ordered, and, at times, controlled than is the case in the United States, where the free play of market forces is thought to produce the most efficient outcome.

On the other hand, the Japanese policymaking process has grown increasingly pluralistic over the past two decades. In addition to the traditional "triumvirate" of big business, the LDP, and the bureaucracy, other actors—new interest groups, the media, opposition parties, for instance—have emerged, exercising considerable leverage on the politial process. In addition, new cleavages have appeared among members of the triumvirate over such issues as fiscal, monetary, industrial, and international trade policy. Japanese automobile companies, for example, have resisted MITI on issues ranging from its attempt in the 1960s to merge all auto companies into only two companies to the voluntary restraint on exports to the United States. Furthermore, big business itself is by no means consistently united. Especially with the internationalization of the Japanese economy, many contemporary issues pit one part of business that stands to gain by a policy against another part that stands to lose.

An overall evaluation, however, leads to the conclusion that corporate power is indeed pervasive and central to contemporary Japan.

One reason for this, of course, is that it fills a vacuum: with no clearly defined political, moral, social, or military vision to guide its future, postwar Japan has engaged in a single-minded pursuit of economic growth. To the extent that this has required cooperation, if not collaboration, among various sectors of the society and polity to construct corporations to pave the way for the creation of national wealth, Japan appears to outsiders to be harmonious, monolithic, and at times collusive. Thus it is not surprising that casual observers would affix the label of "Japan, Incorporated" to describe such a social system. This ideal type is further reinforced by the tendency of Japanese social scientists to proclaim the "uniqueness" and "homogeneity" of their countrymen, and of certain Japanese economists and political scientists to emphasize collusive activity among the country's leadership.

However one ultimately evaluates the role of corporate power in Japan and its relationship to democracy, it is clear that the assessment must take into account the increasing pluralization of Japanese society and the shifting nature of relationships among various actors. No static model can adequately explain the tension in Japan, for instance, between competition and cooperation or between consensus and conflict. Rather than focusing on one aspect to the exclusion of others, examining the dynamic interrelationship between such seemingly opposite—yet coexisting—facets promises to lend a much fuller understanding of the role of corporate power in Japan.

NOTES

I wish to acknowledge the helpful comments by Ellis Krauss and Takeshi Ishida on an earlier version of this chapter.

1. Quoted in Nathaniel B. Thayer, *How the Conservatives Rule Japan* (Princeton, N.J.: Princeton University Press, 1969), p. 70.

2. F. M. Scherer, *Industrial Market Structure and Economic Performance,* 2d ed. (New York: Rand McNally, 1980), pp. 51–52.

3. Caves, Richard E., and Masu Uekusa, *Industrial Organization in Japan* (Washington, D.C.: The Brookings Institution, 1976), p. 18.

4. Miyamoto Ken'ichi, *Gendai Shihonshugi to Kokka* (Tokyo: Iwanami Shoten, 1981).

5. "The OECD Member Countries, 1984 edition," *The OECD Observer,* no. 127 (March 1984).

6. *Asahi Shinbun,* July 14, 1983.

7. Nakamura Takatoshi, *Gendai Nihon no Kyodai Kigyo* (Tokyo: Iwanami Shoten, 1983).

8. Some large company employees, on the other hand, do vote for opposition parties. See Ezra Vogel, *Japan's New Middle Class* (Berkeley and Los Angeles: University of California Press, 1965), chap. 5.

9. See, for example, Edward A. Feigenbaum and Pamela McCorduck, *The Fifth Generation: Artificial Intelligence and Japan's Computer Challenge to the World,* rev. ed. (New York: Signet Books, 1983).

10. This account of the Recruit scandal is based on articles in the *Asahi Shimbun, Yomiuri Shimbun,* and *Nihon Keizai Shimbun,* July 1988 to January 1989.

11. See Gerald L. Curtis, "Big Business and Political Influence," in Ezra F. Vogel, ed., *Modern Japanese Organization and Decision-Making* (Berkeley and Los Angeles: University of California Press, 1975) for the argument that the political influence of business has been much overrated.

12 Industrial Democracy

●

TADASHI HANAMI

Industrial democracy is a term implying, to a greater or lesser extent, the participation of those who work in industry in determining the conditions of their working lives. It is defined as "any theory or scheme as long as it is based on a genuine concern for the rights of workers and industry, particularly their right to share in the control of industrial decisions."[1] The term has been used to describe the removal of arbitrary or autocratic procedures by management and the substitution of machinery in which the workers have an opportunity to present their problems and grievances to management and to receive adequate consideration (here the analogy to political democracy is obvious). The development of collective bargaining is viewed by many as providing the means through which industrial democracy has developed. However, today, particularly in Western Europe, other forms of workers' participation in decision making are becoming increasingly important, such as information sharing, joint consultation, codetermination, and profit sharing. Co-ownership is more frequently found in Eastern Europe.[2]

In the United States, workers' participation in forms other than collective bargaining is less developed but has gradually gained importance in recent years. More and more large and progressive companies are embracing labor-management cooperative programs. They believe it is sound management policy to involve employees in decision making in the workplace. Information sharing, increased worker input, and the relaxation of symbolic barriers between workers and management characterize some of the recent experiments in the auto

281

industry. Significantly, the most pioneering experiment is the General Motors—Toyota joint venture, New United Motors Manufacturing, Inc. (NUMMI), which has turned a problem-plagued plant in Fremont, California, into an efficient factory. This Japanese involvement stimulated the development of "industrial democracy" in the U.S. auto industry and was followed by other experiments such as the ones at the Fiero plant in Pontiac, Michigan, and the virtually company-wide Employee Involvement Program at Ford Motor Company. The U.S. Department of Labor also has strongly supported labor-management cooperation as an important prerequisite to America's return to preeminence in the world marketplace.

This chapter describes and analyzes the degree of industrial democracy in Japan compared to Europe, the birthplace of the concept, and to the more recently developed American pattern.

The Principle of Free Collective Bargaining

The basic principle of the industrial relations system in Japan is that of free collective bargaining, namely, that both parties in industrial relations enjoy freedom of association and autonomy through bargaining. The assumption is that the government should not interfere with their autonomous regulation of labor relations except by setting minimum standards in legislation protecting labor. Parties are encouraged to bargain for better working conditions beyond such minimum standards. Furthermore, workers' rights to organize, bargain, and act collectively are guaranteed as basic human rights by the constitution (article 28).

These workers' rights are protected by legislation against unfair labor practices which was modeled on the American Wagner Act of 1935. Furthermore, the right to bargain is more broadly recognized in Japan since the notion of management prerogative is not generally accepted as in the United States. Further, it is generally accepted in Japan that employers have an obligation to bargain with unions over any subject which may affect the workers' economic situation if it is a matter within the employer's competence. Such matters as plant closing, plant relocation, plant sales, automation, types of subcontracting—subjects of serious conflict in the United States over whether they are mandatory or nonmandatory bargaining subjects—are regarded in Japan as matters of obligatory bargaining.

Consultation and Participation

The German concept of workers' participation has had an influence in Japan since the 1920s and 1930s. In spite of the strong theoretical influence of the German model, however, for a long period Japan never adopted any legal system for workers' participation. In practice, work councils, separate from a collective bargaining system, were established, particularly after World War II, through a number of agreements between enterprise unions and management. Also, some trade union leaders sit on the board of directors or production committee of companies. However, these practices have no legal base and have often been carried out in a very informal way.

Work Councils and Collective Bargaining

According to the 1982 Labor Ministry survey on collective agreements, 59 percent of surveyed unions had work councils. Of these councils, 52 percent were established at the enterprise level, 40 percent at the plant level, and 6 percent were on the workplace level.[3]

Work councils are set up mostly through collective agreements between enterprise unions and management (77 percent of those surveyed). Establishing them through company work rules is not a usual practice, and therefore in most cases work councils are composed of members sent from unions and management. Labor members are often the union president, vice-president, and secretary general in those established at the enterprise level, and other executives in the case of plant or workplace level councils. Because the work council is a product of agreement between union and management, the distinction between functions of work councils and collective bargaining is not very clear. This is because in Japan collective bargaining is carried out mostly at the enterprise level. The above-mentioned survey shows that labor members of collective bargaining sessions are almost identical with those of work councils, that is, they are union officers.

Even some of the issues handled in work councils overlap with issues of collective bargaining. According to the Labor Ministry survey, in 21 percent of the surveyed cases, matters of management and production are not to be discussed in work councils; they can address only working conditions, grievances, and matters of welfare. Seventy-seven percent of the surveyed unions answered, however, that the

principal purpose of work councils was "improvement and maintenance of working conditions." Thus it is no wonder that 13 percent
regard work council deliberations as a preliminary step prior to collective bargaining.[4] In practice, both parties often regard the work council
as a less adversarial step in negotiations, while bargaining tends to be
regarded as more adversarial. The lack of distinction between bargaining and work council procedures in Japan is a striking contrast to the
clear distinction between them in West Germany and other European
countries. There bargaining is carried out industrywide on national or
regional levels by industrial unions, while work council procedures
take place on the enterprise level with most of the council members
elected directly from the employees.

In Western Europe, particularly in West Germany, minimum standards for working conditions are established by collective bargaining,
and work councils cope with the problems arising out of the process
of applying the standards to the individual enterprises or plants. In
Japan, actual working conditions, not just their standards, are to be
established through collective bargaining. Work council procedures
could handle the grievances arising out of the actual application to
individual workers of working conditions established by collective
agreements.

In some cases grievance procedures separate from work councils are
established (39 percent of surveyed unions in the above-mentioned
survey). There are two interesting points about the grievance procedures. Fifty-one percent of the unions with such procedures had had no
actual grievance cases in the three years prior to the survey. Second, the
grievances not solved through this procedure are often settled at work
councils (43 percent) or through collective bargaining (40 percent).[5]

Both work councils and grievance procedures have a Western
origin: the former was taken from European countries and the latter
was adopted from the United States. But the way these actually function is very different from their countries of origin. In Japan, issues
which are not settled through these procedures could be subject to
bargaining and therefore could result in strikes and other industrial
actions. In other words, the use of such procedures does not guarantee industrial peace. This is a striking contrast to "Western legal systems." In Western countries both procedures mean to exclude the
possibility of industrial actions. In the United States the matters
which are not settled through grievance procedures are to be settled
through private arbitration. In European countries, particularly in

West Germany, those matters not settled through work council procedures are to be settled through labor courts.

The Legal Nature of Collective Bargaining and Workers' Participation

The last point is related to the omnipotence of collective bargaining in Japan. The right of unions to bargain and act collectively is guaranteed by the constitution. Collective agreements are given normative effects under the Trade Union Law which makes any individual agreement contradicting the collective agreement null and void. On the other hand, there are no legal provisions concerning workers' participation or grievance procedures in general. In the public sector there is a legal provision which requires managements and unions to establish the joint grievance adjustment board. At the same time the law limits the scope of collective bargaining to cover only matters concerning working conditions and excludes "matters pertaining to the management and operation of the public corporations and national enterprises." The legal structure of the public sector is very close to the general American situation where in both the private sector and the public sector the scope of bargaining basically excludes matters of "management prerogatives."

In the private sector in Japan only a minority claims that management issues are excluded from the scope of bargaining; the majority does not accept this limitation. In other words, it is generally accepted that unions have the right to bargain on all matters which affect the life of workers, *including* management decision making. Unions may demand to bargain over almost all matters except those beyond management's authority such as political issues or the affairs of other companies. Such a broad interpretation of collective bargaining together with legal admission to the right to bargain may cause a degree of confusion in industrial relations in Japan.

What is the legal result when the same issue is to be handled by collective bargaining, grievance procedures, or work councils? Theoretically, matters which were not settled through grievance or work council procedures could be handled through collective bargaining. According to the 1982 Labor Ministry survey, when management and production issues were not settled in work councils, in 12 percent of the cases management was required to suspend implementation for a certain period, and in 48 percent of the cases they had to amend their decisions, taking the union's opinion into account. However, in 12 percent of the cases management was entitled to proceed regardless of the union's opinion.[6] Theoretically it is not clear whether unions may demand further bargaining over such matters and carry out strike actions in unsettled cases. Judging from the strong legal protection of the right to bargain, they may, and unions behave in practice with such an assumption. This is the result of the lack of legal basis for workers' participation in general and for work councils in particular, an important difference in the Japanese situation from many European countries where the work councils are legally constituted and matters are to be settled in a peaceful way without recourse to strike.

Degree of Participation

Since there is no legal provision concerning work councils in Japan there is of course no legal definition of the issues they may handle or the legal nature of the agreements they reach. According to the Labor Ministry survey: "matters of management and production" cover three major areas: (1) management policy and production planning, (2) introduction, abolition, or change of structure of the organization and manpower planning, and (3) introduction of new technology. Of the surveyed work councils, 92 percent dealt with the first, 80 percent deal with the second, and 55 percent deal with the third.[7] Table 1 shows the degree of participation of unions in decision making in each of the three areas where work councils are on different levels. The cases requiring agreement are less than 10 percent in all categories of issues. In most cases, information and consultation, at most, are required. Very generally speaking, the degree of participation tends to be stronger at lower levels, such as the plant level and particularly at the workplace level. The degree of participation is not at all weak but sometimes even stronger in Japan than in Europe where, for the matters referred to in this table, only information and consultation are usually required. On the other hand, matters related to working conditions within an enterprise, for which an agreement with work councils is required in Europe, in Japan are dealt with through bargaining and collective agreements.

The Japanese system, nonetheless, has certain weak points. First, there is no arbitration where the parties fail to reach agreement. Thus it is possible in Japan, in spite of the existence of work councils, that unions could continue disputes and ultimately call a strike. Second, the degree of participation depends entirely on the power relationship between the union and management since there is no legal basis for workers' participation. The Japanese system is therefore flexible and

TABLE 1
Number of Work Councils According to the Degree of Participation and the Level of Work Councils

Area and Degree of Participation[a]	Total		Level							
			Enterprise		Plant		Workplace		Other	
	No.	%	No.	%	No.	%	No.	%	No.	%
Policy and production planning										
1	224	30	139	31	105	31	9	24	1	7
2	229	27	122	27	93	27	8	22	6	43
3	312	37	164	36	125	37	17	46	6	43
4	50	6	28	6	18	8	3	8	1	7
	845	100	433	100	341	100	37	100	14	100
Change of structure in manpower planning										
1	186	25	107	28	70	22	5	15	4	36
2	172	23	86	23	77	24	18	24	1	9
3	314	42	154	40	138	44	16	49	6	55
4	69	9	35	9	30	10	4	12	—	—
	741	100	382	100	315	100	33	100	11	100
Introduction of new technology										
1	151	30	86	35	59	26	6	21	—	—
2	119	24	52	21	58	26	6	21	3	43
3	196	39	85	35	94	42	13	46	4	57
4	38	8	20	8	15	7	3	11	—	—
	504	100	243	100	226	100	28	100	7	100

SOURCE: Rōdō Shō (Ministry of Labor), *Saishin Rōdō Kyōyaku no Jittai* (Newest Survey on Collective Agreements) (Tokyo: Rōmu Gyōsei Kenkyūsho, 1984).

a. 1 = explanation (providing information to the union)
2 = asking opinions (from the union)
3 = consultation (management may proceed if no agreement is reached)
4 = agreement (management may not proceed without agreement with the union)

could be very effective in terms of participation since sometimes unions could have rights of codetermination even in issues such as management policy, production planning, change of structure, or introduction of new technology; the degree of participation, however, depends very much on the power relationship between the parties, and the system as a whole is not very secure in terms of industrial peace.

Workers' Representation on Company Boards and Profit Sharing

There is no law requiring workers' representation on supervisory or directors' boards. In practice there are very few cases of such representation. A Ministry of Labor survey in 1977 shows that only 34 out of 1,700 surveyed unions had representatives on company decision-making bodies. Out of these 34, 4 unions had representatives on boards of directors and other unions had representatives in some kind of body with actual power and influence on the board of directors, such as a management committee, an advisory body to the board of directors.[8] There is no case where unions are represented on the supervisory board. Profit sharing, in which workers receive company stock, is rather frequently found in the larger enterprises. But such practices are mainly meant to be one of the employees' welfare benefits and not a form of workers' participation since in most cases workers' shares are limited and far from influential in company decision making. The widespread practice of awarding handsome bonuses at the year end and midyear is profit sharing in a sense, but the bonuses are regarded as part of wages.

Trends in Formal Participation and the Future

In recent years, especially in the late 1970s, there was growing interest in workers' participation among union and management leaders. This interest was partly influenced by the development of workers' participation in many European countries in the early 1970s. However, it also reflected the growing concern of unions over their loss of influence and the limitations placed on collective bargaining by technological change and change of labor market structure due to the growing importance of female, temporary, part-time, and aged workers. There were even a number of proposals by management associations and some unions to stimulate workers' participation and to introduce legislation for this purpose. However, this trend faded away in the mid-1980s.

The decline of interest in participation could be explained by two closely related reasons. First, the degree of actual participation in Japan is not weak in spite of the lack of formal legal backing. Second, there was the fear that introducing formal, particularly legal, structure might destroy the advantages of Japanese informality. A majority of management leaders are very much concerned about this latter point. Furthermore, a majority of union leaders are afraid that too much emphasis on consultation will undermine their influence through collective bargaining. This last point is related to the peculiar Japanese industrial relations context where bargaining is carried out exclusively on the enterprise level.

Thus, we might predict that the European idea of workers' participation will be extended in the future in Japan, but probably in an informal way, without a legalized formal foundation, unless unforeseen drastic changes occur in Japanese industrial relations.

The Emergence of Informal Participation

Traditional Japanese Harmony?

So far we have seen the difference between European and Japanese systems, mainly focusing on the framework for formal participation. In this section, I will discuss how informal participation was established in Japan and its relationship with industrial peace. It is common knowledge in the West that the performance of Japanese industrial relations is much better than in most of the Western industrialized countries. Table 2 shows that after 1980 only West Germany can compete with Japan in the low level of strike propensity. However, the table also shows that the better performance of Japanese industrial relations is only a recent phenomenon. Until 1975 the Japanese figure is not very different from other countries. In spite of the common notion of Japan as a harmonious society, Japan experienced a good number of serious labor disputes with violent confrontation during the 1940s and 1950s.[9] Thus today's better performance of Japanese industrial relations cannot be explained solely by the traditional culture of the Japanese society and its emphasis on harmony and politeness as a social value.

The agreements concluded by unions in the private sector after the late 1970s showed a strong trend toward forgoing strikes and big wage increases in return for job security and low inflation. The rate of wage increase through *shuntō* (spring offensives) sharply declined af-

TABLE 2
Number of Days Lost by Labor Disputes per 10 Workers in Major Industrialized
Countries

	Japan	U.S.	England	W. Germany	France	Italy
1965	2.0	2.5	1.2	0.0	0.7	7.9
1970	1.2	7.4	4.8	0.0	1.1	22.3
1975	2.2	2.3	2.7	0.2	2.2	16.7
1976	0.9	3.0	1.5	0.2	2.8	15.4
1977	0.4	2.6	4.7	0.0	2.0	9.9
1978	0.4	2.7	4.1	1.9	1.2	6.0
1979	0.2	2.3	12.9	0.2	2.0	15.9
1980	0.3	2.3	5.4	0.1	0.9	9.3
1981	0.1	1.9	2.0	0.0	0.8	5.9
1982	0.1	1.0	2.5	0.0	1.3	10.2
1983	0.1	1.9	1.8	0.0	0.8	7.7
1984	0.1	0.9	1.3	2.6	0.8	—

SOURCE: Japan Productivity Center, *Katsuyō Rōdō Tōkei* (Practical Labor Statistics) (Tokyo: Japan Productivity Center, 1986).

ter 1974. Wage increase percentages dropped from 32.9 percent in 1974 to 13.1 percent in 1975, and then declined further to 8.8 percent in 1976, less than 5 percent after 1983, and less than 4 percent after 1987.

During this same period, workers' participation and cooperative efforts between management and labor increased. The percentage of enterprises having work councils rose from about 63 percent in 1972, to about 71–72 percent after 1977. The percentage having joint committees went from approximately 76 percent in 1972 to about 78 percent in 1984, and those with small circles from about 40 percent in 1972 to about 60 percent in 1984.[10] This trend is attributed to the recent awareness of crisis concerning declining returns, increased competition among enterprises, technological innovation, reform of company structure, and so forth.[11]

Public Versus Private Sector Conflict in Japan

Table 3 shows the interesting fact that the number of disputes in the public sector has grown extensively since 1970 while the total number has been gradually declining. The emphasis on the public sector is even more conspicuous in the figures showing workers' participation rate in disputes. Some of the reasons for this are the

TABLE 3

Number of Labor Disputes with Work Stoppage and Number of Workers
Engaged in Labor Disputes per 1,000 Organized Workers

	Number of Disputes		Number of Workers in Disputes per 1,000	
	All Industries	Public Sector	All Industries	Public Sector
1962	1,696	49 (2.9%)	215	39
1963	1,421	19 (1.3%)	192	29
1964	1,754	58 (3.3%)	169	72
1965	2,359	223 (9.5%)	246	93
1966	2,845	536 (18.8%)	223	260
1967	2,284	10 (0.4%)	120	5
1968	3,167	520 (16.4%)	215	319
1969	4,482	1,133 (25.3%)	273	541
1970	3,783	344 (9.1%)	203	96
1971	6,082	1,696 (27.9%)	307	453
1972	4,996	1,055 (21.1%)	223	294
1973	8,720	3,370 (38.7%)	407	1,034
1974	9,581	2,621 (27.4%)	427	641
1975	7,574	2,645 (34.9%)	366	802
1976	7,240	2,832 (39.2%)	272	893
1977	5,533	2,195 (39.7%)	194	610
1978	4,852	1,984 (40.9%)	168	478
1979	3,492	1,326 (38.0%)	120	341
1980	3,737	1,560 (41.7%)	143	433
1981	7,034	4,488 (63.8%)	234	1,137
1982	6,779	4,428 (65.3%)	190	1,015
1983	4,814	—	—	—
1984	3,855	—	—	—

SOURCE: Ministry of Labor, *Annual Report of Labor Dispute Statistics and Survey* (Tokyo: Ministry of Labor, 1963–1985).

militant unionism in the public sector and the great number of political strikes, including those protesting the prohibition against strikes in the public sector. In addition, it is often pointed out that the public sector unions could afford such disputes even during the period of slower economic growth after the oil crisis (1973) because of the monopoly status of public enterprises. The private sector unions were more conscious of the severity of economic conditions after rapid economic growth stopped, and of international competition. The private sector tried to establish better labor-management relations in order to face and overcome the crisis. Both sides realized that they could no longer afford confrontation. They tried very hard to avoid layoffs and dismissals and to survive without serious damage by creating relationships of mutual understanding and consensus to cope with redundancy by transfer, retraining, change of business orientation, and the introduction of new technology.

Gradually practices emerged to seek consensus through constant and close consultation, information sharing, and negotiation to find a way to survive. In addition to formal consultation or negotiation, various schemes were introduced to facilitate efficiency including quality circles, suggestion programs, and so forth. Such informal daily contacts at the workplace facilitated informal participation. Management came to realize that it needed the support of workers to introduce the drastic structural and policy changes required to cope with growing competition both in domestic and international markets.

Industrial Relations: the United States and Japan Compared

Many see Japanese industrial relations as more conciliatory and amicable than the American, with fewer strikes and litigations, two adversarial modes of conflict resolution.[12] By contrast, in recent years the American industrial relations system has become increasingly legalistic and adversarial. One industrial relations expert, Thomas Rochan, contends that in American industrial relations too much energy and money are wasted defending contractual "rights" and negotiating additional rules to govern the relationship between parties. Unless the system is changed, he warns, "what lies ahead is more polarization and confrontation."[13] According to another labor economist, Harry Katz, the origin of the legalistic approach of the American system can be found in the system established during the New Deal, with its "job control" form of unionism, "highly formalized contracts" through bargaining, and a "quasi-judicial grievance procedure to adjudicate disputes."[14] Thus it is usually agreed that these consequences stem from the adversarial and litigious nature of American traditional culture or the aggressive character of the American people.

I would argue that it is more likely the result of the historical development of the American industrial relations system. The labor law systems of the United States and Japan do not differ fundamentally. Both are based on the principle of free collective bargaining and minimum government intervention, except in the protection of trade union rights through unfair labor practice systems. Neither country has a legal system of workers' participation, unlike most European nations. Informal participation, which is rather prevalent in Japan, has been generally rejected in the United States as an idea that contradicts the basically adversarial approach of the American system. In the United States, conflicts on the enterprise and plant levels are supposed to be settled through grievance procedures and arbitration.

The American grievance procedure and private arbitration system has two distinguishing features. First, it is established through agreements between union and management, similar to the Japanese work council and grievance procedure, and different from the European work council, which is elected by employees. Second, the final settlement is the responsibility of an arbitrator who is an independent third party. This is similar to European councils. It is said that the American arbitration system has a double function: to avoid strikes and to provide a satisfactory alternative to litigation. Thus, it is regarded as a means to avoid both forms of overt conflict. However, it is often pointed out that labor arbitration in the United States today falls short of these goals. Arbitration is becoming more and more expensive, moving slower, and becoming more formalized. The result is a more legalistic and adversarial type of labor relations.

Observers came to realize that American "labor laws, growing out of partisan economic and political strife, not only have proved somewhat deficient in the protection of the public interest, but have also promoted a 'win-lose' mentality that rewards adversarial posturing at the bargaining table and before neutral third parties."[15] In response to such critical observations, the U.S. Department of Labor undertook a study "to review the nation's labor laws and collective bargaining traditions and practices that may inhibit improved labor-management relations."[16] The report, published in June 1986, expressed the department's strong support of labor-management cooperation as an important prerequisite for America's return to preeminence in the world marketplace. According to this report, one-third of the Fortune 500 companies have some form of participative management or quality-of-work-life program in operation, and these efforts have, by and large, resulted in measurably improved employee morale and increased productivity.

Among those recent experimental efforts, one can discern the impact of Japanese ventures in the United States. One of the most auspicious undertakings of this kind is NUMMI, the GM-Toyota joint venture mentioned above. Bruce Lee, regional director for the United

Auto Workers (UAW), described the collective agreement between the UAW and the NUMMI in a letter to the local membership: "We share the risk in that the union agrees to abandon part of its traditional reactive, adversarial role in favor of a proactive, advocacy role, while the company surrenders some of its traditional management prerogative in favor of conferring with the union on important issues."[17]

The Employee Involvement Program at Ford and another cooperative arrangement between GM and the UAW at the new Saturn small car plant in Tennessee share with the NUMMI agreement certain distinctive features. Among these are protection against layoffs, workers' participation in decisions, fewer job classifications, flexible work rules, reliance on team efforts, profit sharing and other reward systems, information sharing, and relaxation of symbolic barriers between workers and management. All these features are exactly what has been emphasized as characteristics of Japanese industrial relations.

Contrary to common belief, such cooperative approaches have been tried in the past in the United States, particularly by some leading companies such as IBM, 3M, and Lincoln National Life Insurance. However, their recent development is significant in that they are now supported by influential unions such as the United Steel Workers Union, the International Brotherhood of Electrical Workers, or the Amalgamated Clothing and Textile Workers Union in addition to the UAW. Moreover, lower absenteeism, higher work ethics and morale, fewer grievances and, as a result, improvement of productivity and efficiency are reported in these attempts.[18] Exactly the same trends are found in many of the Japanese companies and Japanese joint ventures in the United States.[19]

How much such new trends owe to Japanese influence is a question yet to be fully answered. The recent experiences of Japanese ventures in the United States, however, may indicate that they are successful in creating cooperative and amicable industrial relations even without adopting the so-called three pillars of Japanese industrial relations: lifetime employment, seniority, wages and enterprise unionism, not to mention the traditional Japanese mentality of harmony and consensus.

Industrial Democracy and Industrial Peace

I have argued that today's better performance of Japanese industrial relations cannot be explained by traditional Japanese culture and mentality. I have also shown that the Japanese legal system is not basically different from Western ones and does not provide any efficient guarantee for industrial peace; instead it is relatively inappropriate for guaranteeing a peaceful settlement of disputes, particularly at plant level, because of the omnipotence of legal rights to bargain and act collectively. We have seen that in the United States there is a growing interest in Japanese industrial relations because of its better performance, and some see it as a model to be emulated. We have also observed that such features as participation in management decision making, various kinds of joint committees (including quality-of-work-life programs), secured employment, fewer job classifications, information sharing, and so forth, are found both in some efficient American companies and most of the Japanese ventures in the United States.

Needless to say, all these features in essence involve a greater participation of workers in a company's affairs, inlcluding management decision making, and thus a greater degree of industrial democracy. The troubles most of the Western industrialized countries suffered in the 1980s derive from industrial relations based on the assumption of confrontation between labor and management. Industrial democracy thus developed by providing more established formal rules and schemes, including legal schemes. This legalistic approach alienated workers from involvement in management affairs and created a "win-lose" mentality. The degree of alienation in the United States may have been more serious because of its rejection of the European idea of workers' participation.[20] In comparison with the European situation, Japanese participation is more informal, without legal grounding, and thus more flexible. As we have seen, the level of informal participation is fairly high.

Why was Japan able to develop such extensive participation? I have suggested that its better performance is of recent origin and it is only the result of serious efforts of parties to create better relationships based on serious concerns for survival under the threat of growing competition in the world market. The contemporary concerns of American experts are also based on their losing "pre-eminence in the world market." The case of Japan may illustrate that more industrial democracy may equal better performance, and that greater democracy can be created by conscious efforts in the face of crisis.

NOTES

1. H. A. Clegg, *A New Approach to Industrial Democracy* (Oxford: Blackwell, 1968), p. 3.

2. T. Hanami and J. Monat, "Employee Participation in the Workshop, in the Office and in the Enterprise," in *Comparative Labour Law and Industrial Relations,* ed. R. Blanpain, 2d and rev. ed. (Deventer: Kluwer, 1985), pp. 249ff.

3. Rōdō Sho (Ministry of Labor), *Saishin Rōdō Kyōyaku no Jittai* (Newest Survey on Collective Agreements) (Tokyo: Rōmu Gyōsei Kenkyūsho, 1984), pp. 20ff.

4. Ibid., pp. 66ff.

5. Ibid., pp. 79, 82.

6. Ibid., p. 75.

7. Ibid., p. 70.

8. Rōdō Sho (Ministry of Labor), *Saishin Rōdō Kyōyaku no Jittai* (Newest Survey on Collective Agreements) (Tokyo: Rōmu Gyōsei Kenkyūsho, 1979), p. 142.

9. Many cases of such violent disuptes is described in Tadashi Hanami, *Labor Relations in Japan Today* (Tokyo: Kodansha/International, 1979).

10. Rōdō Sho (Ministry of Labor), *Nihon no rōshi Komyunike-shyon no genjyō* (The Present Status of Labor-Management Communication in Japan) (Tokyo, 1985), p. 10.

11. Rōdō Sho (Ministry of Labor), *Rōdō kumiai katsudō jittai chōsa hōkoku* (Report of a Survey on Union Activities) (Tokyo, 1986), pp. 8ff.

12. In Japan the total number of civil labor law cases was 2,179 in 1976; in the United States the number of U.S. district court labor law cases in 1979 was 9,994. For the United States, the number of state court cases is not available and the federal number of 2,719 is not complete since it includes only those classified under "Employers' Liability Act" and "labor law," and many labor cases would be classified under "civil rights."

13. *Business Week,* July 16, 1984.

14. Harry Katz, "Historical Evolution of the U.S. Industrial Relations System," prepared for the Council of Foreign Relations (1984).

15. "Analysis of U.S. Labor Law and Future of Labor Management Cooperation (Text)," prepared by Stephen I. Schlossberg, Deputy Under Secretary of Labor, in BNA, *Daily Labor Report,* no. 116, June 17, 1986, D-1.

16. Ibid., D-2.

17. Ibid., D-3.

18. There are many similar descriptions in American journals. See, e.g., "What's Creating an 'Industrial Miracle' at Ford?" *Business Week,* July 30, 1984, p. 80; "Japan's Way Works in Fremont," *San Francisco Chronicle,* Sept. 25, 1985.

19. "The Difference Japanese Management Makes," *Business Week,* July 14, 1986, p. 47; "Japan's Made-in-America Cars," *New York Times,* March 31, 1985.

20. The Schlossberg report analyzes how the American labor law system is becoming an obstacle for cooperative efforts because of its basic assumption of confrontation between labor and management. It says that the ultimate goal of the study is "to reach consensus on policy recommendations for interpretation or modification of the laws so that they support both the ingredients and the goals of labor-management cooperation rather than conflict with them" (D-1).

13 Democratic Consciousness in Japanese Unions

CHRISTENA TURNER

Democracy is not working in our unions. It should be, but it isn't. It's our job, as leaders, maybe our most important one, to make it work. If democracy cannot succeed in our labor unions, it can't succeed anywhere in Japanese society.

—Union official at a large shoe manufacturer, 1980

The Allied Occupation envisioned the democratization of Japan to involve a variety of interest groups and other voluntary associations, including labor unions, all competing to create a pluralistic democracy while offering ordinary citizens a place to participate in politics in their immediate social environments. Union representation of members' interests has periodically swung from radical to conservative and remains today a politically varied picture. As a whole the Japanese labor movement has pursued the interests of workers in increased democratization and equality with at least enough success to be credited with an important contribution to the achievement of pluralistic democracy in Japan.

The success of labor unions in becoming organizations through which individual members can participate in democracy and have their own interests and concerns heard and represented has been considerably more equivocal. Democracy at this level has significance much broader than the specific politics of a single organization. As Lipset, Trow, and Coleman observed in their classic study, *Union Democracy*, "the extension of democracy in an industrial society requires the extension of control by men over the institutions they

299

depend on."[1] The centrality of industry to the economy and the relatively large portion of the population represented by unions—as compared to other interest groups—makes the internal democracy of the
labor union of continuing interest to an understanding of democracy
in contemporary Japanese society.

The democratization efforts of the Occupation left postwar Japanese workers with extensive legal and constitutional protections and
rights. In just one year the portion of the work force organized into
labor unions jumped from 4.1 percent (1945) to 46.8 percent (1946)
and has remained at about 34 percent for the last thirty years.[2] The
constitution includes specific guarantees of rights "to organize, to
bargain, and to act collectively" (article 11), and three labor laws and a
trade union law detail specific provisions for the protection and operation of labor unions as well as for wages, compensation, vacation, and
other working conditions. These laws are considered by some to be
more comprehensive than comparable American and European legislation.[3] The structure of Japanese unions is, furthermore, formally
democratic. All unions have a constitution which provides for regular
conventions and meetings, for elections by secret ballot of all officials,
and for the establishment of elected legislative and executive committees. In practice, full-time union officers generally outnumber their
American or European counterparts as do the number of meetings
held, and this is itself often taken as evidence of the success of "popular democracy" in Japanese unions.[4] Japanese workers have been living with these institutions and laws for nearly forty years. Younger
workers have experienced no other political system. Workers now
over fifty-five remember very drastic changes. What has democracy
come to mean to them and does it inspire their commitment? Do they
believe that the unions of which they are members, unions which
proclaim their dedication to that ideal, and the organizational relations in which they participate are democratic?

These questions address one of the most important aspects of
democracy: whether or not individuals believe in democracy and believe that their organizations are in fact democratic, that is, the democratic consciousness of ordinary citizens, in this case workers in labor
unions. The democratic processes of politics require some degree of
democratic consciousness and relationship in the institutions of society.[5] Because the American Occupation of Japan intentionally attempted to change social groups like labor unions and to transform
Japanese citizens in a democratic direction[6]—rather than merely rely-

ing on changing the structure of government—this is a particularly important problem in Japan. Has the transition from authoritarian to democratic values, and from passive to active participation, been accomplished in Japanese social organizations such as unions? These are the questions to which this chapter is devoted.

Harmony, Consensus, and Democracy

The attitudes and ideas of the workers described in this chapter differ in some important ways from many of our common assumptions about Japanese workers and companies. The striking success of some Japanese companies both in growing into powerful enterprises following wartime destruction and in weathering worldwide economic crises of more recent history has brought great attention to Japanese industrial relations, which have come to be considered among the most harmonious in the world. Consensus-style decision making employed both within unions and between union and management has been held partly responsible for this harmony and as additional evidence of a healthy democratization of the Japanese organization. Recent work by Japanese and Western scholars has attempted to put this observed harmony and consensus in perspective. Taishiro Shirai strives to bring an appreciation of variation within the Japanese economy to the attention of Western readers, and Tadashi Hanami has tried to introduce us to the highly conflictual, outrageous, and often violent incidents which also crowd both past and present Japanese industrial relations. They emphasize that Japanese industrial relations cannot be summed up in a single generalization like harmony or consensus, even if that generalization is an accurate depiction of some aspects of the system. Shirai points out that our common notions stem from studies of a "limited segment of the Japanese labor market during a limited period of the country's industrializing history."[7]

To a large extent Westerners have focused on very successful, large firms which represent something less than 20 percent of the work force. The harmony and consensus-style decision making which seem to characterize these firms may do so in part because their resources are so great and because basic economic and job security can be guaranteed to at least a substantial portion of their workers. When I asked a Nissan manager about labor opposition to their extensive factory automation he told me that there wasn't any. He attributed the "harmonious" transition to "the expansion of Nissan's markets and operations. When we have to reduce our work force instead of simply relocating or retraining them, we will have problems." In other words, it is not that Japanese culture somehow makes conflict impossible or unlikely, but that for a certain segment of the work force it has been largely unnecessary, and it is on that segment that most of our attention has been focused. The larger segment of that work force has seen much rockier industrial relations, and if we include civil servants and their unions the picture becomes even more varied.

Amid this diversity of workplaces and experiences it is possible to identify a process, one which is likely to be occurring in workplaces of every size. The process of defining democracy, of making democracy meaningful in particular experiences within union and company work structures and dynamics, is ongoing in Japan as elsewhere. Many of the cares, concerns, cynicisms, and problems noted by the workers I spent time with will sound familiar to those with knowledge of workers or unions elsewhere.

The process of making democracy work and of defining and understanding it brings into play both political and social ideas and values. Consequently, when Japanese workers, or recently Chinese or Korean workers, talk about "democracy," they share with American workers the idea of democracy as a form of political equality—freedom from tyranny, and as a voice in the political process—political participation for individuals. What differs across these cultures, however, is the meaning ascribed to these notions of equality, participation, political process, and individualism. The process of making sense of democracy in the context of a particular culture with a specific set of social norms and values is the subject of this chapter. Nowhere is this process more evident than in watching people think and act as they face decisions and conflicts in their own work environments.

The Unions: "Unikon Camera" and "Universal Shoes"

The companies described in this chapter are two smaller and unsuccessful ones, two companies that did not make it through the recent oil crisis. One went bankrupt because the parent company automated and no longer needed it as a subcontractor. The other was bankrupted because of shrinking international markets and a failure to compete in gaining an increased share of the domestic market. The consciousness of the workers in these firms and their unions is interesting because it was changing in response to their experiences while I worked with them and because the workers were facing crises typical of small firms in Japan when the economy slumps and their solvency is threatened.

The unions in both companies were pursuing a still unusual solution to the problem of bankruptcy and loss of jobs: they were operating their own companies under self-management (*jishu kanri*)" while awaiting the conclusion of court cases and negotiations to settle bankruptcy-related labor disputes. The unions at both Unikon Camera and Universal Shoes (neither of these are the actual names of the companies) brought suit charging unfair labor practices, claiming rights to back wages, severance pay, and other benefits due them. They also charged that they had not been given the opportunity to bargain collectively, although under law employers are obliged to accept union offers to negotiate. In turn the unions were sued for obstruction of business and of police enforcement because they refused to evacuate the premises. In these actions the union demanded rights to assets, and set as their goal the reopening of their companies under new management—to be selected and designed by the unions themselves.

At Unikon the dispute went on for just over two and a half years, and at Universal it lasted eleven years. In each case final settlement came through negotiations which ended in a union victory and the establishment of a new company under management designed by the union itself.

Unikon had about one hundred fifty employees during its self-management stage, and just about double that immediately prior to its bankruptcy. Universal had just under fifty. Since both firms had had enterprise unions, as is common in Japan, and both included part-time workers as well as regular employees, these figures also equal the number of union members. The work force was about half male and half female, the women being predominantly middle-aged, part-time employees. The men at Unikon were all in their twenties or early thirties, and the men at Universal were almost evenly divided between middle-aged, full-time employees and elderly, post-retirement employees. These age and sex profiles are typical of workers in smaller firms. Prior to bankruptcy, wages were about average for small firms, lower than that for larger enterprises. (Typically there is a wage differential of just over 20 percent.)[8] The wide range of services and benefits associated with large Japanese companies—housing, low-interest loans, use of vacation facilities—was not available and generally is not in smaller firms. All workers in both unions, except for the very young for whom this was their first job, had had other, sometimes several, jobs. (Such mobility is also characteristic of small firms, which show an annual separation rate of over 30 percent for young and about 15 percent for middle-aged men, as comapred to just 5 percent for large firms.)[9] They therefore had experience in both unionized and non-unionized shops, and in a variety of industries.

The Unikon and Universal workers shared most characteristics with the 70 to 80 percent of the Japanese work force employed in small firms. As workers in a firm facing bankruptcy their situation was not typical, although it was not uncommon either. One of the greatest worries of workers in this section is the threat of bankruptcy, and one of their persistent concerns and a motivation for changing jobs is uncertainty about the continued financial stability of their firms. What is most unusual about these workers is their participation in union-managed firms. While this shows signs of being a growing trend among small firms facing bankruptcy, it is hardly a common practice, although some scholars see it as a new direction in labor relations.[10]

What makes the thoughts and feelings of the Unikon and Universal workers of particular interest is precisely their situation as ordinary people thrown into an extraordinary situation. These rank-and-file workers were forced to make a choice and to act, and once they decided to stay under self-management they were responsible, through their union, for organizing and managing their work as well as their dispute-related actions. The ideals of democracy and equality and the protection of legal and constitutional rights of workers were commonly discussed in meetings held in both unions, and within the unions all members were said to be equal and united. Such a setting of self-proclaimed democracy and equality provided a unique opportunity to study democratic consciousness through the discussions and the actions of people directly confronting these issues in their daily lives.

Because Japan is a non-Western, historically and culturally different society, the degree to which the ideals of democracy or its very definition resemble our own is a matter more for investigation than for assumption. In order to study ideas and values in the context of experience, my research was designed as participant observation, allowing me to interact with people at work and in home and recreational environments on a daily basis for a period of one year.[11] I did not rely on interviews, but rather on recollections, personal reflections, and spontaneous discussions in which I sometimes participated and other times simply listened. I found that three definitions of democracy (*minshushugi*) occurred in the everyday conversations of the Unikon and Universal workers: (1) the absence of tyranny; (2) the pursuit of the interests of the workers through the labor movement; and (3) participation in discussion and decision making within their organizations.

Democracy as the Absence of Tyranny

The word *minshushugi* is used frequently with reference to history or historical change, primarily in memories of older workers as recounted to younger co-workers or to their own families. For the younger workers there are no memories of Japan as anything other than a democracy. For those in their fifties and above, however, the memories of prewar and wartime society not only color their own ideas about contemporary society, but also emerge forcefully and frequently in discussion at home and at work.

In addition to the memories of older relatives and co-workers, younger people also have their own education, the popular press, and the entertainment media to elaborate on their image of Japan's past. As a result, for the "average person," as they most often refer to themselves, contemporary democracy is defined largely in contrast to the tyranny experienced by the "common person" in the past. Furthermore, since the ruling power was the military in the most recent past, it is also contrasted with militarism. Consequently, workers frequently link tyranny with the daily coercion experienced by workers and militarism, all of which are often juxtaposed and placed, as such, in opposition to "democracy" and "freedom."

A seventy-five-year-old former textile worker responded to her daughter-in-law's complaints about the lack of democracy in her shop by saying how much worse things used to be. She spoke of twelve-hour days, fences to keep the girls inside, working conditions which actually led to death for many of her co-workers, and a system whereby no one was allowed to even visit with their families until their "contract" was complete. She followed this with a detailed description of the way men her own age had been beaten to keep them in line after being drafted into the army. She concluded that "thanks to losing the war," "democracy" and "freedom" came to Japan, and things improved greatly. When used in this way, democracy is described more by implication than by specific reference to institutions or democratic processes, whereas the tyranny which it replaced is recounted in elaborate and personal detail. The resulting vagueness of the concept allows it to be used as a powerful symbol of what is hoped for in postwar Japanese society. Almost everything that people associate with increased freedom is labeled at one time or another "democratic." For instance, "We poor people have been greatly helped by the democratization . . . of Japan. We used to need a new suit, a bath, and hair cream just to go [downtown]! . . . If you couldn't afford it . . . you just had to stay home."

Democracy in this sense means increased freedom and decreased susceptibility to arbitrary power for the average citizen. It is associated with other ideals like equality and freedom, but not with any particular system or institution, representing expectations and hopes rather than concrete goals or criteria. It is illustrated more by what it replaced than by what it ushered in, and contemporary problems are quickly attributed to remnants of an undemocratic tradition, even while institutions and procedures which constitute the structure of Japanese democracy are looked upon with some cynicism.

The Labor Movement as a "Struggle for Democracy"

The Unikon and Universal unions referred to their disputes as "struggles for democracy," and the ideals of democracy, equality, and freedom—and the protection of constitutional and legal rights of workers—were explicitly emphasized both with reference to the labor movement's role in society and to the union's management of the firm and its members internally. While the rank and file supported these ideas in general, they were by and large participating in the struggles less out of an ideological desire to transform their workplaces or their society than to protect their jobs and their right to a decent livelihood.

Workers have a good grasp of the laws and institutions in their society, the political apparatus, and the operation of politics both in general and within their unions and union federations; knowledge of contemporary political issues is extensive. The idea, however, that the maximization of democratic goals is to be achieved through these structures or the political process at this level is not popular, and very little faith is placed in this method.

Rank and file cynicism toward the political process and its institutions nevertheless is combined with involvement in political action as union members. Even prior to the bankruptcy disputes which I observed, and during these disputes as well, they participated in actions aimed at furthering the interests of the workers as a whole. *Shuntō* (Spring Labor Offensive) demonstrations and May Day parades are only two examples. Their meetings, celebrations, and demonstrations all involved speeches and slogans emphasizing the role of the labor movement in furthering democracy in Japanese society. The threat of antilabor policies of the conservative government and big business was also portrayed convincingly as something against which workers must, through their unions, wage a stubborn struggle. The specific problems of Universal and Unikon, and their efforts to fight against losing their jobs were also represented by union leaders as part of the greater labor movement, of relevance to Japanese workers as a whole and even to workers internationally.

The majority of Japanese unions are aligned with political parties, and Universal is so aligned with the Socialist party, while Unikon remains "nonaligned" but "supported by" both Communists and Socialists. The rank and file recognize the necessity of these connections in order to gain necessary political strength at the national or local level. Their own political preferences are not, however, always in line with their union's, and they show no signs of making any efforts to change that. Differing political preferences are not spoken of in front of union leaders, although among co-workers such inhibitions are largely absent. At both Universal and Unikon, workers were all supporters of opposition parties, and shared at least an anti-conservative party orientation.

Both unions are affiliated with Sōhyō, the General Council of Trade Unions of Japan, as well as with the appropriate trade union federations. Unikon belongs to the All Japan Metalworkers Federation and Universal to the All Japan Leatherworkers Federation. Because they are small unions, the officials of these federations play a relatively strong role in guiding their policies. Also because they are small, they are financially weak and thus depend on the larger network of unions for support. Their size is also seen as the reason for their disadvantaged position within both the federations and Sōhyō, and the leaders complain about Sōhyō's lack of concrete support for smaller unions.

Rank and file members recognize the necessity of affiliation with union politics and national politics at this level. The collective weakness of the opposition parties is seen as related to the weak position of workers in Japanese society, and the parties' relative strength or weakness at any given time is even thought to have some impact on the speed with which particular union disputes are settled. Affiliation with political parties, with federations, and the presence of Diet members at union functions receive only equivocal support, however. Because participation is so indirect at this level, through representatives, people do not feel they have a clear sense of just how things are handled. They evaluate the political process by its achieved benefits, of which they characteristically feel they do not get an adequate share. They believe that benefits go primarily to workers in large firms whose unions are stronger and more financially sound, and who are taken more seriously by government and big business as industry leaders.

While leadership continues a concerted effort to arouse interest in and commitment toward the labor movement as a force for furthering the interests of workers and thus Japanese democracy, the rank and file persist in a sort of well-informed apathy tinged with cynicism. This attitude contrasts sharply with the deeply felt commitment to the ideal of "democracy" in general and to the goal of individual participation in decision making within their own unions.

Democracy as Participation in Decision-Making

At Unikon and Universal, democracy most often inspires conversation and arouses emotion when conceptualized as participation in decision making, usually understood to be involvement in discussion. Other forms of participation in union politics, like voting or attending meetings, while taken advantage of, do not evoke high expectations for maximization of democracy in their unions. Attention is focused instead on discussion, debate, and consultation. The word *democracy* itself comes up occasionally in informal discussion and more frequently in formal addresses, but it is far more common for people to discuss the issue without using the term. "Democracy," people told me, means "being able to speak up, be listened to, and be taken seriously."

At both Universal and Unikon, the failure to achieve this kind of democracy was more obvious and received more attention than the successes, particularly among rank and file and even among the leaders. The trade union federation representatives and Sōhyō officers involved with these unions told me, furthermore, that these unions are not unusual. A man in his sixties with thirty years' experience working with Sōhyō affiliated unions said, "There isn't any real democracy in Japanese unions anywhere, not if you mean real participation of the average member in making decisions and forming policies." One of the officers from Universal's affiliated federation thought the reason for this lack was to be found in the newness of the democracy in Japan. Rank and file would agree, but they do not believe the solution lies in educating the membership. Instead they focus on the attitudes and political practices of union leaders. A Universal worker explained it this way: "Democracy doesn't work because our leaders act like *samurai*. As soon as they get any power, they start acting superior and stubborn. They don't even want to hear differing ideas, and they are scared that their own power might be weakened if differing opinions come out in the open. Consequently, they try to suppress any debate. You can't have democracy with that kind of attitude!"

Union leaders continue their efforts to overcome the attitude among rank and file that it is either too risky or too futile to speak up. They emphasize that important decisions must not be left to executive committees and advisory committees composed of officials, but must be made with the cooperation of all union members. The officials themselves consider unions to be one of the "foundations of Japanese democracy," and they worry that not enough progress has been made in increasing actual participation of members in policy decisions. Many say that they are battling a tradition of political passivity and apathy among workers. The union members do not typically feel these expressisons of concern to be completely sincere.

While democratic participation in principle is recognized as important, it is also, and perhaps more commonly, linked to more concrete goals. The leaders see discussion and the expression of personal opinion to be important in building a unified membership and a strong union and in guaranteeing the organization's responsiveness to its members. Their efforts and goals center on education, improvement of members' consciousness as workers, and assessment of their needs. For the rank and file, the benefits are almost exclusively seen in terms of having their needs and their point of view heard, understood, and taken into account in the formation of union policy.

Participation at Universal

At Universal, despite some occasional, temporary improvements, workers did not feel that democratic participation had ever been fully realized. The earliest stages of union management were somewhat better, probably because the relative chaos of that period inspired informal meetings in which people were able to air their opinions and participate more directly in decision making. As their dispute and self-management continued, however, they felt the gap between themselves and their leaders to be ever widening. A tension developed between these two sides which neither seemed capable of breaking through. This situation was perceived by both to be detrimental to their union and to be a source of weakness which accounted in part for the length of time it took to reach a settlement.

Universal's leadership was somewhat idealistic and tended toward a commitment to socialism, self-management, and the creation of a "democratic," "egalitarian," and "cooperative" workplace. To these ends, discussion and debate among all members were repeatedly stressed both formally at gatherings and informally. These themes were employed constantly, for example, at the union's twenty-fifth annual convention; but each request for discussion met with silence from the members. This was a meeting which lasted some four and a half hours and involved extensive reporting on past and future policy. In the end, the members made no comments of any kind, although afterward there was abundant informal discussion, lasting for a couple of weeks, about new strategies and policies announced at this meeting.

Prior to this particular meeting, the people with whom I worked warned me not to expect much of it, even though it was a major gathering. "Wait and see," they said; "there won't be a peep from any of us. We'll just keep quiet. It's always like that." There were, in fact, distinct disagreements on some issues and misgivings on others. But they were aired out of earshot of leaders during work or at lunch or tea breaks, or while walking to and from the train station, or at snack bars after work. If such a discussion were underway when one of the union officers approached, people would simply quiet down until he left. The tension between leadership and rank and file remained, and the silence of the latter was largely unbroken in spite of widespread agreement about the importance of discussion and expression of opinion.

Participation at Unikon

At Unikon the situation was somewhat different. The union had, for a time, achieved what looked to many observers, and felt to many workers, like democratic participation. The workers boasted about being able to "say whatever you think," and the leaders characterized their union as one in which workers were so vocal, committed, and well-informed that they were sometimes "frightening." Officials of other unions called Unikon "a union with real discussion, real unity, and real strength," and held it up as an example for their own.

Nevertheless, as Unikon neared final solution of its dispute and entered the critical concluding negotiations which would determine the precise conditions under which it would settle and reopen the company, things began to change. The rank and file were not consulted and information ceased to flow down to them. The important decisions concerning new working conditions and other matters actually leaked out as rumor before they were even announced. There was no room for any sort of decision.

The new working conditions, when finally announced, were actually much worse than people had expected. As a result, some workers quit and many who stayed were bitterly disillusioned. Both groups agreed that the real problem was not just the specific new working conditions, but the way in which things were handled. Whatever decisions needed to be made, they felt that they should have been involved and, at the very least, should have had access to relevant information. People began to reassess their union, and in hindsight questioned whether or not they had really been participating in decision making at all. They had been encouraged to air their opinions, but in the end, they reflected, things had always ended up going in the direction that the leaders had planned. They sometimes blamed themselves for having been too trusting, and many concluded that they should have defended their own interests more vigilantly.

What these workers did do was to have extensive discussions and to encourage each other through informal get-togethers and conversation at work. Many of these conversations were very emotional, with anger and tears commonplace, and most people spoke at one time or another of losing their sense of purpose. At meetings, however, they were utterly quiet. They did make sarcastic comments aimed at individual leaders when the leaders were within earshot, but they never made any kind of organized or formal statement of opposition and never requested explanation or defense from their leaders. They said that they had to deal with the problem themselves and to handle their feelings about things privately.

The Nature of the Problem

To explain the unsatisfactory level of discussion and debate in their unions, leaders tend to focus on the workers' inexperience in democracy or their political apathy or passivity. The rank and file present a different picture. Their interpretations of the problem center on (1) powerlessness, (2) personal insecurity, (3) inequality, and (4) formality. These four aspects of their situation combine to create an "atmosphere" in which people say it is unwise to speak up and sensible to remain silent. This is neither an atmosphere of harmony and consensus nor one of authoritarian subordination. It is rather a well-calculated acquiescence, a response which cultural orientations and political realities make sensible to these workers.

Powerlessness

Perception of themselves as politically weak, both as individuals and as an interest group, is one of the most pervasive elements within the social consciousness of these workers, and one with a particularly strong impact on their understanding of their own potential to be active participants in a democratic political process. It is a widely used notion, providing explanations for why workers must organize on their own behalf and why they cannot possibly do so, for why they must defend their own interests and for why it is often futile to try.

This sense of powerlessness or weakness is a relative one, conceptualized within the context of certain relationships where workers see themselves as the weaker partner. The four of relevance here are (1) rank and file— leadership, (2) union—management, (3) (small) union—federations/Sōhyō, and (4) workers—government/big business (or capitalists). In each of these the participation of the weaker side in a democratic process of decision making, policymaking, or collective bargaining is seen as possible and desirable. The initiative and responsibility to create specific mechanisms for participation is believed to lie, however, with the stronger side. Any perceived failures in achieving democracy at these levels are therefore considered to be the fault of the stronger partner.

The weaker side, with which workers inevitably identify, is not only free of blame or responsibility, it is also thought to have very limited possible responses. When I challenged some of the workers with the idea that if they spoke up, things would no longer be a "one-way street," as they so often complained, people laughed and joked that that might work in America, but in Japan the leaders aren't smart or skillful enough nor do they know how to behave democratically. Further, they argued, "We aren't given a chance to say anything. They just say what they want to say and all we can do is keep quiet and go along with it." The idea that they have "no opportunity" to speak is understandable only in light of two widely held common sense assumptions: that their own behavior is in response to their leaders' action and therefore dependent on it, and that the leaders are responsible for consulting and encouraging discussion.

What many workers openly object to is a set of circumstances over which their leaders have control and which represents to them both leadership power as well as insincerity concerning real rank and file participation. The leadership controls information, the timing of its release, and the meeting agendas. Because members have no say in any of these areas they say they are always reacting to decisions which have already been made and that they never have the necessary information prior to a final decision. In short, they feel like subjects rather than participants.

Their attitudes are filled with paradoxes. They recognize the need for the leaders to lead, to have first and greater access to information, to represent them in the outside world, and to make many decisions without daily consultation with the entire membership; they themselves want to delegate much to their leadership and content themselves with their daily work and home life. On the other hand, they feel that it is precisely in the decisions that most directly affect their daily lives that they should, but rarely do, have a say. They are frustrated about not being consulted on these matters, but they do not feel obligated or even able to insist upon it and prefer instead to blame their leaders for being old-fashioned, undemocratic, and acting only in their own personal interests. These rank and file feelings of frustration, anger, or betrayal are, in turn, generally dealt with informally and apolitically.

There is another sense in which the notion of powerlessness makes its appearance in discussions about democratic participation. When speaking of the broader social structure, workers tend to divide people into two groups, "the strong" and "the weak." Specific identities change with the context, but again, workers always identify with "the weak." They also call themselves "commoners" and identify with various historical tendencies which they group under the general "Japanese tradition." After seeing plays and movies about the Dickensian conditions of peasants or Meiji era female silk workers, for instance, people commented on how "our company is just like that."

However impossible it is to believe that conditions can be as bad now as they were in feudal or prewar times, it is an important aspect

of the consciousness of workers that they see enough continuity of
weakness and victimization at the hands of "the strong" to refer to the
past of the Japanese commoners, workers, or peasants when explaining their own inability to act, or their own position of weakness or
difficulty. Seeing themselves as contemporary bearers of a tradition of
powerlessness, coupled with a concrete sense of their weakness
within their unions, helps them explain their own political passivity.
The consequence of these self-images is a feeling of political sovereignty in the abstract sense of belief in the ideals of democracy, but
with a very low level of political efficacy in their daily encounters
with the political processes within their own unions.

Personal Insecurity

The importance of their families to Japanese workers is probably
impossible to overestimate. In addition to natural ties of affection,
the responsibility to provide them a "bright and cheerful life," an
omnipresent slogan at demonstrations and parades, is a basic motivation for much of their action. At both Universal and Unikon,
workers talked about work itself, and their participation in their
unions and in the labor disputes, as being "for the sake of my
family." Yet when people discussed their participation in union politics, they also cited their families as central reasons for their silence
or hesitation.

At one informal shop floor meeting at Universal, for instance,
"the problem of people not speaking up" at general meetings was
introduced by the foreman for discussion. There were several brief
comments followed by unanimous agreement, to the effect that
"everyone has a family, so what can you do?" The other common
response to the question was "raising children is a big responsibility."
The link, which to everyone seemed self-evident, between keeping
quiet and having a family is insecurity, a repeated theme throughout
conversations about participation in their unions. "You don't want to
end up in an insecure position—you don't want to be argued with,"
concluded one man.

Ultimately the source of this feeling is the fear of losing their jobs.
I asked one of the men I worked with why he thought people were so
quiet even though they had so many opinions of their own and were
willing to express them informally. "People just don't want to stick
their necks out [medatsu] especially the older men. They can't afford
to." While it seems unlikely that speaking out would lead to losing

your job, it is a very real concern to these workers. They see uncertainty in the low growth rate of the Japanese economy in recent years, especially following the oil crises of the 1970s, in the threat of bankruptcy to their own small companies, and in the fierce competition among small enterprises in the Japanese economy. Workers in this sector, they say, are "perpetually worried about their jobs and about their livelihood."

There is also a personal dimension to this fear of being fired or forced into quitting. At Universal there is a story about a well-liked man who tried some years ago, before the bankruptcy dispute, to make his views known. He spoke out and expressed himself well at meetings even when he disagreed. The consequence was that he was bullied and given such a hard time that eventually he was forced to quit. Part of what people experience as insecurity is, of course, a result of their unions being enterprise unions and not trade unions. Because employment at the company equals union membership, being out of favor with their own union also means that there is at least the possibility of losing their jobs.

There is yet another source of insecurity for these workers in the meager social services in Japanese society.[12] People say that they have to rely solely on themselves, on their own resources. Housing is expensive, old age pensions are small, health insurance programs are limited, and their children's education can be expensive. All of this adds up to a heavy sense of responsibility. As one Unikon worker put it: "For those in large companies, their companies provide everything for them. For us, as soon as we leave at five o'clock we are on our own. You are all by yourself and no one is there to help you." With all this responsibility and a sense that there is nowhere to turn for help, you cannot afford to risk losing your job.

To understand the workers' feelings of insecurity, it is necessary to understand their belief that it is impossible for expressions of opinion to lead to discussion, compromise, and decision making in a peaceful democratic process. What people envision when they talk about speaking out is essentially a fight. In responding to either an abuse of power or simply a policy or decision with which rank and file do not agree, a polarization of alternatives occurs. Workers feel that they must choose between either inactivity accompanied by suppression of their own ideas and feelings, or extreme opposition. Extreme opposition, when conceived as an individual effort or an unorganized effort of a small group, promises great risks in personal security for those involved.

Opposition as an organized effort is dismissed as too complex a task to undertake, and in a small union just too impractical, in part because the only members skilled in political organization are already operating as leaders. To oppose them, it is thought, is to fail simply due to ignorance of and inexperience in the political process.

The consequence of this polarization of alternatives is severe constraint on any democratic participation which would include legitimate expression of divergent or opposing views. People point to the so-called minority unions or breakaway unions in large companies as the only form which internal differences of opinion can feasibly take. When the total disruption of their own union is either not desired or not considered feasible, the most sensible alternative is quiet, calculated acquiescence.

The Distance Between "Top" and "Bottom"

The distance between "those on top" and "those on the bottom" is considered to be at once the source and the consequence of vast differences in goals, ways of thinking, and strategies between leadership and membership. In addition to what is considered a "natural" distance necessitated by their different roles within the organization, the pursuit of personal power and status, available only through the union hierarchy, is also seen to give leadership a very different set of goals. "Without the labor movement there isn't any way for them [leaders] to become or to associate with big shots [*erai hito*]. They don't want to do things simply; they want to show off their positions and act powerfully to outsiders." "They" are seen often to be "just going their own way," "taking detours," and "not really caring what we think." This "us" (*oretachi* or *watashitachi*) and "them" (*mukō*) terminology is by far the most common way for rank and file to refer to themselves and their leaders in conversation. Included in "them" as in the "top" and "big shots" are members of the executive committes and all higher officers as well as the affiliated federation and Sōhyō officers.

Basic to the perceived distance are the differences in "ways of thinking" and the "unwillingness" of their leaders to really listen to their ideas. Leaders announce things, request cooperation, explain policies and strategies, and try to convince rank and file that they are right. People feel that they do not really listen. Encouragement of expression of opinion is often simply the first step in pressuring rank and file to approve the leaders' decisions. "Even when you do speak up, the discussion is still a one-way street going wherever the leaders have already decided it's to go."

If the rank and file feel that they are being coerced into consensus, the leaders, on the other hand, feel that if they don't work hard to maintain some semblance of control over the members, chaos will result. In response to the expression of opinion from the rank and file, which they themselves encourage, leaders see their responsibility to be "education." They commonly perceive the average Japanese worker to be egotistical, selfishly individualistic, and lacking in consciousness, concerned only with the most personally relevant social issues, and with their own personal benefits. "All they care about," one leader complained, "is what the union can offer them. They have no concern with the labor movement itself or with strengthening their own unions." One Sōhyō advisor I spoke to saw American individualism as tempered with a sense of civic responsibility, but his own country's individualism as unrestrained, with workers who lacked any sense of "social responsibility." Leaders widely believed, therefore, that they must "manage discussion" and lead it in a productive direction.

Union leaders are as concerned as members with this gap and try in a variety of ways to overcome it or at least lessen inhibitions about communicating across it. Paradoxically, their efforts often reaffirm the vertical distance even while denying it. A speech by an official at a general meeting, for instance, urged "equality" in the following way: "In our union we are all the same. We are all equal union members and equal as workers—all of us—from the president all the way down to the part-time women." Their efforts are further impeded by the polite and deferential attitude and language which common sense dictates in interaction between persons of unequal status. Workers say that you should not speak too much or disagree too openly with your "superiors" and that you must use "correct language." While appropriate discussion and even disagreement is a possibility, it is a linguistically and socially sophisticated one which most do not feel the confidence to attempt. Lacking that confidence, workers tend to avoid situations where it is necessary and, failing that, cope by speaking as sparingly as possible.

From both sides of the gap comes the notion of great distance between them in terms of goals and strategies. From both we get a feeling of near futility in closing that gap. Leaders make frequent efforts—some sincere and some not—to achieve real participation, but in their very efforts they often demonstrate their own stubborn unwillingness to listen. Their own belief that democracy is somehow to be achieved by denying or even ignoring material self-interest contradicts the rank and file belief that democracy is meant at least in part to serve them in achieving an improved livelihood. Complicating this distance even further is the perception that leaders are themselves, while espousing higher purposes of the labor movement, actually striving for their own personal power and status within that movement and using their membership to those ends.

Formality

The unions' general meetings are held at least twice a year and sometimes more often in order to allow the rank and file to approve policies and decisions made by their officers and executive committees. Although the formality of these affairs is assumed to be appropriate to the occasion, it is in and of itself disliked and the members participated with considerable ambivalence. It is to the carefully planned and absolutely predictable structure of these meetings that rank and file refer when they talk about it being "impossible" to speak out.

The complete lack of any kind of spontaneity in these gatherings is itself a mandate against membership participation. The agenda, printed up and handed out as people enter the room, is strictly followed and the meetings begin and end on a very predictable note. Since the officers and guests draw up the agenda and prepare speeches in advance, their participation contributes to the orderliness of the proceedings. Rank and file see the agenda for the first time on entering the meeting room, and if they have something to say or ask they must do so on the spot. They "haven't time," they complain, "to work out just what we want to say" and consequently they nearly always remain silent.

The order of speakers is a further inhibition. Greetings and addresses are given in order of status, with Diet members speaking first; leaders of affiliated labor movement organizations next, and then their own officers. Proposals and opinions are offered first by these people in the form of speeches to the membership. In addition, these proposals are printed up and handed out at the door in pamphlet form. It is only after thirty minutes to an hour of such addresses that rank and file are encouraged to express their opinions and ask questions. Following their almost inevitable silence, they are asked to approve policy proposals by voice vote or applause. The fact that proposals are already approved by higher authorities according to accepted procedures, that they are offered already in print, and supported by well-prepared speeches by high ranking officers, in lucid and correct language, all combine to create the "atmosphere" of which rank and file repeatedly speak, in which it is "impossible to say anything."

These meetings are, nonetheless, taken seriously by rank and file in one sense. They are seen as a necessary show of solidarity and unity when the union is struggling to win a dispute. The meeting recalled a performance, and it is here that harmony comes most directly into conflict with democratic participation. Workers take great pride in the success of these affairs, and they reflect with good-natured humor on their own competence in depicting harmony, unity, and solidarity. Their purpose is to display strength, and since conceptually harmony is linked directly to strength, a show of dissension would defeat what for the rank and file appears to be the only real purpose of the gathering. The addresses all emphasize unity, solidarity, and strength, as well as universally relevant themes like improvement of livelihood and protection of jobs. The utter impossibility of shattering the image by standing up and disagreeing with some issue is understood by everyone as a kind of unquestioned common sense. To do so would be like an actor in a play suddenly discarding his role and asserting his own personality.

Large meetings, which include outside guests, are inevitably difficult. They are on the one hand displays of determination, strength, and unity, and on the other one of the most important business meetings held by the union. They are vital for the dissemination of information and are meant to be important forums for at least limited discussion. There seems to be a feeling that argument and debate suggest conflict, and an organization with open conflict is weak. Naturally, this attitude encourages the suppression of the open and relatively uninhibited discussion required for participation.

What rank and file suggest as a solution to this dilemma is, in their words, a "seminar" (*zeminaru*), an informal gathering where information would be made available and issues discussed prior to actual decision making. The proper timing for such sessions is critical, since one important complaint is that nothing is ever discussed until decisions are already made. The agenda would also be flexible, with an opportunity for rank and file to introduce topics of concern. Results of these sessions would then be reported to union officers and the opinions integrated into policies at that level. This suggestion itself, while held very widely and with some enthusiasm, has never been put formally to officials—because workers "have never been given a chance to do so."

Conclusion

To return to the questions with which I began, democratic ideals and values have had considerable success in penetrating the consciousness of the rank and file worker. The ideals of democracy have been embraced so enthusiastically that the word itself sometimes has the awesome ability to represent almost anything that is good about post-war Japanese society. The democratic structures of the polity, however, have come to be taken for granted after nearly forty years. And, while workers' constitutional and legal rights, political institutions, and union organizations are considered basic to the operation of the political process, they are not by and large considered sufficient to the realization of democracy.

The operation of politics itself is given the most cynical of interpretations, stemming largely from a certain attitude not toward formal institutions but toward power within the social world of the workers. As Unikon and Universal workers see it, relationships of power determine the uses made of democratic institutions and procedures, not the other way around, and these structures of democracy are not widely considered capable of checking the misuses of power which the rank and file observe around them. While formal procedures may guarantee informative and expressive opportunities, they cannot guarantee real participation and involvement because they are not capable of altering or even substantially moderating the critical structuring relationships, "power relationships," or "the system."[13]

To these workers it looks as though the further realization of democracy in contemporary Japan is being threatened by traditional Japanese power relationships surviving relatively unchanged within the formal structures of capitalism and democracy. It is not that the traditional norms of harmony and consensus inhibit their voicing of opinion, thus stalling democracy, but that the really important decisions are made by power holders behind the scenes without involvement or even consultation. Too often what passes for consultation is little more than an orchestrated expressive opportunity designed to appear democratic, the substance being handled somewhere out of reach. Unikon and Universal workers made these generalizations about politics at all levels as it pertains to workers, from the national arena to their own shop floors. Within their unions, responsibility for initiating democratic participation, discussion, or debate is seen to belong to the leadership. On the national level, they rely on representation by federations and resign themselves to their relatively disadvantaged and underrepresented position as small firm workers within these organizations.

Political protest is one way in which workers have been very successful in speaking out and guarding their own interests. Political participation in this form is largely a veto of already decided or enacted policies and is an important check on abuse of power or neglect of rank and file interests. And it is here that the success of Japanese democracy is abundantly evident: in the unquestioned notion that it is possible for workers to fight for their rights and that they will even be likely to win if they do. However, the satisfaction of the average union member with this form of participation is not high. Protest often requires more time and effort than people can give. They prefer negotiation, consultation, and discussion prior to decision making. Furthermore, organizing a protest either by a union or within a union is seen as involving political skills not possessed by rank and file in small unions and entailing many risks for people in their social and economic position.

The goal of democracy for most rank and file is the improvement of their own and their families' well-being. Within their unions this means an almost exclusive focus on economic and related political concerns. Efforts by union leaders to expand the power of the labor movement or secure a more advantageous organizational position for their unions are commonly criticized as involvement in tangential issues or as representing their desire to expand their own personal power and stature. Rank and file focus instead on the importance of finding a way for average workers with a sincere but limited political commitment to have a say in union decision making prior to the actual formation of proposals.

At present the consciousness of Unikon and Universal workers is characterized more by a series of competing motivations and attitudes than by consistencies. They act out of a calculated acquiescence as often as out of a committed consensus, believe more in the ideals of political sovereignty than in their own political efficacy, and strive for political participation without demanding political equality. Harmony within their unions is more a strategy for showing strength and achieving certain goals than it is an end in itself, and their commitment to their union stems in large part from a sense of individual vulnerability.

Their sense of inevitability, of futility, and of resignation is an outgrowth of cultural assumptions about the nature of power relationships and of an appraisal of their own past. Japan has come so far so fast, and workers have already achieved so much, that there is a certain contentment—although an increasingly uneasy contentment. It is too soon since feudal times and too soon since the end of World War II to expect democracy to be fully realized. On the other hand, after some forty years it is too late, and people have come to expect too much, to feel wholly comfortable with the level of democratic participation in their unions today.

NOTES

1. Seymour Martin Lipset, Martin Trow, and James Coleman, *Union Democracy* (New York: Anchor Books, 1956), p. 462.

2. Kazutoshi Kōshiro, "Japan's Labor Unions," in *Politics and Economics in Contemporary Japan,* ed. Hyōe Murakami and Johannes Hirschmeier (Tokyo: Japan Culture Institute, 1979), p. 148.

3. Tadashi Hanami, *Labor Relations in Japan Today* (Tokyo: Kodansha, 1981); Lawrence Ward Beer, *Freedom of Expression in Japan* (Tokyo: Kodansha, 1984); Sheldon M. Garon, "The Imperial Bureaucracy and Labor Policy in Postwar Japan," *Journal of Asian Studies* 43 (May 1984): 441–57.

4. Norikuni Naitō, "Trade Union Finance and Administration," in *Contemporary Industrial Relations in Japan,* ed. Taishirō Shirai (Madison: University of Wisconsin Press, 1983), p. 154.

5. Gabriel Almond and Sidney Verba, *The Civic Culture* (Boston: Little, Brown and Company, 1963).

6. Garon, "Imperial Bureaucracy," p. 450.

7. Taishirō Shirai, ed., *Contemporary Industrial Relations in Japan* (Madison: University of Wisconsin Press, 1983); Tadashi Hanami, *Labor Relations,* and "Conflict and Its Resolution in Japanese Industrial Relations and Labor Law," in *Conflict in Japan,* ed. Ellis S. Krauss, Thomas C. Rohlen, and Patricia G. Steinhoff (Honolulu: University of Hawaii Press, 1984).

8. Kazuo Koike, "Workers in Small Firms and Women in Industry," in Taishirō Shirai, ed., *Contemporary Industrial Relations,* p. 92.

9. Ibid., p. 97.

10. Hideo Totsuka, "Chū-shō Kigyō no Rōdō Sōgi" (Labor Disputes in Small and Medium-Sized Industry), *Chūō Rōdō Jihō*, no. 4 (1980): 2–13.

11. The findings reported here are part of my Ph.D. dissertation research. Field work was carried out in 1980–81.

12. Robert Cole, *Work, Mobility, and Participation* (Berkeley and Los Angeles: University of California Press, 1979), pp. 245–46, discusses the link between worker commitment in large firms and the "structured dependency relationship" between worker and firm, the need for which is created by limited public services. Shirai, "Japanese Labor Unions and Politics," in Taishirō Shirai, ed., *Contemporary Industrial Relations*, p. 342, cites insufficient "social infrastructure" as one of the most persistent complaints among both white- and blue-collar workers.

13. The notion that a strong exercise of power within an organization can be compatible with formal opportunities for participation and consultation is stressed in ibid., p. 203, in the context of labor-management relations in large firms.

Conclusion

14 Japanese Democracy in Perspective

•

ELLIS S. KRAUSS and TAKESHI ISHIDA

As the preceding chapters have made clear, in the forty years since World War II Japan has made the transition from a devastated and defeated nation with an authoritarian political system to an industrialized society with a democratic polity. Japanese democracy, on a relative scale, compares favorably with the industrialized democracies in North America and Western Europe. As in the Western democracies, however, democracy in Japan has particular strengths and weaknesses. No one-dimensional characterization of Japanese democracy can accurately capture its complexity. Nor will all observers necessarily agree on what is a strength or a weakness.

Further, as in all countries, aspects of democracy that some consider weaknesses often go along with the strengths. This is the approach we take here in trying to provide a short evaluation of Japanese democracy. We will summarize the major accomplishments and failings of Japanese democracy in the postwar period as described in greater detail by our contributors and, where appropriate, indicate how at times the positive and negative aspects may be closely related to each other.

As we suggested in chapter 1, it may be helpful to evaluate democracy by organizing discussion around four elements: representation and accountability, participation, equality, and stability. In this discussion, we will also place the development of contemporary Japanese democracy into historical perspective. Afterward in our concluding section, we will evaluate the recent stereotypes that view Japan as a model for democratic postindustrial or developing societies.

Representation and Participation

One of the most successful aspects of Japanese democracy has been the way in which important democratic values and institutions have been accepted and established. We tend to forget that just forty-one years ago, not a long period in historical perspective, millions of Japanese were ready to sacrifice themselves for their belief in an emperor-system that legitimized an authoritarian military regime. Thus, the very fact that an overwhelming majority of Japanese people today believe in democracy and take it for granted as the ideal system for Japan is a major accomplishment.

The widespread and deep acceptance of the structure of democracy—a constitutional order based on the sovereignty of the people, representative institutions, civil liberties, free and competitive elections, and the other aspects of political pluralism—is even more remarkable if we recall that this system was imposed on the Japanese by a foreign, occupying power. Certainly there were democratic elements and tendencies in prewar Japan upon which the Occupation could build, and this may help account for some of the postwar success of democracy in Japan. Whatever its origins, with the exception of fringe groups on the right and left, the institutions and basic values of democracy as the concept developed initially in the West have been accepted and institutionalized in postwar Japan.

Beyond the structures, the process of politics too has become more democratic and acquired legitimacy. Leading politicians, as John Campbell makes clear (chapter 6), are at least as influential as the still powerful bureaucrats in policymaking. An active press has taken upon itself the role of disseminator of information as well as critic of authority, as Lawrence Beer suggests (chapter 4). Political activity by interest groups had shallow organizational roots and dubious legitimacy in the early postwar period, but now has acquired both stronger bases and respectability.

Also acquiring popular support have been the basic ideas upon which pluralist democratic politics rest: the idea of "rights" has gained currency in a culture that formerly stressed political obligation; open public conflict among political parties has become increasingly accepted in a culture that previously emphasized consensus; the concepts of local autonomy and citizen input into government, as Terry MacDougall writes (chapter 7), have acquired positive value in a society where a tradition of elite rule and modernizing centralization previously predominated. In other words, the cultural norms on which many Western observers would argue democratic process must be based have filtered down to the mass level.

One of the most salient characteristics of predemocratic Japanese political culture was the extent to which ordinary citizens felt themselves "subjects" of political life, rather than active participants in it. No longer is this the case among large segments of the public. Not only do the institutions and legal framework provide for popular participation in government, but the social and economic resources to channel participation into effective group action have also grown. The affluence and high mass educational attainments of the past two decades have given the individual Japanese the "resources" associated with a greater tendency to participation in public life. With the high rate of participation in social organizations comes the potential for more effective political participation through collective group mobilization.

Consciousness of one's ability to take advantage of those opportunities and resources—and sometimes go even beyond them—too has proceeded apace: protest, both within and outside the law, has been a frequent occurrence in postwar politics (see Patricia Steinhoff, chapter 8). Also increasing has been grass-roots participation in social and not just political organizations: as Tadashi Hanami shows (chapter 12), informal participation of workers in company decisions has advanced recently. This trend is not the automatic result of traditional Japanese cultural notions of harmony, but of conscious efforts in the face of economic crisis, and it undoubtedly represents the increasing acceptance of democratic values in all spheres of life.

Unquestionably, all the above developments—political, economic, and social—suggest a nation with a healthy democratic system in many respects. But there is a more negative side interwoven amidst these accomplishments.

The very acceptance of democratic ideals has contributed in some quarters to a cynicism toward the political process because the expectations for democracy are either impossibly high or are seen not to have been adequately rooted in the individual's daily life. Christena Turner's discussion (chapter 13) of the beliefs about democracy of some workers and their alienation from their own unions suggests a deep well of political cynicism about leaders and politics in Japan. It is also a vivid reminder that the growing informal participation of workers in large company decisions, as described by Hanami, is not necessarily duplicated in the small and medium enterprises in which a majority of

Japanese work, nor even in organizations whose rhetoric proclaims them to be working on behalf of democratic causes.

Similarly, it is the acceptance of democratic norms that has under-lined the inherent unfairness of apportionment of Diet seats between urban and rural districts in Japan, discussed in detail by J.A.A. Stockwin (chapter 5), and created dissatisfaction in the press and among some urban salarymen with the inability of the government to reform the system as quickly as they would like. The problem of electoral malapportionment constitutes one of the major problems of democratic structure and basic legitimacy remaining in the postwar system. It is by no means an insurmountable problem—as the Liberal Democratic party has successfully shifted its policies to gain more support among the urban middle class, it may continue the process of gradual reform because reapportionment will no longer threaten its ability to stay in power.

The growing respectability of interest groups and their influence on politics may be a mixed democratic blessing. For example, the close relationship between big business and the ruling LDP has led some to become particularly cynical about the influence of money on politics and the opportunities for corruption it has provided. Further, the polarized pattern of interest groups' relationship with political parties, whereby the interest group tends to support one party almost exclusively, can create special problems in Japanese democracy. Al-though most major interest groups have some degree of influence on policy through various channels, organized labor has been aligned primarily with parties opposed to the long-ruling LDP, and its influ-ence in politics has therefore been much less than in any other postwar democratic country. Whether this has resulted in more rational eco-nomic policies in Japan or not is a subject that many will debate; we merely ask whether the diminished influence of such an important segment of modern society is completely functional for the develop-ment of a stable democracy.

Even the increased influence of some interest groups and politicians on policymaking in recent years has not been without its problems. When combined with the severe competitive segmentation of the Japa-nese bureaucracy, this trend has sometimes produced a fragmented political process in which coordination among alliances of certain po-liticans, interest groups, and ministries against other similar alliances has become difficult. The centralization of power in a prestigious and elite bureaucracy creates one type of problem in democracy—elitism;

but the permeation of policymaking by political considerations and the existence of competing centers of power can create another kind of problem—lack of policy coordination. As Campbell argues, the decline in technical efficiency and effectiveness and in coherence of the policy process is sometimes the price paid for the greater "democratic" influence on social groups and elected representatives on policy, a problem Japan as well as other Western democracies must wrestle with.

A fragmented policy process may also create another type of difficulty—the need for a "fixer" or informal coordinator able to bring together and manipulate the diverse power centers and interests. The rise in the 1970s of such a "fixer" as Tanaka Kakuei, the former prime minister under indictment for bribery who nonetheless continued to be a major political force because of his skills in party and bureaucratic politics, perhaps represents the leadership vacuum created by the diversification and pluralization of interests and power in Japanese politics during this period. In other words, trends which seem to be more democratic may have unintentional negative consequences for the ideal democratic system.

Finally, even the higher level of informal worker participation and integration in the companies that Hanami describes may have a negative side. As they are more strongly integrated into and identified with the company, Japanese workers may find that their ability to behave politically outside the company becomes increasingly limited. This may be because they have less need for political action when they can achieve their goals through participation in the company decisionmaking process (this, after all, is one of the main ideas behind moderate trade unionism); but Glen Fukushima's examples of company attempts to influence or even intimidate their employees politically (chapter 11) remind us that there may be a price for having one's political role subsumed into one's company role.

Equality

Japan represents a paradox to Western stereotypes of egalitarianism. Its cultural values and norms of social interaction contain such nonegalitarian aspects as deference to those of higher social status, hierarchy, and seniority. Its governmental leadership since the end of the Occupation has consistently been drawn from elite conservative groups opposed to ideologies of egalitarianism. Its industrial structure is more concentrated, as Fukushima shows, than that in the United States. And yet, as Margaret McKean demonstrates (chapter 9), Japan has one of the most equal distributions of wealth and income among the industrialized democracies. Access to the key resource in modern society—education—also is open and based primarily on merit and achievement (see Beauchamp, chapter 10).

In other ways too the egalitarian dimension of democracy seems to present fewer problems in Japan than in Western democracies. A remarkably homogenous society with a tradition of tolerance and ecclecticism toward religion, Japan has had few of the minority challenges that arise in the democratic countries of the West and destroy the political fabric of many developing countries.

Minority discrimination and egalitarian problems do exist, however. Discrimination against outcastes, Koreans, and women is deep-rooted in Japan, as Beauchamp shows. Perhaps because of the very homogeneity of the society, and its history of hierarchical cultural traditions, such discrimination has not been confronted in the public arena as much as one might expect and sometimes remains unacknowledged by the homogeneous majority. Nor was discrimination as readily discredited and attacked as was segregation in the American South in the 1960s.

Protests by outcastes in the 1970s did briefly become a political issue in Japan, and material grievances were often responded to by local governments. The root issue of the status and equality of Burakumin, however, was not directly addressed and has again become almost taboo as a topic for public debate. Although some individual Koreans have assimilated into Japanese society, the Korean minority as a group remains neither completely assimilated nor completely accepted as full-fledged, if different, Japanese. The problem may be that whereas American minorities such as blacks have often acquired substantial influence through alliance with the white majority and have thus been "incorporated" into the political process, in Japan alliance with the majority and incorporation into the local and national power structures have not followed from the protest of such groups.[1] The cultural isolation of minorities from the majority in Japanese society may serve as a significant obstacle to such incorporation.

Women's rights movements appeared for a short period in the 1970s, but never made the same advances that they did in many Western democracies. A law enacted to support equal employment rights for women is designed more as an example than a means to root out discrimination since it contains few enforcement provisiosn. Women have gradually made some advances in Japanese society—one recent example is the election of a woman to lead the Socialist party—but they are largely of an individual or symbolic nature. Large groups of women have not made great strides through the political process. The traditional sexual division of labor, with male supremacy in many areas of home and public life, remains perhaps to a greater degree than in other industrialized democracies. Japan thus presents the paradox of a relatively equal democratic society (in material terms) with some persistently unequal components (in cultural terms); of a pluralist society and democratic polity without a salient public ideology legitimizing and spurring greater equality and pluralism.

On this dimension, too, Japan appears simultaneously to be both more and less "democratic" than some other countries in the West.

Stability and Responsiveness

The fulfillment of democratic ideas in a society must be accompanied by a degree of political stability or that fulfillment may cause severe conflict and a chaotic political process that ultimately can undermine those ideals. Viewed from one perspective, Japan is a very stable democracy. Democratic ideals, as we have seen, are widely and deeply accepted by most Japanese. The political and social institutions of Japanese society work, and more often than not elicit respect and loyalty. One political party, the LDP, has been in power for over thirty years and has brought a consistency of governing style and policy not often found in democratic countries. The "creative conservatism" of that party has produced a fair degree of responsiveness to a wide range of groups, thus distributing enough benefits to enough segments of society to keep them at least minimally satisfied.[2] Protest, while frequent, in recent years has either not involved a broad section of the population or, if it has, has not been aimed against the system itself but rather at the solution to a particular problem such as pollution.

This stability was not always the case. It is instructive to remember the very valid questions asked by observers of Japan in the wake of the 1960 treaty crisis. One perceptive study of Japanese politics as revealed in that crisis expressed concern about the stability of Japanese democracy, given the failure of democratic and Japanese cultural norms to become integrated; about the ability of Japanese politics and leaders to respond to the emergence of democratic mass society; and about the widespread alienation from democratic institutions that motivated extraparliamentary radical behavior.[3]

These fears were not groundless; but they have turned out to be unfulfilled, as we have seen. Japanese culture and democratic values have proved increasingly compatible, the Japanese political elite has responded flexibly to changing socioeconomic conditions, and democratic institutions and practices have become firmly established. The reasons for these developments are complicated, but undoubtedly involve a combination of a political learning process by the political elite, an increasingly affluent economic base, and Japanese leaders and citizens becoming more accustomed to legitimate democratic processes over time.

Yet questions remain. Stability deriving from one-party domination has potentially negative implications. To the extent that the LDP has been responsive to changing socioeconomic conditions and to the opinions of various segments of society, it has done so in part because it felt itself in very real competition with the opposition parties. For example, the LDP demonstrated perhaps its greatest flexibility and responsiveness in the 1970s when it deemphasized rapid growth and gave priority to environmental quality and social welfare. Yet this was largely the consequence of the threat to its control over major metropolitan areas and Diet seats posed by the opposition and citizens' protest movements.

With little prospect of the opposition gaining power in the foreseeable future following the LDP's 1986 landslide election victory, will there be sufficient incentive to keep it responsive to change and the concerns of a wide strata of the population? It was exactly such dominance in the 1960s that led the LDP to ignore growing problems of pollution and welfare that were addressed only after grass-roots protest and defection. In other words, in Japan's dominant party system, some responsiveness has been both late and under pressure; it has not been a consistent and normal part of the democratic process resulting from alternation in power by different parties through short-term changes in election results.

On the other hand, some opposition influence is built into Japan's dominant party system. The LDP's unwillingness to ride roughshod over the minority despite its great majority of seats provides the opposition with a form of leverage. It can use procedural delays to force the LDP to choose between getting its legislative agenda passed or making some concessions (including postponing or dropping bills very offensive to the opposition). Given the short legislative terms in Japan and the hesitancy of the LDP to appear in the public's mind as too arrogant or unconsensual in the exercise of power, these tactics can give the opposition at least some influence in the process. For example, in 1987, despite the LDP's overwhelming majority of seats, Prime Minister Nakasone had to abandon plans to pass a nationwide sales (value-added) tax when it was vigorously challenged by the opposition, among others.

In most parliamentary democracies, alternation in power means that the opposition generally does not influence policy while out of office, but once in power may pass whatever it wants; in Japanese-style parliamentary democracy, the opposition has a little influence most of the time. In other words, *alternating power* is replaced by *simultaneous, shared, but unequal influence.* Is one type more democratic than the other? What are the consequences of such "simultaneous" but minimal opposition influence? When one party is perpetually in power, are there built-in consequences such as a tendency toward political corruption and the perennial alienation of segments of the population who support political parties that have no chance of ever holding office?[4] Or does the opposition have enough influence to keep the government relatively honest and its constituents satisfied with political life?

This brings up the basic question of the long-range stability of a system like Japan's. Do the opposition parties and their supporters have enough influence to tie them to the democratic system? To make them into effective and responsible parties? Japan is now riding the crest of its enormous economic achievements and affluence. Should this favorable economic climate ever change in the future (through precipitous events such as "trade wars" and protectionism, or international economic collapse, or through gradual economic decline), would opposition parties and their supporters, who have never been given the chance of power nor disciplined by the realities of governing, remain loyal to the democratic system and act responsibly? Under such circumstances, would both the opposition parties and the governing party be able to resist using antidemocratic nationalism as an easy symbolic method of either gaining or maintaining power? The question of whether a one-party dominant system fits the definition of democracy is an interesting theoretical question. Even if one concludes that such a system can be democratic, the question of the extent of real long-term stability and responsibility is one only the future can answer.

Japan as a Model: Consensus and Democracy?

As Japan has risen to economic prominence, it has attracted great attention as a model of a successful postindustrial society.[5] Many have come to see the admitted accomplishment of Japan—the creation of a modern, affluent society that "works"—as deriving from the vaunted Japanese ability to fashion a social and political consensus to solve its problems, to achieve the Japanese ideal of "harmony" in practice. The fact that this harmony has been accomplished in the context of a democratic political system has had a powerful attraction for Western observers perhaps troubled by the immersion of their own democratic systems in deep conflicts and their inability to solve contemporary problems. So too for some leaders of the Third World looking for an alternative model to the democratic but alien systems of the West, or the authoritarian and equally alien Communist systems. Japan has come to symbolize a non-Western culture the emulation of which might produce democracy without conflict, development without disorder, through the combination of Westernization and tradition. Are these accurate perceptions of Japanese democracy? Does it approach these stereotypes of a democratic system based on harmonious consensus, a modern democracy that has managed to easily incorporate both Westernization and traditionalism?

We are skeptical of some of the stereotypes of Japan on which the above views are based and also, despite its admitted achievements, of making Japan a generic model of democracy and progress for other democratic nations. First, we believe that many of these conceptions are based on a superficial understanding of the development of Japanese democracy in the pre- and postwar eras. As many of the preceding chapters make clear, Japanese political and social development has been anything but completely harmonious. Deep and serious conflicts have characterized Japan's history, particularly its political history in the postwar period. To see Japanese democracy as resting on a completely harmonious base is possible only by ignoring its past and present realities.[6]

Second, although Japan has handled certain postindustrial problems better than some Western nations, Japanese democratic and economic achievements have not been without their costs, trade-offs, and characteristic problems.

Third, the successful resolution of problems often has been the result not of achieving harmony and consensus, but of conflict. The intense conflict over the 1960 treaty, for example, may have stimulated Japanese leaders to attempt to resolve their political differences through the democratic process rather than force the political dialogue to the verge of a major breakdown.[7] Environmental pollution was tackled and to an extent brought under control because of widespread protest and conflict in the 1970s. Similarly, the appalling lack of welfare services in Japan became an issue only through criticism and conflict. It was a severe economic downturn and the prospect of increasing international competition, as Hanami points out, that increased worker participation and industrial peace, not traditional consensus. This is not to say that conflict always helps solve problems—it can also cause problems or pose obstacles to their solution. But it does perform the useful function of raising issues that need to be addressed, drawing attention to problems that have been ignored, and stimulating solutions. Conversely the appearance of harmony sometimes may reflect an attempt to avoid conflict rather than a successful response to a problem.

Fourth, an argument can be made that the very idea of a complete integration of harmony and democracy is in fact an impossibility. Democracy presumes conflict. The very concept of democracy presupposes a diversity of antagonistic interests, views, and opinions in society and assumes that these conflicts should be expressed, represented, and ultimately managed through the political process, not suppressed. A harmonious society and polity to the extent portrayed in some of the stereotypes of Japan would not be democratic. To the extent that Japan is democratic, it must inevitably fall short of such perfect, harmonious ideals.

As with the fallacious idea that Japan has perfectly combined harmony and democracy, so with the notion that it has managed to smoothly blend Westernization and tradition in developing democracy. It has not been that simple. Western ideas have been used in Japanese history to justify both democracy and authoritarianism. In prewar Japan, the goal of "catching up with the West" in terms of material modernization was used by political leaders to justify suppression of democratic rights even as other Western ideals were used by opponents of the modernizing regime to justify the necessity for expanding democracy. In postwar Japan, traditional values have been used by some conservatives to justify greater obedience and conformity and to prevent the expansion of democratic ideals in the Western sense; but traditional ideas have also been used by the left to protest the strict application of such Western ideas as majority rule, on the grounds that it violates the traditional norm of "consensus."

The fact is that both Western ideas and traditional ones have been used at various times by different, often hostile groups to justify their particular goals and interests. There has not been any simple or smooth "blending" of Westernization and tradition in the development of Japanese democracy.

It is for these reasons that we urge caution in interpreting Japanese democracy as a model for the integration of harmony and democracy, or of Western and Eastern traditions. Japan presents an example of a successful democracy, but one with conflicts and problems. Japan has its own unique history and tradition that has managed to adopt the value and institutions of democracy, an idea that originated in the West; but this adoption has not always been easy and has resulted in a political process with both comparable and idiosyncratic processes and conflicts. In this sense, Japan is not so much a model as a representative case of what all nations experience when they embark on the great adventure in self-rule we call "democracy."

NOTES

1. See, for example, Rufus P. Browning, Dale Rogers Marshall, and David H. Tabb, "Protest Is Not Enough: A Theory of Political Incorporation," *PS* 19 (Summer 1986): 576–81.

2. T. J. Pempel, *Policy and Politics in Japan: Creative Conservatism* (Philadelphia: Temple University Press, 1982).

3. Robert A. Scalapino and Junnosuke Masumi, *Parties and Politics in Contemporary Japan* (Berkeley and Los Angeles: University of California Press, 1962), esp. chap. 5.

4. The implications of dominant party systems, including Japan's, for democracy and policymaking are explored in T. J. Pempel, *Uncommon Democracies: The Politics of One-Party Dominance* (Ithaca, N.Y.: Cornell University Press, forthcoming). Many of the questions raised above are addressed in this volume.

5. For example, see Ezra F. Vogel, *Japan as Number One: Lessons for America* (Cambridge, Mass.: Harvard University Press, 1979).

6. For a detailed examination of the extent of conflict in postwar Japanese society and politics, see Ellis S. Krauss, Thomas P. Rohlen, and Patricia G. Steinhoff, eds., *Conflict in Japan* (Honolulu: University of Hawaii Press, 1984).

7. See Ellis S. Krauss, "Conflict in the Diet," in ibid.

Notes on Contributors

Edward R. Beauchamp is Professor of Education at the University of Hawaii where he teaches history of education and comparative education. A specialist on education in the United States and northeast Asia, he has taught and lectured at universities and research institutes worldwide. In 1988 he served as Fulbright Lecturer at Eotvos Lorand University in Budapest.

Lawrence W. Beer, a native of Portland, Oregon, is Fred Morgan Kirby Professor of Civil Rights at Lafayette College. He is chair of the Committee on Asian Law of the Association for Asian Studies and served as Fulbright Professor in the Faculty of Law, Hokkaido University, 1986–87. His books incude *Freedom of Expression in Japan; Constitutionalism in Asia;* and *The Constitutional Case Law of Japan* (with Hiroshi Ito).

John Creighton Campbell has taught political science at the University of Michigan since 1973. He is the author of *Comtemporary Japanese Budget Politics* and is writing a book about theories of policy change and Japanese public policy toward the elderly.

Glen S. Fukushima is Deputy Assistant U.S. Trade Representative for Japan and China in the Office of the U.S. Trade Representative, Executive Office of the President, Washington, D.C. He is a graduate of Harvard Law School and studied government-business relations at Harvard Business School, in the Ph.D. program in sociology at Harvard, and as a Fulbright Fellow at Tokyo University.

Tadashi Hanami is Professor of Labor Law and former dean of the Law School at Sophia University in Tokyo. He served for eleven years as a public commissioner for the Tokyo Metropolitan Labor Relations Commission and has taught at Catholic University of Leuven and Harvard Law School as a visiting professor. He has written numerous articles on industrial and labor relations and law in both English and Japanese. Among his books in English are *Labor Relations in Japan Today* and *Labor Law and Industrial Relations in Japan*.

Takeshi Ishida is Professor Emeritus at the University of Tokyo, where he was Professor of Political Science and the director of the Institute of Social Science. He is the author of two books in English, *Japanese Society* and *Japanese Political Culture: Change and Continuity*, and fifteen books in Japanese. His current research concerns the historical development of major political concepts in modern Japan.

Ellis S. Krauss is Professor of Political Science at the University of Pittsburgh. He is the author of *Japanese Radicals Revisited* and co-editor of *Conflict in Japan* and of *Political Opposition and Local Politics in Japan*. His current research interests include television news and politics in Japan, Japanese political elites and policy-making, and U.S.-Japan trade friction over public works construction.

Margaret A. McKean is the author of *Environmental Protest and Citizen Politics in Japan*. In recent years she has been writing about the design of cooperative solutions to collective choice problems in Japanese society, from traditional village management of common forests to modern economic regulatory policy.

Terry Edward MacDougall is Associate Professor of International Relations and Political Science at Boston University. He is editor of *Political Leadership in Contemporary Japan* and author of "Yoshida Shigeru and the Japanese Transition to Liberal Democracy," "Lockheed and the High Costs of Politics in Japan," and a forthcoming book on politics and policy in urban Japan.

T. J. Pempel is Professor of Government and Adjunct Professor in the Johnson School of Management at Cornell University. From 1980 to 1985 he was also director of Cornell's East Asia Program. His most recent books are *Policy and Politics in Japan: Creative Conservatism* and *Japan: Dilemmas of Success*.

Patricia G. Steinhoff is Professor of Sociology and director of the Center for Japanese Studies at the University of Hawaii. In addition to her research on conflict, ideological conversion (*tenko*), and the Japanese Red Army, she is editor of the *Directory of Japan Specialists and Japanese Studies Institutions in the United States and Canada*.

J.A.A. Stockwin is Nissan Professor of Modern Japanese Studies and director of the Nissan Institute of Japanese Studies at Oxford University, having previously taught in the Department of Political Science, Australian National University, Canberra. He is the author of *The Japanese Socialist Party and Neutralism* and *Japan: Divided Politics in a Growth Economy,* and co-author of *Dynamic and Immobilist Politics in Japan.*

Christena Turner is an anthropologist and Assistant Professor in the Department of Sociology at the University of California at San Diego. She works on culture and consciousness in contemporary organizations and has done fieldwork in a variety of Japanese companies in Tokyo. She is preparing a book on Japanese unions.

Index

Pitt Series in Policy and Institutional Studies
Bert A. Rockman, Editor